An introduction to Islamic archaeology

The New Edinburgh Islamic Surveys
Series Editor: Carole Hillenbrand

TITLES AVAILABLE OR FORTHCOMING

Contemporary Issues in Islam   Asma Asfaruddin

The New Islamic Dynasties   Clifford Edmund Bosworth

Media Arabic (2nd Edition)   Julia Ashtiany Bray

An Introduction to the Hadith   John Burton

A History of Islamic Law   Noel Coulson

Medieval Islamic Political Thought   Patricia Crone

A Short History of the Ismailis   Farhad Daftary

Islam: An Historical Introduction (2nd Edition)   Gerhard Endress

A History of Christian–Muslim Relations   Hugh Goddard

Medieval Islamic Science   Robert Hall

Shi'ism (2nd Edition)   Heinz Halm

Islamic Science and Engineering   Donald Hill

Muslim Spain Reconsidered   Richard Hitchcock

Islamic Law: From Historical Foundations to Contemporary Practice   Mawil Izzi Dien

Sufism: The Formative Period   Ahmet T. Karamustafa

Islamic Aesthetics   Oliver Leaman

Persian Historiography   Julie Scott Meisami

Pilgrims and Pilgrimage   Josef Meri

The Muslims of Medieval Italy   Alex Metcalfe

An Introduction to Islamic Archaeology   Marcus Milwright

Twelver Shi'ism: Unity and Diversity in the Life of Islam   Andrew Newman

Muslims in Western Europe (3rd Edition)   Jørgen Nielsen

Medieval Islamic Medicine   Peter E. Pormann and Emilie Savage-Smith

Islamic Names   Annemarie Schimmel

The Genesis of Literature in Islam   Gregor Schoeler

Modern Arabic Literature   Paul Starkey

Islamic Medicine   Manfred Ullman

Islam and Economics   Ibrahim Warde

A History of Islamic Spain   W. Montgomery Watt and Pierre Cachia

Introduction to the Qur'an   W. Montgomery Watt

Islamic Creeds   W. Montgomery Watt

Islamic Philosophy and Theology   W. Montgomery Watt

Islamic Political Thought   W. Montgomery Watt

The Influence of Islam on Medieval Europe   W. Montgomery Watt

An introduction to Islamic archaeology

MARCUS MILWRIGHT

EDINBURGH UNIVERSITY PRESS

Edinburgh University Press Ltd
22 George Square, Edinburgh
www.euppublishing.com

Typeset in Goudy by
Koinonia, Manchester, and
printed and bound in Great Britain by
CPI Antony Rowe, Chippenham and Eastbourne

A CIP Record for this book is available from the British Library

ISBN 978 0 7486 2310 5 (hardback)
ISBN 978 0 7486 2311 2 (paperback)

Published with the support of the Edinburgh University
Scholarly Publishing Initiatives Fund.

Contents

Figures

NOTE The maps have been prepared by Chris Mundigler

Acknowledgements

Much of the initial research for the book was undertaken in 2006, during fellowships at the Aga Khan Programs for Islamic Architecture at Harvard University and the Massachusetts Institute of Technology. I would like to express my gratitude to Gülru Neçipoglu and Nasser Rabbat for their hospitality during my time in Cambridge, MA. Grants from the Social Sciences and Humanities Research Council of Canada have allowed me to undertake fieldwork in the Middle East, Britain and Greece.

In assembling the illustrations for this book I have relied upon the generosity of many scholars. It is a pleasure to acknowledge those who have contributed site plans, diagrams and photographs, as well as information on where images could be located. The following list is doubtless incomplete: James Allan, Antonio Almagro, Ruth Barnes, Yuval Baruch, Alessandra Cereda, Keith Challis, Katya Cytryn-Silverman, Michael Danti, Erica Dodd, Denis Genequand, Véronique François, Oleg Grabar, Stefan Heidemann, Julian Henderson, Mark Horton, Jeremy Johns, Richard Jones, Kenneth Jonsson, Ruba Kana'an, Robert Mason, Alastair Northedge, Konstantinos Politis, Kay Prag, Julian Raby, Charles Redman, Mariam Rosser-Owen, Lisa Snyder, Cristina Tonghini, Luke Treadwell, Antonio Vallejo Triano, Bert de Vries, Donald Whitcomb, and David Whitehouse. I have also benefited greatly from scholars who have shared with me their archaeological expertise. Aside from those already mentioned above, the following are due particular thanks: Glaire Anderson, Robin Brown, Lynda Carroll, Joseph Greene, Mahmoud Hawari, Stephen McPhillips, Chase Robinson, and Dede Fairchild Ruggles. The maps in this volume were prepared by Chris Mundigler. I also thank Mike Huston for his invaluable help in preparing many of the images for publication; and I thank the staff of the Maltwood Museum and Special Collections, McPherson Library, at the University of Victoria.

I am most grateful to Carole Hillenbrand for the invitation to write this volume and for the comments that she and Robert Hillenbrand have offered on earlier drafts. My editor, Nicola Ramsey, has been a fount of knowledge about the publication process, and I salute her patience as I made the final preparations to submit the manuscript.

Lastly, I thank my family. My mother, Mary, read and corrected a draft of the manuscript. I could not have written this book without the love and support of my wife, Evanthia. In addition to providing much thoughtful criticism of my work, she shouldered the responsibilities of caring for our children, Loukas and Clio, during stages of the research and writing. This book is dedicated to her.

Notes on transliteration and dating

Confronted by the range of languages employed for personal and place names across three continents, this book adopts a pragmatic approach. Personal names and technical vocabulary in Arabic and Persian are transliterated according to the *International Journal of Middle Eastern Studies*, but without the macron over the long vowels and the dots under selected consonants. I have not employed the plural forms of Arabic and Persian terms; plurals are indicated by the addition of an unitalicised s. The spellings of place names are generally as they appear in published archaeological reports, although I have sometimes provided ancient, medieval or modern alternatives. I have, however, imposed some standardisation: the Arabic definite article is always given as 'al-', and the Persian *izafa* as –'-i'. Words that appear commonly in toponyns are also rendered in a consistent manner. Thus *tal* is preferred to *tel*, *tell* or *tall*; *khirbat* is preferred to *khirbet*; and the Maghribi *qsar* is, in accordance with its spelling elsewhere in the Arabic-speaking world, given as *qasr*. The geographical scope of terms such as Greater Syria, Ifriqiya, and Khurasan is explained in the glossary. The years and centuries mentioned in the book are given according to the Common Era, with *Hijri* dates added in cases of objects or buildings with dated inscriptions.

Abbreviations

ADAJ	*Annual of the Department of Antiquities of Jordan*
BAR	*British Archaeological Reports*
BASOR	*Bulletin of the American Schools of Oriental Research*
BSOAS	*Bulletin of the School of Oriental and African Studies*
DOP	*Dumbarton Oaks Papers*
JESHO	*Journal of the Economic and Social History of the Orient*
JRA	*Journal of Roman Archaeology*
OSIA	*Oxford Studies in Islamic Art*
PEQ	*Palestine Exploration Quarterly*
PSAS	*Proceedings of the Seminar for Arabian Studies*

I

Introduction

We dug out a well in the region of the Banu Wurayq. We were unaware of anything (exceptional) existing in it until we noticed the mark of old excavations, which informed us that the place had been dug out at some previous date. Our excavations led us to a huge rock. Turning it over, we found underneath the corpse of a man in a sitting posture and looking so unlike the dead that one would think he was engaged in conversation. Above his head we found the following inscription: 'I am Qidir ibn Isma'il ibn Ibrahim, the friend of the Compassionate God. From among a people whose king is unbelieving I fled carrying the torch of the true faith. I testify that there is no god but Allah; I associate none with Him and turn to no other than Him for help.' Thereupon we restored the place to its former condition.

Attributed to one Salim al-A'raj, this report is contained within a collection of anecdotes about the antiquities of southern Arabia entitled al-Iklil and written by Hasan ibn Ahmad al-Hamdani (d. 945).[1] In this description of the discovery of a male burial during the digging of a well, the excavators are startled by the pose of the body – standard Muslim practice would require a supine position with the head turned towards the qibla – although the inscription above the dead man's head, with its profession of the oneness of God (shahada), evidently persuades them to leave him undisturbed and, presumably, to sink the well at a different location. This brief account is interesting for the 'archaeological' approach apparently adopted by the excavators: first, they are alerted to something unusual by the signs of earlier digging into the soil; second, they note the strange arrangement of the corpse; and, third, they decipher an inscription as a means to come to a conclusion concerning the confessional allegiance of the dead man.

The surviving parts of al-Iklil abound in descriptions of the exhumation of ancient tombs, often providing entertaining observations about the remarkable preservation of bodies, the clothing of the corpses, the precious artefacts, and the associated inscriptions. Al-Hamdani also gives accounts of famous monuments of southern Arabia, including the massive Ma'rib dam, parts of which survive to the present, and the lost palace of Ghumdan. He was not the only Islamic author to be intrigued by the material record of pre-Islamic Arabia (known by Muslims as the jahiliyya, or 'time of ignorance'); for instance, the Kitab al-Asnam of Hisham ibn al-Kalbi (d. 821–22) contains numerous descriptions of idol stones that were employed in the pagan practices of Arabia prior to the revelation of Islam.[2] Muslim rulers and their courts were evidently fascinated by the monuments of earlier centuries. In 955 the Buyid sultan, 'Adud al-Dawla (r. 949–83), visited the Achaemenid city of Persepolis in southern Iran and, according to accounts of the event, had the ancient inscriptions read to him by the Zoroastrian high priest.[3] The Egyptian author, Ahmad ibn 'Ali al-Maqrizi (d. 1442), describes an excavation in 1342 that followed the accidental unearthing in the vicinity of Bab al-Luq of what was identified as an ancient mosque. A scoundrel named Shu'ayb claimed it to be the burial place (*qabr*) of a companion of the Prophet Muhammad and enterprisingly charged fees to the dignitaries of Cairo for conducting them around the 'shrine'.[4]

Did the discovery of the grave of Qidir ibn Isma'il ibn Ibrahim actually occur and, if so, did the events unfold as they are recounted in *al-Iklil*? There is, of course, no way to answer these questions definitively, but a general assessment of the character of *al-Iklil* gives cause to doubt the veracity of the account of the discovery of Qidir. The frequently fanciful details accompanying al-Hamdani's descriptions of ancient tombs or palaces such as Ghumdan locate *al-Iklil* within a well-established Arabic genre of *belles lettres* (*adab*), though the text certainly also contains important observations about Arabian monuments of the pre-Islamic period (as well as giving an idea about the attitudes expressed towards them by tenth-century Muslims). There is no denying that al-Hamdani offers an intriguing demonstration of analytical technique in his description of Qidir's burial, one which is perhaps not so different from the writings of early British antiquarians.[5] The same complex dynamic between literary intent and the objective reporting of past events is evident in other descriptions of excavations. Thus al-Maqrizi's decision to recount in his *Kitab al-Suluk* the story of Shu'ayb and of the 'shrine' at Bab al-Luq is not motivated primarily by an interest in archaeological method, but by a desire to use the episode moralistically to highlight the ways in which unscrupulous individuals prey upon human gullibility. That said, al-Maqrizi's other great work, *Kitab al-Mawa'iz wa'l-i'tibar bi-dhikr al-khitat wa'l-athar* (*Exhortations and Reflections on the History of Urban Quarters and Monuments*), shows that he was indeed passionately interested in the historical topography and monumental architecture of his native city.[6]

In other words, despite these authors' evident interest in the past, the responses to the material record of earlier phases of human history given by al-Hamdani, Ibn al-Kalbi, al-Maqrizi, and other pre-modern Islamic authors should not be accepted at face value. They employed literary forms that would have been readily identifiable to their intended audience and they viewed the past, particularly the pre-Islamic past or the 'age of ignorance', subjectively, from their viewpoint as Muslims, the recipients of the complete revelation of Allah through His Prophet Muhammad.

The present book is also about the material culture recovered from excavations in the Islamic world, but it is concerned with a specific type of engagement with the past, that of archaeology. In recent decades the sub-discipline of archaeology that devotes itself to the study of Islamic occupation phases (i.e. those periods when a given locality was under the control of an elite that professed the faith of Islam) has come to be known as 'Islamic archaeology'. Before moving to the presentation of the history and achievements of this area of study, it is important to establish a working definition of what is meant by Islamic archaeology. How is it to be distinguished from the antiquarian approach to the past of the Islamic authors already discussed, and what is its relationship to other forms of modern scholarly interrogation of the Islamic past, most importantly the disciplines of history and art history?

Today the phrase 'Islamic archaeology' is used to encompass a wide variety of scholarly activities. Most obvious among these are the recording of artefacts, architectural features, and other aspects of human activity recovered from systematic excavation and regional surveys, but the list can be expanded to include the analysis of aerial and satellite photography; geophysical survey; the reconstruction of the phasing of buildings through the analysis of construction techniques ('buildings archaeology'); and marine archaeology, the examination of shipwrecks and other undersea features. Like other areas of archaeology, ethnography and anthropology also provide comparative information for the explication of past practices. Beyond these modes of collecting 'raw' data, there is a multiplicity of 'post-excavation' techniques that allow for the interpretation of the material record. These range from the conventional, but still essential, activities of typological study (drawing, describing, dating, and identifying comparanda from other sites) to forms of scientific analysis of manufactured artefacts, human and animal bones, and plant remains. Many of these techniques are discussed in this book, but it is worth asking what holds them together under the umbrella of Islamic archaeology. Furthermore, can a working definition of Islamic archaeology simply comprise a list of the scholarly pursuits now practised in the field?

If one takes this approach of formulating a definition based on a list of activities or techniques, then it is also necessary to include other modes of study of the artefacts and buildings recovered through archaeological research. For instance, two forms of study often categorised as 'archaeological' in the study of the Islamic past are epigraphy (most pertinently, monumental inscriptions) and numismatics. To take another example, the history of Islamic art and architecture, particularly that of the first four centuries of Islam, would be notably poorer if it did not include excavated material. While one should acknowledge that the boundaries between art-historical and archaeological approaches to excavated material are porous, the two disciplines have rather different priorities in their analytical processes (although their ultimate goals may be similar). What distinguishes archaeological enquiry – and this represents the principal criterion for the selection of the published data discussed in the remainder of the book – is its focus on the spatial and temporal relationships between things. It is this overriding concern with context that forms the basis of the archaeological interpretation, and this means that the archaeologist is, theoretically at least, equally interested in all physical traces of human activity from a given period, from macro-level ones (for instance city layouts, canal networks, field plans, and habitation patterns) to specific ones (for instance a single structure, an artefact, or the carbonised material from a hearth). It is certainly true that many early excavations of Islamic sites privileged the more aesthetically engaging artefacts in their collection procedures and final publications, but more recent projects are as likely to devote attention to mundane aspects of everyday life, from unglazed ceramics to discarded animal bones.

This is not to say that more 'art-historical' concerns with technique, style, iconography, and patronage are not of interest, but they should be considered of secondary importance in archaeological research. Likewise, inscribed artefacts and coins are discussed in this book, but attention is given to their physical characteristics and to the information contained in them (particularly dates, names, and locations) rather than to palaeographic or philological issues. Through this focus upon temporal and spatial context, I hope that the studies presented in the following chapters demonstrate the rich potential of archaeology to illuminate social, economic, and cultural practices in the Islamic past, from the seventh to the early twentieth century. For instance, where art-historical analysis can provide valuable data concerning the original meanings attributed to the specific designs on an artefact, the archaeological study of the spatial distribution of similar artefacts allows for a consideration of the mechanisms of regional and international trade in a given period.

Like other branches of archaeology, Islamic archaeology attempts to reconstruct past practices through the interpretation of physical evidence. This concern with the material record distinguishes it from the principally text-based study of history, though, again, the boundaries between history and archaeology are increasingly hard to define. On the one hand, the evolution of what is now termed 'historical archaeology' (see below) encourages archaeologists to engage with contemporary textual sources as a means to explicate patterns of data retrieved from excavations and surveys. On the other hand, many historians are making use of numismatic and archaeological information as a means to address lacunae in the written sources. Archaeology can, of course, be subsumed into the larger category of history, but there are important ways in which an archaeological conceptualisation of the passage of time might differ from that constructed by a textual historian. To make a crude generalisation, information in pre-modern Islamic archival documents, chronicles, geographical works, and other written sources tends to be focused on short-term events rather than on phenomena that occur over long periods. Written from an urban perspective and largely devoted to the lives of the political and economic (and literate) elite, these sources provide a record of the past that is clearly defined in chronological and geographical terms. In other words, they abound in the dates and locations at which events occurred. The record of the past retrieved by archaeologists seems rather nebulous in comparison. With the exception of sudden cataclysms such as the 749 earthquake, which buried pack animals, humans, and their personal possessions beneath collapsed buildings of towns and villages in the south of Greater Syria,[7] excavations tend to reveal human occupation over the course of decades or centuries.

This 'archaeological' past does not represent time as it was directly experienced, and it is unlikely to correlate closely with the information culled from chronicles and archival sources.[8] This is equally true of the material record left by successive phases of occupation within an individual building and of the slowly changing patterns of settlement within a larger region. The evolution of the historical discourse espoused by the *Annales* school provided opportunities to bridge this divide. Of central importance is the recognition that social, economic, demographic, and cultural processes may occur at different rates, from the short term (*événements*) to the middle term (*conjonctures*) and to the longer term (*la longue durée*).[9] Reconstruction of longer-term processes necessitates a different approach to the information contained within the written record, as well as a search for other, non-textual data. Naturally enough, this has prompted historians to make greater use of archaeological data. Islamic historians are also becoming increasingly interested in the lives of non-elite groups in urban and rural environments. These developments have considerable implications for Islamic archaeology. First, there is now much greater potential to engage with theoretical models proposed by historians, and one can point to several examples of *Annales*-influenced archaeology.[10] Second, with the growth of non-elite historical studies, archaeology cannot simply justify itself as the sole means for accessing the everyday lives of the urban and rural poor. Third, now more than ever archaeologists have a responsibility to communicate their findings in a clear and comprehensible manner to a wider non-specialist audience.

That the employment by Islamic historians of data from excavations and surveys has not always been successful is, in some part, the fault of archaeologists.[11] Three issues are worth highlighting. The first is the sometimes opaque language of the published archaeological reports themselves. Archaeology is no different from other academic disciplines in its reliance upon technical terminology; the requirement for precision in the description of, for instance, excavated stratigraphy necessitates a rather dry prose style.

That said, it is not uncommon to find the wider implications of the raw archaeological data left unexplored, a situation which leaves the non-specialist reader to wonder why such effort has been expended on the formation of pottery typologies or on the reconstruction of the sequence of floor layers within a building. A second problem lies in the record of publication, which in the field of Islamic archaeology leaves much to be desired. Many excavated sites are known only from preliminary reports (the final publication never appearing), while others remain unpublished. Recently there have been valiant attempts to recover information from long-completed and partially published excavations, though problems are obviously encountered in the interpretation of old or fragmentary field notebooks, site plans, and drawings.[12] A third and related problem lies in the failure, until relatively recently, to synthesise information in order to draw out larger generalities – either regionally or chronologically defined – in the archaeological record. The need to employ preliminary reports or personal knowledge of unpublished material represents a challenge in this respect, as does the linguistic range of the available publications and the diversity of journals in which the reports appear. Thankfully this is now changing, and the last ten years have witnessed an increasing number of books and articles devoted to the archaeology of specific time periods and regions.[13]

Is there anything intrinsically 'Islamic' about Islamic archaeology? Taken at face value, Islamic archaeology is no different from Islamic history or Islamic art history in that all are cultural and historical labels indicating that the subjects in question deal with aspects of the past in regions where the ruling elite has professed the faith of Islam. In this sense, Islamic archaeology, like Islamic art history, addresses the things made and used both by Muslim and by non-Muslim communities within these historically defined regions and periods. This material culture encompasses artefacts and buildings that have specific functions in the practice of faith – Islam, Christianity, Judaism, Buddhism, and so on – as well as the larger corpus of material culture employed for other aspects of daily life (what can broadly be termed the 'secular' domain). To tell the story of Islamic archaeology, it is also necessary to address the areas of continuity with earlier phases of human history prior to the birth of Islam, particularly the period known as 'late antiquity' (chapter 2). Turning to other areas of archaeology, one comes across a variety of labels of convenience, which express often loosely defined cultural, political, or geographical commonalities – Roman, medieval, post-medieval, and crusader archaeologies, to name but a few.

This cultural–historical definition of Islamic archaeology is employed in the remainder of the book, and readers will find some sections devoted to the religious practices of non-Muslims in the Islamic world, as well as to the archaeology of many aspects of the 'secular' environment, ranging from irrigation and urban water systems to manufacturing and international trade. In this respect, the archaeologists whose work forms the subject of the present book tend to adopt methodologies and theoretical standpoints that exhibit close correspondences to archaeological practice in other periods and regions.[14] Clearly the interpretation of the evidence is informed by specific environmental and historical factors, but in general Islamic archaeologists have not chosen to develop a distinct body of theory. An alternative to the cultural–historical model has been proposed by Timothy Insoll in his book *The Archaeology of Islam* (1999) and in other writings.[15] For Insoll, it is possible to investigate the archaeology of a religion – meaning here both the explicit practice of faith and the integration of religious values into everyday life – through the material record. Insoll employs a much wider range of sources than is usually encompassed by conventional archaeology, from anthropology, ethnography and sociology to art and architectural history. While he is certainly sensitive to the existence of the different branches of Islam and of the various adaptations of religious values as Muslims came into contact with other cultures and religions, his thesis is predicated upon the concept that Islam represents a 'structuring code' conditioning the daily practices of Muslims throughout the world.[16] In other words, there is the potential that material culture – such as the organisation of the domestic space, the decoration of an artefact, or the butchering marks on an animal bone – can be used to identify the presence of Muslim communities in the archaeological record.

At first sight it seems difficult to disagree with this point of view. Any visitor to the Islamic Middle East, North Africa or Central Asia is struck by the ubiquity of mosques and other forms of Muslim religious architecture, while Qur'anic verses and invocations appear both on buildings and on portable artefacts. In their private lives, Muslims are required to abstain from alcohol and certain types of food, while the practice of the pilgrimage to Mecca (*hajj*) might be celebrated with the painting of a mural around the doorway to one's house. To what extent, however, can religious identity be reconstructed in the archaeological record, particularly if this is applied to the more restricted definition of excavations and field surveys? Of course, mosques and artefacts associated with Muslim ritual practice are readily identifiable signs of Islam, but even in this explicitly religious domain there exist problems of definition. The presence of a mosque does not in itself define the religious affiliation of the majority of the surrounding population. Shrines also present significant difficulties of interpretation; for instance, what can one say of the religious 'identity' of a shrine visited by local Christians, Jews, and Muslims on the supposed birthday (*mawlid*) of the saint?

To take some examples from the portable arts, one might consider the wine jars painted with the images of Christian priests recovered from excavations in a ninth-century palace in Samarra, or the inlaid metal basin carrying Christian motifs made for the Ayyubid Sultan al-Salih Ayyub (r. 1240–49).[17] Does the presence of Christian themes in each case lend the objects and their owners a 'Christian' cultural identity? The metal vessel known as the Innsbruck plate (Fig. 1.1) poses further challenges: decorated in enamel – a typically 'Byzantine' technique – and probably made by a Georgian craftsman, it carries in the central roundel a depiction of the ascension of Alexander the Great. While one might expect this to have been manufactured for a Christian patron with a taste for classicising themes, this interpretation is challenged by the presence of Arabic and Persian inscriptions. The Arabic text includes titulature and personal names associated with the Artuqids, a Turkish Muslim dynasty ruling areas of southern Anatolia, Syria and north-eastern Iraq from the beginning of the twelfth century.[18] Whether this piece was made for one of the Artuqids (perhaps as a diplomatic gift) or for a Georgian client is unclear, although it is worth noting that classicising themes and overtly Christian ones appear on Artuqid copper coinage. Turning to written sources, the Innsbruck plate can be located within a long process of cultural assimilation and adaptation among different populations – defined by ethnicity, language, and religious belief – which occurred in the Hellenised lands of Anatolia after the victory of the Saljuq Turks over the Byzantine army at the battle at Manzikert in 1071.[19]

While one could argue that the artefacts discussed above represent exceptional cases, they provide reason enough for exercising considerable caution in assigning overarching religious identities to excavated material, whether in the Islamic world or elsewhere.[20] These problems are particularly acute on the borderlands between Islamic and non-Islamic polities – for instance in Anatolia, Sicily, Spain, northern India, and Central Asia – but it should also be remembered that the Islamic world has always contained within it substantial populations of non-Muslims. Predictably, the arts and wider material culture of the Islamic world reflect cross-cultural exchange between different confessional, linguistic and ethnic groups over the course of centuries. I do not wish to minimise the significance of religious belief in the negotiation of individual and collective identity – indeed religious belief and its physical manifestations in the archaeological record are discussed in chapters 2, 3 and 6 – but I believe that the intrinsic limitations of archaeological data necessitate an interpretive strategy which acknowledges our inability to recreate the complex interplay of faith, language, ethnic or tribal affiliation, socio-economic status, world-view, and personal choice – factors which operate in the determination of that sense of identity. Thus the present book takes as its starting point the archaeology itself, allowing the wider interpretations to evolve from the results of excavations, surveys and other forms of archaeological investigation.

This book aims to deal both with the principal discoveries of the archaeological research carried into the Islamic period and with the practice of Islamic archaeology. In other words, I felt it was necessary to address not simply the

contributions made by archaeology, but also the methods employed and inferences made by archaeologists in the interpretation of data collected from excavations and surveys. One result of this focus on archaeological methodology is
the discussion of the historiography of the sub-discipline itself (the final section
of this chapter). The other result is the case studies gathered in the remaining
chapters of the book. The latter usually focus on a small number of excavations
or on the wider examination of a single topic. This approach is designed to allow
for the presentation of the significant results, the means by which scholars reach
their conclusions, and the reasons why there might be differences of opinion
concerning the interpretation of the evidence. The highly uneven coverage of
excavations and surveys militated against a chronological/dynastic or regionally
based discussion of the evidence; instead, the approach adopted in the book
draws on the methodological questions outlined above and concentrates upon
recurrent issues that, in the opinion of this author, are most important in Islamic
archaeology as it has developed in recent decades.

A few comments are needed concerning the methodological, chronological,
geographical, and linguistic limits established during the preparation of this
book. As already stated, this book concentrates upon evidence drawn from excavations, surveys, and post-excavation analysis. I have tried to avoid references to
unpublished data, preferring to cite published work that is accessible in research
libraries. In an effort to avoid replicating material found in surveys of Islamic
art and architecture, the book does not analyse standing structures – except
in the context of spatial distribution or of analysis of the construction phases
within individual monuments – or present the aesthetic and iconographic study
of excavated artefacts.[21] Although many of the works mentioned in this book
are informed by theoretical models developed in other fields of archaeology,
such models are not discussed explicitly. This decision was taken in order to
make it possible for the bulk of the book to be about the data of Islamic archaeological research. The preponderance of studies relating to architecture and
ceramics (and, to a lesser extent, metalwork, glass, and textiles) was necessitated
by the nature of the published evidence. While areas such as archaeobotany,
zooarchaeology, environmental archaeology, and physical anthropology are all
now vital components of Islamic archaeology (and selected projects have been
discussed in later chapters), they still represent a small fraction of the available
books, chapters, and articles.

The chronological boundaries of the book are broad – ranging from the
fourth to the early twentieth century – but each century does not receive equal
coverage. The considerable focus among archaeologists on the transition from
the late antique to the early Islamic centuries warranted greater discussion of this
period than some other phases of Islamic history did. Looking at the Islamic past
from a dynastic perspective, it also becomes clear that some empires or polities

offer much more archaeological data than others: compare for instance the huge assemblage of archaeological information from Greater Syria in the Mamluk period with the relative paucity of published excavated material relating to the 'Great Saljuq' period in the Islamic East (1040–1194). In geographical terms, this book does not attempt to encompass all regions that are usually defined as the 'Islamic world', nor does it deal with the archaeology of post-Islamic phases in regions such as the Iberian peninsula, Sicily, or Greece. Confronted by the vast geographical range of past and current archaeological projects, I decided to limit the focus of this book: largely omitted from consideration are sub-Saharan Africa, south-east Asia, the Muslim regions of western China, and the Indian subcontinent. I emphasise that these omissions do not mean that I view the archaeology of these areas to be unimportant. Rather, the decision to concentrate on the so-called 'central Islamic lands' reflects the expertise of the author, and, I believe, the dominant focus of Islamic archaeology throughout the twentieth century (Fig. 1.2). That Islamic archaeology is constantly broadening its geographical focus is much to be welcomed, and it seems likely that very different surveys of Islamic archaeology will be attempted in future years. Lastly, publications on Islamic archaeology are written in a myriad of languages – English, French, German, Spanish, Arabic, Persian, Turkish, and Russian being perhaps the most important – so that they are beyond the skills of any single archaeologist. For some regions and languages I have relied upon summary articles written by specialists. Of course, these summaries represent only a glimpse of the wealth of archaeological research in a given area and become increasingly out-of-date in the years after their publication.

The book is divided into three parts. The first part (chapters 2 and 3) deals with the archaeology of the transition from late antiquity to the early Islamic period; that is, from the fourth to the tenth century. Chapter 2 starts with a presentation of the earliest artefacts that bear definable traces (that is, epigraphy, motifs or representations) of the new religion of Islam or of the political structures of the nascent Islamic state, then it moves to a consideration of late antiquity in North Africa and in the Middle East. The case study that forms the final section of the chapter examines the palatial residences of Umayyad Greater Syria and questions the extent to which these structures should be considered an extension of practices encountered in the archaeological record of the fifth and sixth centuries. Chapter 3 focuses on the ways in which the archaeology of the early Islamic period (principally between the eighth and the tenth century) starts to diverge from the patterns of late antiquity. This question is addressed from the perspective of expansion, synthesis, and innovation. The last theme is taken up in a case study that looks at the evolution of the mosque and of the *dar al-imara* (governor's palace) in the urban environments of the expanding Islamic empire.

Many of the themes introduced in chapter 3 are dealt with in greater detail in the second part of the book (chapters 4–8). This part is concerned with the archaeological approaches to the different environments and human practices within the Islamic world. The main focus is on evidence from the eleventh to the fifteenth century, though examples are also drawn from earlier and later phases of Islamic history. The first two chapters assess the archaeological approaches to the human environment, dividing them broadly into the countryside (chapter 4) and urban life (chapter 5). Chapters 6–8 are focused on human practices: religious life (chapter 6), crafts and industry (chapter 7), then trade and other forms of exchange (chapter 8). The third part of the book (chapter 9) reviews the archaeological contributions to the study of the later Islamic centuries, placing a particular emphasis upon the engagement with western Europe between the sixteenth and the early twentieth century.

A brief history of Islamic archaeology

When did Islamic archaeology come into being as a distinct mode of investigating the Islamic past? No single event represents a turning point, though one could reasonably isolate the last years of the nineteenth and the first decade of the twentieth century as a crucial phase in the early evolution of this sub-discipline of archaeology. For instance, employing the new stratigraphic recording techniques pioneered by Flinders Petrie, Frederick Bliss and Robert Macalister were able to distinguish levels dating to the Islamic centuries in their excavation (from 1899) of the multi-period site of Tal al-Safiyya near Gaza.[22] Their published report of 1902 devotes only a brief section to the 'Arab' artefacts from the digs (their interest being focused on more ancient phases), although there is evidence that other archaeologists were seeking out sites where the sole or most conspicuous phase of occupation belonged to the Islamic centuries. Notable among the published excavations of this period are those of the Qal'a of the Bani Hammad in Algeria (1898–1909), and of Rammadiyya and Madinat al-Zahra' in Spain (1909–10); while the hugely influential work of Friedrich Sarre and Ernst Herzfeld at Samarra commenced in 1910. Excavations were also conducted by Russian archaeologists in Samarqand as early as 1885 and by the Ottoman authorities in the Syrian town of Raqqa (1905, 1906, and 1908), though neither project was published at the time and their impact on subsequent archaeological debate was slight.[23]

While a contemporary archaeologist searching for comparative material would be unlikely to have much recourse to books or articles printed prior to 1900, this does not mean that Islamic artefacts did not appear in earlier publications or that nineteenth-century scholars were uninterested in the material culture of the Islamic period. Muslim burials were apparently recorded by excavators in the North African port of Carthage in the 1860s, and Islamic pottery (not always correctly identified as such) appears in the publications of early excavations such as Ephesus and Jerusalem.[24] Doubtlessly Islamic artefacts were cast away unrecorded, both on illicit and on more controlled nineteenth-century digs elsewhere in the Middle East and North Africa. Although they were not to be subjected to systematic excavation until the twentieth century, the waste heaps of Fustat attracted the attention of European scholars, and samples of glazed and unglazed pottery were published by Stanley Lane-Poole, Henry Wallis, and Nicholas Fouquet. Ceramics were also gathered from surface deposits in Damascus and other sites in Syria. The glazed dishes (known as *bacini*) attached to the façades of churches in Pisa were analysed by Charles Fortnum.[25] More than a century earlier, another class of artefact – coinage – formed the subject of perhaps the earliest published 'archaeological' study devoted to an Islamic theme. Written by George Kehr and printed in Leipzig in 1724, the *Monarchiae asiatico-saracenicae status* was the first of what became a popular field of study in eighteenth and nineteenth-century Europe (one which has continued to the present day). A more general interest in Arabic epigraphy can be detected in the writings of Carsten Niebuhr, Josef von Hammer-Purgstall, and J. T. Reinard.[26]

The study of standing architecture and the decipherment of monumental inscriptions are often included under the general category of archaeology. Leaving aside the voluminous body of written descriptions and drawings of Islamic buildings left by European travellers to Muslim lands from the medieval to the early modern period, one can trace the emergence of a more systematic engagement with the forms and evolution of Islamic architecture in the late eighteenth century. The first publications were devoted to the monuments of Spain; studies of Islamic architecture in Sicily, North Africa, and Egypt appeared in the early nineteenth century. Further east, French scholars such as Charles Texier and Xavier Hommaire de Hell dealt with the Islamic architecture of Anatolia and Iran during their travels of the 1830s and 1840s. The most important early contribution to the study of monumental inscriptions was made by the Swiss scholar Max van Berchem in a series of publications from 1886 onwards. While much of this story revolves around the work of Europeans, it should be emphasised that Muslim scholars in the Islamic world were not indifferent to their architectural heritage; a striking example is the meticulous examination of the buildings of Delhi written in Urdu by Sir Sayyid Ahmad Khan and first published in 1847 (fifteen years before the establishment of the Archaeological Survey of India by the British). In addition, the Ottoman authorities sponsored a Turkish–French–German book on Ottoman architecture published in Istanbul in 1873.[27]

Some significant issues can be highlighted from this review of scholarly activities before 1900. First, this broadly defined area of archaeological study was, with some important exceptions, the domain of European scholars. Predictably, the early evolution of archaeology in North Africa, the Middle East and Central Asia was tied up with the expansion of European economic and political interests in the Islamic world. Thus the multi-volume *Description de l'Egypte* (1809–28) owes its existence to Napoleon's expedition to Egypt. The long-standing French engagement with Islamic North Africa can be traced from the invasion of Algeria in 1830 and from the declaration of Tunisia as a protectorate in 1881. Russian colonial expansion into Central Asia (1863–74) was soon followed by the dispatch of scientific expeditions into the newly captured territories. The establishment of archaeological societies, although not directly controlled by governments, often followed in the wake of territorial gains, as is the case of the Egypt Exploration Fund, established after the British occupation in 1882. Others – such as La Délégation Scientifique Française en Perse (1897) and the Deutsche Orient-Gesellschaft (1898) – are examples of archaeology's dependence upon alliances between European and Muslim states (in these cases, between France and Qajar Iran and between Germany and the Ottoman Empire respectively). The visit of Kaiser Wilhelm II to the Ottoman sultan 'Abdul Hamid II even resulted in the transportation of the decorated façade of the eighth-century palace of Mshatta to Berlin in 1903. Another important dimension of the archaeological societies was their promotion of ancient history, which was privileged over the recovery of more recent – particularly Byzantine, Sasanian, and Islamic – occupation phases. For instance, it was an interest in the material culture of the biblical past that stimulated the foundation of the Palestine Exploration Fund, the American Palestine Exploration Society, and the Deutsche Palästina-Vereins. At an institutional level, notable exceptions to this pattern can be seen in the establishment of the Committee for the Conservation of Monuments of Arab Art (1881) and of the Museum of Arab Art (1884) in Cairo.[28]

The dominant focus upon the ancient cultures of the Middle East has important implications for the approaches adopted to Islamic buildings and artefacts recovered from excavations. When these later phases were recorded at all in published reports, the scant comments usually reflected an implicit view that the 'Arab' period represented a phase of decline by comparison with the glories of the more remote past. In the rush to access the more ancient levels, the phases of Islamic occupation were often removed without making proper records. Sadly, this practice remained common through much of the twentieth century, and even persists on a few current excavation projects. A secondary ethnographic theme emerges in the discussions of the material culture of the contemporary (that is, nineteenth-century) Islamic world, particularly of rural areas. From the volumes of the *Description de l'Egypte* and on well into the twentieth century, many European scholars were struck by the apparent continuity in craft practices between the ancient world and the occupants of the modern villages around excavated sites.[29] Collapsing huge time periods (without accounting for lacunae of centuries, or even millennia) and denying the dynamic nature of localised manufacturing practices, comments from such scholars, frequently encountered as they are, create a picture of intellectual and technological stagnation. There were, however, European ethnographers and native observers of the late nineteenth and early twentieth century who sought to record actual craft activities of towns and cities of the Islamic world as well as to note the adaptations that occurred as traditional practices faced competition from industrially produced European commodities.[30]

The crafts – textiles, metalwork, glass, glazed ceramics, rock crystal, and ivory – of the Islamic world have long been prized in Europe. Objects made their way to Europe throughout the medieval period by means of trade or diplomacy, as booty, and among the personal possessions of travellers and pilgrims. The growth in the trade of classical antiquities in the late seventeenth and eighteenth centuries stimulated the activities of dealers in the eastern Mediterranean, and by the second half of the nineteenth century some dealers and patrons (both private and institutional) were concentrating their attention on purchasing Islamic artefacts. The European and North American market for the Ottoman glazed wares of Iznik is well documented, many objects being bought from houses on the Greek islands and in Damascus.[31] The emerging interest in Islamic visual culture in the second half of the nineteenth century and the concomitant growth in the trade of artefacts are certainly reflected in the collections of museums in Europe, North America, and Egypt. While this process clearly had beneficial effects, namely an increasing public awareness of the artistic achievements of the Islamic world, its impact on Islamic archaeology was more mixed. Crucially, the trade in Islamic 'antiquities' encouraged illicit digging of sites to feed the demands of connoisseurs and museums. As a result, the recovered items were separated from their archaeological context; frequently even their provenance remains doubtful. Furthermore, the arbitrary privileging of some classes of Islamic artefacts as *objets d'art* led many archaeologists, at least in the first half of the twentieth century, to devote their energies to urban sites (where the richest finds would be located) and to the publication of only the most decorative items.

Although the excavations and related studies conducted in the first half of the twentieth century must be seen in the light of the difficulties noted above, there were notable achievements that were to have a fundamental impact on the subsequent evolution of Islamic archaeology, and their influence was also felt in the fields of art history and, to a lesser extent, Islamic history. Reviewing the publications from the first two decades of the twentieth century, one is struck by the geographical range as well as by the diversity of the sites. As already noted, some of the earliest excavation projects were located in Spain and Algeria. While much of the concentration was on architecture, pottery and other portable artefacts were also published in the final report of the excavations of the Spanish palace of Madinat al-Zahra'. The ceramics found at the Qal'a of the Bani Hammad were treated in a separate monograph by Georges Marçais in 1913. A year later Alfred Bel published the study of a ceramic workshop discovered at Tlemcen in Morocco, while Marçais contributed further to the understanding of Islamic pottery through his publication of material from Bougie and of the glazed lustre tiles from the congregational mosque of Qayrawan.[32] That pottery had been manufactured on a large scale at Fustat was recognised in the late nineteenth century, but it was not until the 1910s that formal excavations were conducted on the site by 'Ali Bahgat. The first publication of ceramic kilns appeared in 1914 and was followed by a book coauthored with Félix Massoul in 1930. The extensive excavations of the site also resulted in the recovery of many other types of artefact, including fragile materials such as paper, papyrus, leather, and textiles. Equally significant was the publication in 1921 of a number of sophisticated multi-storey domestic structures, together with evidence of major hydraulic engineering.[33]

Greater Syria was the focus of considerable archaeological activity in this phase. In Palestine excavations of multi-period sites led to the recovery of Islamic material, and small assemblages of pottery were published from sites such as Ti'innik, Tal al-Mutasallim, Tal al-Sultan, and Jerusalem. More influential, however, were the excavations occurring further north, particularly at Ba'albak (published by Friedrich Sarre in 1925) and Raqqa.[34] Although the Ottoman excavations were not published, the architecture and portable artefacts of early Islamic Raqqa were brought to wider scholarly attention through their inclusion in Sarre and Ernst Herzfeld's four-volume *Archäologische Reise im Euphrat und Tigris Gebiet* (1911–20). Glazed ceramics from Raqqa were highly sought after in Europe and North America, and a number of articles addressed themselves to matters of style, typology, and provenance. It was not until the commencement of controlled excavations by Syrian, German and British teams from the 1950s onwards, however, that it became possible to recover the evolution of the urban environment and of industrial activity in Raqqa. Friedrich Sarre was also involved in the excavations of Miletus in Turkey, the results of which were published in the 1930s. His focus on the glazed pottery and on evidence of ceramic production anticipates the detailed examination of the Ottoman period kilns of Iznik later in the century. In Iran, the Islamic ceramics from the excavations of Susa were published by Raymond Koechlin.[35]

Archaeological reconnaissance in Greater Syria was also making advances in the study of early Islamic architecture, most importantly in the discovery of the 'desert castles' (usually known now as the *qusur*) of the steppe lands in the east of Jordan and Syria by scholars such as Alois Musil, Antonin Jaussen, and Raphael Savignac.[36] Further east, Oskar Reuther produced the first study of the monumental late eighth-century palace of Ukhaidir in 1908, while in the 1920s and 1930s André Godard and others investigated the Saljuq and early Islamic architecture of Iran.[37] Sarre and Herzfeld's journey through Mesopotamia in 1906–8 convinced them to undertake what was to become the most significant excavation of the early twentieth century in the Abbasid city of Samarra. The huge ruined city on the Tigris river had been known to European scholarship since the mid-nineteenth century. Limited surveys and excavations had already been made by Léon de Beylié and Henri Viollet, but Sarre and Herzfeld's project succeeded in bringing to wider attention the gargantuan palaces and mosques, the modes of decoration (particularly the carved and moulded stucco), and the diversity of the material culture. The results of the excavations were published in six volumes between 1923 and 1948: four by Herzfeld and one each by Sarre (ceramics) and Carl Lamm (glass).[38]

The influence exerted by the excavations at Samarra on the study of early Islamic art and architecture can hardly be overstated, but Sarre and Herzfeld's work also posed considerable problems for subsequent scholarship. Perhaps most significant was Herzfeld's failure to publish a full analysis of the architecture and stratigraphy recovered from the excavation. This meant that it was impossible to discern the structural history of crucial buildings like the Dar al-Khilafa. The analysis also limited the potential to integrate the stratigraphy with the excavated finds. In the study of portable arts – particularly glazed ceramics and glass – the erroneous assumption that the finds recovered from Samarra belonged solely to the period between the foundation of the city in 836 and its abandonment by the caliphs in 892 (the so-called 'Samarra horizon') led to inaccuracies in the chronological parameters established for many classes of artefact. More recent archaeological work conducted in Iraq has established that many 'Samarran' ceramic wares were circulating prior to 836.[39] Tardy publication and failure to correlate the stratigraphic data with excavated artefacts have also compromised the results of major projects undertaken in the 1930s. In Iran, Erich Schmidt's excavations in Rayy were only published in some short preliminary reports. The Metropolitan Museum of Art project at Nishapur resulted in a series of books on architecture and portable artefacts, published between 1973 and 1995. These books represent significant contributions to the understanding of Islamic urban culture in Khurasan (chapter 5), but the emphasis on uncovering large tracts of the city at the expense of the careful examination of the occupational history inevitably reduces the accuracy of the dating, both of the architecture and of the excavated finds.[40]

Similar problems are apparent in the Danish excavation of the multi-period citadel at Hama. Although stratigraphic records were kept, the publication of the excavated artefacts several decades prior to the final report on the Islamic architecture of the site makes it difficult to establish accurate chronologies for the ceramics, glass, and metalwork.[41] In common with Nishapur, the final publications have tended to emphasise the complete and decorated artefacts, with no statistical analysis of the totality of the excavated finds. Despite their evident limitations, the publications from Hama, like those of Antioch to the north, provide valuable insights into the diversity of material culture in the cities of Greater Syria, particularly in the period from the eleventh to the end of the fourteenth century. Islamic material also appeared in the publication of other multi-period sites in Greater Syria, but more important than these was the renewed focus on the archaeology of the Umayyad *qusur*. The excavations of Khirbat al-Mafjar by Robert Hamilton and of Qasr al-Hayr West by Daniel Schlumberger were crucial to the study of this phase in Islamic palatial architecture.[42] Important later excavations of Umayyad sites in Greater Syria include those of Qasr al-Hayr East and of the citadel of 'Amman. This focus on the architecture of the earliest phases of Islamic history can also be seen in the Iraqi excavations of the *dar al-imara* at Kufa and of the congregational mosque of Wasit (chapter 3).[43] Crusader military architecture and material culture were investigated on sites such as Pilgrim's Castle ('Athlit) on the Palestine coast and Port St Simeon (Mina) near Antioch. While the development of crusader archaeology is beyond the scope of the present book, it is worth noting that these and other sites provided the means to begin an examination of the changes which occurred in material culture as a site was shifting from Frankish occupation to being used by indigenous populations.[44]

The volume of archaeological projects greatly increased in the post-war period. This upsurge in activity was paralleled by a growth in the range of archaeological techniques applied to the phases of Islamic occupation and by an expansion of the geographical coverage of the projects. Published excavations now encompass all regions of the Islamic world, from Indonesia to the Iberian peninsula. The archaeology of sub-Sahara and East Africa has experienced considerable growth since the 1960s, the excavation of sites such as Kilwa, Manda, and Shanga contributing greatly to the understanding of the processes of Islamisation and of Indian Ocean trade.[45] International trade has also been studied in the distribution of Islamic artefacts beyond the borders of the Islamic world, ranging from tombs in China to coin hoards in Scandinavia and to glazed ceramics excavated at medieval ports in Europe (chapters 3 and 8). Another significant change has been the shift from the concentration upon sites associated with the political and economic elites to the examination of the lives of the less affluent, both in towns and in villages. The archaeology of the countryside is also being approached through the use of regional surveys. As the rest of the book is largely concerned with excavations and other projects published since 1945, it is unnecessary to present a chronological evaluation of the major achievements of these decades. Instead, the following paragraphs assess the principal trends in archaeological scholarship during this time.

In common with many other branches of archaeology, regional survey has become an important tool in the interpretation of the Islamic past. Representing a cost-effective means to evaluate the patterns of human occupation and land exploitation over extended periods of time, surveys may be designed to address specific research questions or to complement excavations. Surveys may combine remote analytical strategies (such as the analysis of aerial or satellite photography) with field walking in order to record architectural or engineering features and to pick up artefacts. The results are, of course, contingent upon the techniques employed, upon the intensity of the field walking and of collecting artefacts, and upon the availability of independent chronologies for the recovered artefact types (most commonly ceramics). While it is certainly important to acknowledge the methodological difficulties inherent in the interpretation of survey data (chapter 4), the undoubted value of surveys is the insight they give into the longer-term dynamics of settlement and agricultural practices. These longer-term patterns are often invisible in the primary written sources of the pre-modern Islamic world. Perhaps the most influential archaeological survey was that conducted by Robert Adams in the Diyala plain in southern Iraq in the 1960s.[46]

Countries that have undergone extensive survey work include Spain, Tunisia, Israel, Jordan, Syria, and Iran, while in recent years the Ottoman phase in Greece has been productively approached in this manner (chapter 9). Some general comments can be made concerning the interpretation of data from these surveys. Political or cultural biases in the host country – particularly the tendency to privilege the study of specific phases of national history – and the personal research interests (or prejudices) of the project director are clearly factors that affect the recording of data as well as the shape of the final published reports. These factors can have serious consequences for the study of the Islamic centuries, as the material dating after the seventh century may be ignored or only partially published. Within the Islamic period itself, the later centuries (especially after c.1500) have received least attention, though this is changing with the growth of 'Ottoman archaeology'.[47] The question of dating is also highly significant, as precise chronological indicators (monumental inscriptions or coins) are rarely encountered, while rural domestic architecture tends to be conservative in nature and hydraulic technology often remains in use for centuries. In this context, ceramics take on a vital importance in the process of interpretation.

Although the study of standing buildings may be seen more obviously as the domain of architectural history, several monuments in the Islamic world have benefited from an archaeological approach concentrating upon establishing the phases of construction. Such approaches are particularly valuable in the analysis of long established mosques and of castles or other forms of military architecture. An early example of this approach is Robert Hamilton's study of the Aqsa mosque in Jerusalem. Similar techniques have been applied to other ancient mosques (chapter 6). The detailed analysis of standing walls allows for the reconstruction of complex sequences of construction, destruction, and renovation, which are often encountered in Islamic and crusader military architecture. These techniques may also be combined with excavation, the reading of monumental inscriptions, and the examination of the contemporary historical record. Examples of this integrated methodology are the projects at Qasr al-Hallabat and Shawbak (crusader Montréal) in Jordan, and the Shayzar castle and the Damascus citadel in Syria.[48] The spatial distribution of standing and fragmentary monuments is another aspect of archaeological interpretation. This area of study has focused on the placement of buildings within the landscape (frequently assessing the proximity to water sources), on relationships to major trade or pilgrimage routes, and even on considerations of land ownership or of relationships between elites and the bedouin (chapters 2 and 8).

Middle Eastern archaeology was relatively slow to recognise the importance of recording occupation phases dating to the Islamic period; it privileged instead more ancient periods of human history. Within the study of the Islamic centuries, the same process can be detected: the most recent centuries (namely the ones after c.1500) are often neglected. This situation has been changing in recent years, particularly in regions formerly encompassed by the Ottoman Empire (late thirteenth century to 1924), and the phrase 'Ottoman archaeology' is now commonly employed for the study of this period (chapter 9). This development can be fitted into the wider trend of what is known as 'historical archaeology'.[49] Although the latter phrase can simply refer to research that seeks to integrate material culture and contemporary textual sources, its more common usage relates to the archaeology of various regions in the centuries after the European discovery of the Americas in 1492. The rationale behind using this date as a watershed is that it marks the beginning of a new phase of European colonial expansion and the establishment of international trading systems. Archaeology is also able to examine the impact upon traditional societies of advances in military technology and of competition with mass-produced European and North American commodities. These questions have been addressed in projects for regions as diverse as Morocco, the Persian Gulf, Greater Syria, Turkey, and the Red Sea. Particularly noticeable is the nuanced picture provided by archaeology, a picture which shows the persistence of native industries and localised trading networks in the face of pressure from European polities.

Like other branches of archaeology, Islamic archaeology has also become increasingly sophisticated in its collection and analysis of material culture. In contrast to the focus on complete and decorated artefacts which is apparent in excavations undertaken during the early twentieth century, modern projects are likely to formulate procedures that allow for the recovery of man-made artefacts (organic and inorganic), plant materials (such as carbonised seeds), and animal bones. Soil cores may be taken in order to examine such issues as the pollen composition or heavy metal contamination in different phases of a site, while geophysical surveys allow for the non-destructive analysis of underground structures. Naturally, this expanded range of collected data also means that modern archaeological projects are collaborative in nature, bringing in specialists from a wide variety of disciplines. This expansion of post-excavation techniques has greatly enhanced the ability of archaeology to offer interpretations of past human activity, as well as allowing for the study of an individual site to be placed into a wider environmental context. Archaeobotany and zooarchaeology have made important contributions to the study of diet and nutrition and to practices of cultivation and animal husbandry in the Islamic period (and they also established points of continuity with earlier phases). Past environments – including processes of desertification or the use of irrigation technology – can be studied through changes in weed species, particularly those reflected in pollen samples. Man-made artefacts can also be subjected to a wide range of scientific analyses designed to establish their age (for instance the carbon-14 dating of textiles), their provenance, and the methods of their manufacture. The study of ceramics, a key component of archaeological research, has been revolutionised by the employment of petrographic and neutron activation analysis. Other analytical techniques allow for the study of glazes and glass (chapter 7).[50]

Lastly, it is a sign of the increasing maturity of Islamic archaeology – and of archaeological research over all periods within Islamic regions – that scholars are investigating from a historical viewpoint the excavations conducted during the nineteenth and twentieth centuries. Importantly, these historiographic studies bring into clearer focus the ideological foundations of archaeological work and the intersections between archaeology and European and North American colonialism. Also significant in this context is the use of archaeology and of ancient sites in the formation of national identity.[51] A self-critical awareness of the history of archaeology is valuable to all the aspects of the framing of projects, from the formation of larger research goals to the minutiae of collection procedures and the presentation of published results. While it is reasonable to assert that the archaeology of Islamic regions has been dominated by European, Soviet/Russian, and North American scholars, it is important to recognise the numerous significant contributions made by indigenous scholars to the study of Islamic archaeology (particularly after 1945) in countries such as Iran, Iraq, Jordan, Syria, and Turkey.

Notes

1 Hamdani (1931), 199. Slightly adapted from the translation of Nabih Faris in Hamdani (1938), 107.
2 Ibn al-Kalbi (1969).
3 The visit to Persepolis is discussed in Rogers (1974), 16–18.
4 Shu'ayb wisely chose to abscond with the money he had collected before the arrival of the authorities. Predictably, the shrine was found to be a fabrication. See Maqrizi (1934–72), 2.2: 249–50. This episode is discussed in Shoshan (1993), 9.
5 For instance, see sources discussed in Hodder (1989).
6 For an appreciation of al-Maqrizi's *Khitat*, see Rabbat (2000).
7 On the dating of this event, see Tsafrir and Foerster (1992). A vivid demonstration of the impact of the earthquake is provided by the excavations of Pella in Jordan. See McNicoll et al. (1992), 1: 123–41, 2: pls 46, 47, 56.
8 Smith (1992), 26–7.
9 For the application of these ideas in archaeology, see Sherratt (1992).
10 For instance Johns (1995a); Insoll (1999); Milwright (2008a). For the related concept of 'resilience theory', see Redman and Kinzig (2003); Walmsley (2007), 146–7.
11 The problems encountered in the synthesis of archaeological evidence are well demonstrated in the essays by Michael Morony and Donald Whitcomb in Bierman, ed. (1995).
12 For instance the final reports on excavations in Qasr-i Abu Nasr (Old Shiraz), Hama, Samarra. See Whitcomb (1985), Pentz (1997); Leisten (2003). For selected material from excavations at Rayy, see Treptow (2007).
13 Ugo Monneret de Villard was perhaps the first author to write a book devoted to the topic of Islamic archaeology (of the Umayyad period), though his attention is largely focused on architecture. See Monneret de Villard (1966). More recent surveys of archaeological data from the late antique and Islamic periods in different regions include: Hodges and Whitehouse (1983); contributions by Donald Whitcomb, Alan Walmsley and Alison McQuitty in MacDonald, Adams and Bienkowski, eds (2001); Kennet (2005); Rosen-Ayalon (2006); Walmsley (2007). For an introduction to the geographical range of archaeological projects currently being conducted in the Islamic world, see also the 'Focus on Islam' series in *Antiquity* 79, 2005.
14 For recent trends in archaeological theory, see Hodder et al., eds (1995); Bahn and Renfrew (2000), 461–96.
15 Insoll (1999) and (2004); Insoll, ed. (2001). For different perspectives on this issue, see the introduction and contributions in Whitcomb, ed. (2004).
16 Insoll (1999), 9.
17 Rice (1958); Ward (2004).
18 The long accepted attribution of this vessel to Rukn al-Dawla Abu Sulayman Dawud (r. 1114–42) is not supported by the revised reading of the Arabic inscription in Redford (1990), 119–24.
19 Kafadar (2007).
20 For instance, on the difficulties of establishing confessional allegiance in rural areas of Norman Sicily, see Johns (1995b).
21 Introductions to the history of Islamic art and architecture include: Ettinghausen, Grabar and Jenkins-Madina (2001); Blair and Bloom (1994); Hillenbrand (1994).

22 Bliss and Macalister (1902). For the Islamic pottery from the site, see their pl. 65.
23 The historiography of Islamic archaeology has been discussed (with extensive bibliographies) in Rogers (1974) and Vernoit (1997). On early developments in Islamic art, see also contributions in Vernoit, ed. (2000). On the Ottoman excavations at Raqqa, see now Jenkins-Madina (2006), 22–6, 192–3.
24 On the early study of these sites, see: Vitelli (1981), 5–6, 17–20; Canby (2000), 128–31; Johns (1998), 74 n. 41; Milwright (2001a), 20.
25 The works of these and other early European scholars of Islamic ceramics are collected in Tonghini and Grube (1989); Atasoy and Raby (1994), 71–4; Milwright (2001a).
26 On this early phase in the study of Islamic visual culture, see Bloom (1996).
27 Rogers (1974), 37–46; Hillenbrand (1986); Vernoit (1997), 1–2. On the *Usul-i Mi'mari-i Osmani / L'architecture ottomane / Die Ottomanische Baukunst* and the early study of Islamic architecture, see Bozdogan and Neçipoglu (2007), 3, n. 15. For an abridged translation of Khan's *Asar al-sanadid*, see Khan (1979). I owe my knowledge of this text to Fatima Qureishi.
28 Rogers (1974), 46–58; Vernoit (1997), 2–4; Erzini (2000). See also Silberman (1982).
29 For instance, Vivant Denon remarks of the water jars he had seen in use in Egypt, 'de temps immémorial elle est d'un usage général dans toute l'Egypte pour clarifier et rafraîchir l'eau du Nil. J'ai vu les mêmes vases dans les peintures antiques, employés au mêmes usages.' Denon (1802), 2: xxviii (text accompanying pl. 94, nos. 1–7, in vol. 2). For a later treatment of this idea, see Crowfoot (1932).
30 For instance Gatt (1885); Einsler (1914); Qasimi, Qasimi and al-Azem (1960). Other ethnographic studies are discussed in chapters 7 and 9.
31 Atasoy and Raby (1994), 71–4.
32. Marçais (1928). For a bibliographic survey of other studies of North African ceramics, see Vitelli and Pringle (1978). See also the bibliography in Benco (1987).
33 Bahgat and Massoul (1930). The bibliography for the domestic architecture at Fustat is presented in Scanlon (1970) and in Kubiak and Scanlon (1973).
34 Publications are reviewed in Tonghini and Grube (1989); Milwright (2001a).
35 Wulzinger, Wittek and Sarre (1935); Koechlin (1928). On the excavation of the kilns of Iznik, see Aslanapa, Yetkin and Altun (1989); Atasoy and Raby (1994), 50–64.
36 On the early study of the *qusur*, see Urice (1987), 6–23 and Fowden (2004), 1–30. Comprehensive bibliographies can be found in the footnotes for individual sites in Creswell (1969). See also Creswell and Allan (1989).
37 Hillenbrand (1986). On the archaeology of Islamic Central Asia, see Pugachenkova and Rtveladze (1986).
38 Herzfeld (1923–48); Sarre (1925); Lamm (1928). For a bibliography of archaeological scholarship on Samarra, see Northedge (2005b).
39 On these issues, see: Northedge and Kennet (1994); Northedge (1996) and (2005a), (2005b).
40 Treptow (2007), 13–18; Wilkinson (1973 and 1986); Allan (1982); Kröger (1995).
41. Riis, Poulsen and Hammershaimb (1957); Pentz (1997).
42 Schlumberger (1939); Hamilton (1949).
43 Creswell (1969), 1.1: 48–58 (Kufa: citing the excavations conducted by Muhammad 'Ali Mustafa), 132–8 (Wasit: citing the excavations of Fuad Safar); Safar (1945); Creswell and Allan (1989), 10–15, 40–1.

44 Johns (1935). For surveys of crusader archaeology, see Benvenisti (1970) and Boas (1999). On the early history of this field of archaeological study, see Ellenblum (2007), 32–9.
45 Chittick (1974 and 1984); Horton (1996). For a wide-ranging survey of Islamic archaeology in sub-Saharan Africa, see Insoll (2003).
46 Adams (1965 and 1981).
47 Baram and Carroll, eds (2000), 1–35. Also Silberman (1989), 228–43.
48 Faucherre (2004); contributions in Kennedy, ed. (2006).
49 For different perspectives on historical archaeology, see contributions in: Small, ed. (1995); Funari, Hall and Jones, eds (1999). For specific projects, see Orser, ed. (2002).
50 For different analytical techniques applied to inorganic objects, see Henderson (2000).
51 Silberman (1989); Vernoit (1997); Bozdogan and Neçipoglu (2007); Kohl, Kozelsky and Ben-Yehuda, eds (2007).

Early Islam and late antiquity

There can be no doubt as to the momentous nature of the Arab conquests of the seventh and early eighth centuries. A vast territory stretching from Central Asia in the east to the Iberian peninsula in the west came under the dominion of the Rashidun and Umayyad caliphs. The Arabian peninsula was largely under the control of the Prophet Muhammad before his death in 632, and virtually all of the Byzantine territories of Greater Syria and Egypt were captured by the early 640s. Arab armies went on to besiege the capital of Constantinople for the first time between 674 and 680. The battle of Qadisiyya (635 or 637) marked the beginning of the campaigns against the Sasanian state; by 651 the last shah, Yazdigerd III, was dead and his empire was consigned to history. The conquests continued west into North Africa, with a Muslim expeditionary force led by 'Uqba ibn Nafi' which reached the Atlantic Ocean in 680 and with the fall of the key port of Carthage to the Arabs in 697. In 711 an army of Arabs and Berbers crossed the straits of Gibraltar and, later that year, inflicted a decisive defeat over the forces of the Visigothic king, Roderick. To the east the expansion continued into Central Asia, the city of Samarqand coming under Arab control after 710. Not all the campaigns were fought for the acquisition of new land, however; this crucial period of Islamic history was also marked by civil wars (*fitna*) in 656–61 and 683–92.

The arrival of the new religion of Islam and the formation of an Arab Muslim political elite brought changes to the physical environment of these conquered territories. New settlements (*misr*, pl. *amsar*) were constructed to house the Arab garrisons. Early examples include those of Basra and Kufa in Iraq (c.635 and 638 respectively), Fustat in Egypt (641–2), and Qayrawan in Tunisia (670).[1] Each *misr* was furnished with a congregational mosque for the Muslim community. This concept of designating a space for communal prayer can be traced back to the arrival of the Prophet Muhammad and his followers in Medina after the migration (*hijra*) from Mecca in 622. Whether this praying place (*musalla*) in Medina also functioned as the dwelling place of the Prophet and his family has recently been questioned, though it is reasonable to assume that the idea of orienting the Muslim faithful to the *qibla* (first towards Jerusalem, and then in 624 towards the Ka'ba in Mecca) was fixed upon during the lifetime of the Prophet. Rudimentary mosques were founded in the *amsar* during the 630s and 640s.[2] Through the remainder of the seventh century, many of the key components making up what is known as the hypostyle mosque – a rectangular walled compound comprising a central courtyard, which is surrounded by arcades and a covered area in front of the wall facing the *qibla* – were established. The other significant architectural innovation found in the *amsar* is the governor's residence, or *dar al-imara*.

The evolution of these two building types will be discussed in greater detail in the following chapter, but the key point to make at this stage is that our knowledge of the earliest decades comes almost exclusively from written sources. As excavations are not permitted in the 'holy cities' of Mecca and Medina, there is no prospect of recovering physical evidence of the seventh-century architectural fabric and material culture of these cradles of early Islam. The Dome of the Rock, constructed by caliph 'Abd al-Malik (r. 685–705) in Jerusalem, marks a decisive turning point in the study of Islamic art and architecture. Not only does the Dome of the Rock retain its seventh-century plan and elevation; its interior also preserves substantial amounts of the original decorative programme. This building and the other structures on and in the immediate vicinity of the Temple Mount (Haram al-Sharif) certainly signal the new sense of artistic ambition among the Umayyad political elite. A massive construction project of this nature required the existence of a sophisticated bureaucracy for the provision of skilled labour and materials to the site. The lavish mosaic decoration of the Dome of the Rock is notable for the presence of Arabic inscriptions in gold on a blue ground running some 240 metres around the interior. These inscriptions represent the largest corpus of extant Qur'anic verses from the seventh century, and they also contain the date of 691–2/72. This is usually assumed to be the year of the completion of the building, though it may be a foundational date.[3]

What, then, can archaeology tell us about the Muslim community in the formative period between 622 and the 690s? Apart from its intrinsic interest for the study of Islamic art history and archaeology, this question takes on an additional importance when seen in the context of the historiography of early Islam. One of the central problems confronting scholars of this period is that, apart from the *Qur'an* itself, there are no contemporary Muslim accounts of events in Arabia during the lifetime of the Prophet and of the subsequent expansion of the Islamic state under the Rashidun and early Umayyad caliphs. The earliest extant chronicles, biographies, and collections of the sayings of the Prophet and his companions (*hadith*) date from the eighth century and later, and modern historians have to remain ever mindful of the tendency of written sources to recast both past events and the attitudes expressed by seventh-century figures to suit the expectations of later Muslim audiences. Attempts to fill this gap in our understanding of early Islam with contemporary historical accounts written by non-Muslim authors have met with limited success.[4] Thus the recovered objects and buildings from this phase possess the potential to act as an independent source of evidence for reconstructing aspects of the first stages in the growth of the Islamic state.

According to Muslim tradition, the first canonical recension of the *Qur'an* was compiled during the caliphate of 'Uthman (r. 644–56). While no 'Uthmanic manuscripts are known to survive, there exist several parchment folios from *Qur'ans* that have been dated to the mid-seventh century on the basis of the style of Arabic script (a precursor of Kufic known as Hijazi).[5] Some rock-cut inscriptions in Arabia have been assigned to the seventh century on palaeographic grounds, but there are others which carry either dates or identifiable names. Probably the earliest is a *graffito* located at Qa' al-Mu'tadil, near al-Hijr in Saudi Arabia, which refers to 'the death of 'Umar'. Given the lack of any further elaboration around this name, it is safe to assume that it probably refers to the second caliph, 'Umar b. al-Khattab, who died on the last day of 23 AH (643 CE) and was buried on the first day of 24AH. Mu'awiya is the next caliph to appear on an Arabic inscription carved on a rock near Ta'if in Saudi Arabia recording the construction of a dam in 678/58. His name is also included on a Greek text in a mosaic pavement from a bath at Hammat Gader in Israel (662–3/42), as well as on coins and papyri (see below). Significantly, the references to Mu'awiya – whether in Arabic, Greek, or Persian – are accompanied by the phrase that was to become the standard honorific of all later caliphs, *amir al-mu'minin*, or 'Commander of the Faithful'.Other evidence for seventh-century Muslim religious practice can be seen in the invocations that appear on an Egyptian gravestone made for 'Abd al-Rahman ibn Khayr (February 652/ Jumada II, 31 AH). This begins with the phrase that opens each *sura* of the *Qur'an: bism allah al-rahman al-rahim* ('in the name of God, the Merciful, the Compassionate'), and later it asks for the forgiveness of Allah. The abbreviated form *bism allah* appears on silver coins (sing. *drachm/dirham*) imitating issues of the Sasanian shahs Khusraw II (r. 590–628) and Yazdigerd III (r. 632–51) minted from 651/31. 'Arab–Sasanian' *dirhams* minted in different regions of Iraq and Iran in the 660s and 670s contain additions to the simple *bism allah* of such words as *rabbi* ('my Lord') and *al-malik* ('the possessor [of everything]', see *Qur'an* 3: 26). While the existence of these variants may appear rather trivial, it is worth noting the very public character of coinage and the role such inscriptions have in the transmission of political and religious ideology. What is most remarkable about the coins and other inscribed artefacts of this period, however, is what they omit: neither the name of Muhammad nor his status as the Prophet (*rasul*) of Allah is mentioned. It is only in the phase from 685–6/66 to the minting of the first fully epigraphic Islamic coin in 696–7/77 that one encounters the complete profession of faith (*shahada*) asserting the oneness of God and the prophethood of Muhammad. From 691–2/72, a series of experimental coins include so-called 'orans' *dirham* and 'standing caliph' *dinar* (Fig. 2.1 a–c).[6]

Documents written on papyrus also illustrate the process of formalising the standard Muslim invocations and caliphal honorifics, as well as other aspects of the development of the Islamic state. The earliest complete papyrus is written in Greek and Arabic and records the receipt of sixty-five sheep from Christophoros and Theodorakios, sons of Apa Kyros, in the Egyptian settlement of Herakleopolis (Fig. 2.2). The beasts were slaughtered to feed the soldiers of the *amir* 'Abd Allah and, according to the note on the reverse, were regarded as a downpayment for the annual taxes. Written by two scribes, one in Greek and the other in Arabic, the document also carries dates according to the Byzantine indiction year (30th of the month of Pharmouti in the first indiction) and to the Muslim calendar (Jumada I, 22 AH = 642). The Arabic text opens with *bism allah al-rahman al-rahim*, while the Greek employs the shorter form 'God, in the name of God'. No mention is made of Muslims, but the Greek text employs the Genitive plural *sarakhenon* (σαρακηνῶν, Saracens) and the Dative plural *magaritais* (μαγαρίταις), the latter perhaps deriving from the Arabic, *muhajirun*, or 'those who undertook the *hijra*'. Although the event recorded on the papyrus is of little historical import, the format of the document is highly significant; the requirement for both Arabic and Greek and the reference to the Byzantine indiction system indicate the extent to which the Muslim authorities were reliant upon existing administrative practices in their newly conquered regions. Later papyri excavated from Nessana in the Negev date from the reigns of Mu'awiya and 'Abd al-Malik, while another cache of documents from an Egyptian village called Aphrodito continued through to the time of al-Walid I (r. 705–15). Recording the payment of taxes in the form of transfers of agricultural produce and provision of labour as well as of money, the papyri indicate the increasing sophistication in the bureaucracy of the Islamic state, particularly during the rule of 'Abd al-Malik. It is during his caliphate that Arabic was established as the sole language employed in official communications.[7]

Architecture provides very little evidence; prior to the construction of the Dome of the Rock we lack any buildings – either standing structures or those recovered through excavation – that carry inscriptions, and the dating is based on circumstantial historical evidence. Apart from the minimal traces of the mosque discovered in the Iraqi *misr* of Kufa, the only other candidate for a seventh-century dating is the Aqsa mosque in Jerusalem. Founded as early as 638, the present building may retain elements of a building programme instigated by Mu'awiya (chapter 6). The most famous example of secular architecture is the *dar al-imara* in Kufa (Fig. 2.3). Excavations in the 1930s revealed a large brick building surrounded by an *intervallum* and a fortified wall on the *qibla* side of the mosque. The *dar al-imara* itself was constructed in three main phases, the earliest of which may have been c.670, although the evidence is far from conclusive. The earliest positive dating of the Umayyad residences (in Arabic *qasr*, pl. *qusur*) in Bilad al-Sham (Greater Syria) consists of an inscription dated 700/81 naming 'amir al-Walid, son of the Commander of the Faithful' (that is, Caliph al-Walid I) at Qasr al-Burqu' and a *graffito* of 710/92 in Qasr al-Kharana; but recent research has provided plausible evidence for two palatial structures of the seventh century.[8] The first one is Khirbat al-Karak in northern Israel – one which may have been a palace, known in Arabic sources as Sinnabra or Sinnabris, employed by both Mu'awiya and 'Abd al-Malik. The second one is Bakhra', located to the south of the Syrian desert city of Palmyra. Having been a Roman *castrum* of the period of the Tetrarchate (293–305), the structure was remodelled into an Islamic *qasr* through the addition of a fortified annex (Fig. 2.4 a–b). This addition is probably the work of Nu'man b. Bashir, who died in 684.[9]

In summary, the extant objects, inscriptions, and buildings dating between 622 and 692 represent too small and too fragmentary a body of data on which to formulate an independent vision of the earliest phase of Islam. For all their interpretive problems, Arabic chronicles and related texts of the late eighth century onward still represent the best means for understanding this key phase in Islamic history (with the study of Arabic papyri becoming an increasingly important aspect of historical research). That said, the material record suggests some interesting lines of inquiry. Monumental inscriptions and those formulae placed on coins and papyri suggest that the Muslim community took some decades to agree upon the appropriate format of its principal religious invocations. While the standard phrase 'in the name of God, the Merciful, the Compassionate' already appears on an Egyptian papyrus of 642/22 and on a tombstone of 652/31, it took longer for this phrase to be adopted in its complete form on coinage. No specific mention of Islam, Muslims, or the Prophet Muhammad appears until coin the issues from 685–6/66. Experiments with the wording of the *shahada* occur repeatedly on Arab–Sasanian *dirhams* minted by the two competing factions during the second civil war – an intriguing example of the linkage of political and religious ideology that is so often a feature of art and architecture produced by later Islamic dynasties. Mu'awiya appears to be a key figure in the propagation of the title, 'Commander of the Faithful', and this correlates well with historical accounts to the effect that he sought to invest the position of caliph with attributes of imperial authority borrowed from Constantinople and Sasanian Iran. It is unclear from the papyri and coins the extent to which Mu'awiya moved the administrative framework of the nascent Muslim state from its reliance upon existing Byzantine and Sasanian practices. It is only during the reforms of 'Abd al-Malik in the 690s that one encounters conclusive evidence of the formation of a coherent Arabic bureaucracy.

Archaeology provides some important insights into this formative period of Islam, but it is worth placing this small group of portable artefacts, inscriptions, and buildings into a larger context. Most importantly, the extensive archaeological investigation of the seventh century in recent decades has recovered remarkably little evidence of the new Muslim community in the material record. This can be demonstrated by the ceramics (the most abundant category of portable artefact recovered in excavations and field surveys) in regions such as Jordan and Palestine. The seventh century was evidently a period of conservatism in this craft, exhibiting considerable continuity with the vessel forms and decorative practices of the previous century. None of the political upheavals of the initial Arab conquest and of its aftermath can be discerned in pottery production, and it is only in the eighth century that significant new forms evolve in the ceramic repertoire. The virtual absence of a 'Muslim' material culture is also attested in excavated contexts dating to the decades after the Arab conquests of North Africa, Spain, and Central Asia. It should be remembered that, even though they were the new political elite of an expanding empire, Muslims would have constituted a small minority of the population in each conquered region. The initial wave of conquests brought Christians, Jews, Zoroastrians, and the adherents of other religions under Islamic rule. Muslims did not become the largest confessional group in many parts of the Islamic world until the tenth century, if not later.[10] In this context it is hardly surprising that the material record of the seventh century exhibits so much evidence for continuity with the decades and centuries which precede the Islamic conquests. A comparison – albeit generated by very different political circumstances – could be made with the scarcity in the archaeological record of recognisably 'Christian' artefacts in the first two centuries of the Common Era.

Of interest in the present context is the period known in modern scholarship as late antiquity and usually defined as lasting from the third/fourth to the seventh century. In the next section some comments are made concerning the broad characteristics of late antiquity in the archaeological record of the Middle East and North Africa, with particular emphasis upon urban life and patterns of international trade. The important issues of crop cultivation and irrigation technologies are addressed in chapter 4. The last section of the present chapter is devoted to a discussion of the archaeology of the *qusur* of the Umayyad period. This case study considers the extent to which the construction and location of these buildings can be understood in the context of the resources, trade routes, and architectural practices of late antique Greater Syria.

The archaeology of late antiquity

Profound changes can be witnessed from the fourth century in the cities and towns of the Middle East and the Mediterranean basin. The classical city (*polis*, pl. *poleis*) of the Hellenistic and Roman periods was characterised by its civic institutions, its large public spaces (*fora*), and its colonnaded streets. Monumental buildings included temples, theatres, meeting halls, and public baths. Typically, the major thoroughfares were arranged perpendicular to one another, with the crossing of the *cardo* (north–south) and the *decumanus* (east–west) marked by a monumental structure known as a *tetrapylon*. The paved streets were usually wide enough to accommodate wheeled transport, and they incorporated shops facing onto porticoed walkways. Numerous classical cities are preserved in the Middle East and North Africa of which Jarash (Gerasa), Bet Shean/Baysan (Scythopolis), Palmyra (Fig. 2.5), Busra, Apamea, Lepcis Magna, and Carthage are impressive examples. The contrast with the narrow winding streets, courtyard houses, and maze-like markets of the traditional 'Islamic city' is clear enough, and it raises two questions that have preoccupied archaeologists, historians, and geographers: first, when did this evolution of the urban environment occur; and, second, what do these physical changes tell us about the social, political, and economic organisation of towns and cities in the late antique and early Islamic periods?

Searching for remnants of classical urban planning within the existing urban fabric of Syria, Jean Sauvaget was one of the first scholars to recognise the archaeological evidence for this process of transformation. In a famous diagram he showed how the colonnaded streets of Latakia and other Syrian towns and cities were gradually encroached upon by private commercial and domestic architecture. A thoroughfare that had been wide and straight became narrow and crooked, only passable by pedestrians and pack animals (Fig. 2.6).[11] Sauvaget assumed that the breakdown of the classical street plan occurred after the Arab conquests of the seventh century, but there is now general agreement that these changes were already under way by the fourth century. Although the precise chronology varies with each urban centre and aspects of 'classical' urban planning were imposed on urban centres such as Jerusalem as late as in the sixth century (see also the eighth-century foundation at 'Anjar, chapter 5), certain general points can be made about the fate of public architecture on the basis of historical studies and excavations.[12] Temples and theatres were no longer constructed, and those that remained fell into neglect, sometimes being reused for industrial purposes (chapter 7). While the bathhouse continued to be a feature of the late antique urban landscape, it tended to be smaller than in earlier centuries. At the same time, there was a massive expansion in church building, even modest settlements boasting several places of worship (chapter 6). Lastly, the cities of late antiquity increasingly incorporated an encircling defensive wall with fortified gates; within the Roman empire, at least, this had only been a feature of frontier settlements.[13]

These significant changes to the physical layout of the cities of the Middle East and North Africa were evidently shaped by numerous socio-cultural and economic factors. Most obvious in the regions of the Byzantine Empire was the increasing dominance of the church in the lives of city dwellers. This was manifested not merely in the erection of places of worship, but also in the closing of pagan temples and the eradication of theatrical performance as a form of public entertainment. The failure to protect public spaces from encroachment by private building can be attributed partly to the inability of the civic officials to exercise their authority, although the disappearance of the wide colonnaded streets and spacious fora probably also reflects the fact that city dwellers no longer prized these amenities. The centres of late antique cities were more focused upon mercantile activities than their classical forerunners, and this new emphasis upon trade and manufacturing placed increased pressure upon existing public spaces. The abandonment of wheeled transport in favour of pack animals was a phenomenon that affected an area stretching from the Atlantic coast of Africa to Central Asia from as early as the second century. Its relevance in the present context is that the winding, narrow streets of many late antique cities represented a genuine impediment to the passage of an ox cart, but could be negotiated easily by a laden camel or mule.[14] In other words, there is no reason to assume that the loss of the wide, colonnaded streets is a physical manifestation of economic stagnation. Rather, this was a dynamic environment in which new religious and economic values were reshaping urban spaces and institutions.

Moving to somewhat smaller settlements, one encounters evidence of considerable regional diversity. One type of small urban unit has been identified in marginal agricultural regions such as the Negev in southern Israel, the basalt desert (Hawran) of northern Jordan and south-east Syria, and the limestone massif of north-west Syria. The first area is well illustrated by Shivta, a town that prospered between the fifth and the eighth or ninth century. Notable is the absence of the orthogonal planning, the street plan being largely dictated by the organic development of domestic architecture. Shivta contained a small central public space, and the most monumental structures are the churches. Similar features can be identified in the Byzantine town of Umm al-Jimal in northern Jordan, although this settlement also incorporated a defensive wall, a *praetorium*, and a *castellum* (Fig. 2.7). The urban plan of the Jordanian town is characterised by clusters of courtyard buildings (perhaps reflecting tribal or clan affiliations), often endowed with their own small church. Like the populations of the Negev, the inhabitants of Umm al-Jimal and its surroundings relied upon an impressive system of cisterns, water channels, and other hydraulic engineering.[15] The so-called 'dead cities' of the Syrian massif also adopt this organic urban development, with little sense of planning in the arrangement of housing, religious architecture, hostels, and agricultural installations.[16]

Increasing agricultural productivity played a part in the transformation of towns further west in Tunisia. This process is demonstrated by Uchi Maius (now known as Henchir al-Douamis), where the forum, with its equestrian statue of Septimius Severus, and the main streets were invaded by a cistern, an olive press, and – later – a lime kiln. Dated on archaeological grounds to after 364–75, this adaptation of the public spaces of the town correlates well with the wider evidence for the promotion of agriculture during the Vandal occupation of North Africa. Following the Byzantine reconquest in 533, control over lucrative activities such as the production of olive oil was ceded to the church. Like Umm al-Jimal, Uchi Maius developed a more defensive aspect with the construction of a citadel in the sixth century. In common with many of the smaller towns of North Africa, Uchi Maius was abandoned prior to the seventh century; the first phase of Islamic urban development did not occur until the tenth or eleventh century. Continuous settlement through the seventh and eighth centuries can only be identified in the cases of Sétif and Rougga, perhaps suggesting a large-scale abandonment of urbanism in favour of nomadic or semi-nomadic lifestyles.[17]

The tendency toward the greater use of defensive features – city walls, fortified gates, citadels, and so on – appears to be widespread in the late antique world. While Roman frontier settlements like Dura Europos on the Euphrates had long been provided with defensive walls, from the fourth century on there was a greater tendency to fortify towns elsewhere in the empire. The eastern defences were supplemented from the third century onwards by the construction of lines of forts (limes), and recent archaeological work is pushing the date of some forts as late as the sixth century.[18] On the Arabian peninsula and the northern coast of the Persian Gulf there is extensive evidence for the construction of fortified enclosures between the second and the fourth or fifth century (Fig. 2.8). The ancient trading entrepôt known today as Qaryat al-Faw in the southern part of Saudi Arabia has a fortified complex (adopting the basic plan of the Roman castrum) surrounded by less formally arranged domestic and commercial architecture. Similar structures at sites such as Mlayha and Dur on the Gulf coast may have been constructed by Arab-speaking tribal groups who were settling the area. The reasons for the abandonment of these fortified sites remain unclear, but archaeological evidence suggests that few were in operation by the sixth century.[19]

Forts were also being erected by the Sasanians on the coast of Iran at sites such as Siraf (probably by Shapur II in the fourth century), although the shahs also established larger ports such as Bushihr, founded by Ardashir I (r. 224–41).

Impressive fortifications were also a feature of great Sasanian cities such as Veh Ardashir ('New Seleucia') and Ctesiphon, both on the east bank of the Tigris. Founded by Ardashir I and probably intended to replace the existing Hellenistic city of Seleucia, located on the west bank of the Tigris, the circular city of Veh Ardashir comprised a citadel, a prison, a fire temple and a rabbinical academy. Archaeological investigations inside the southern perimeter wall (some ten metres thick) revealed mud-brick courtyard houses separated by streets, as well as evidence for metalworking and glass-making. A substantial church was also excavated on the site. To the east, the city of Merv in Turkmenistan had been fortified since Achaemenid times, and the maintenance of the citadel (Erk Kala) and outer defences continued under Sasanian rule.[20] Forts built within the Atrek valley in Khurasan also probably date to the Sasanian period. Among the most impressive remnants of the defensive systems are the lines of walls defending the entrance to the Sasanian lands east and west of the Caspian Sea. The so-called 'Alexander's wall', running some 175 km from the Gurgan plain into the mountains, is studded with forts along its southern side, one of the most impressive of which is Turang Tepe (occupied from the Sasanian into the early Islamic period).[21]

Two major spheres of late antique commercial activity are relevant to an understanding of the archaeology of international trade in the Islamic period. The first is the maritime trade in the Mediterranean. There can be little doubt that the volume of traffic in both raw materials and manufactured goods was considerably lower in the fifth and the sixth centuries than it had been during the first and second centuriesCE. In Europe the political, social, and economic disruptions caused by the breakdown of the Roman Empire and rise of the Gothic polities must have been a factor in the diminishing levels of trade. That said, the demand for luxury commodities from the east – notably papyrus and fine textiles – did allow for the maintenance of some channels of trade. Indeed, papyrus was still being employed by the Merovingian court several decades after the Islamic conquest of Egypt (the principal source of this writing material), and official documents from Italian cities such as Ravenna as well as bulls issued by the papacy in Rome provide evidence for the continued use of this material as late as the early eleventh century.[22] Amphora production is another indication of long-distance trade. Used for the storage of such commodities as wine and olive oil, amphorae were manufactured on a large scale during the fifth and sixth centuries in Middle Egypt and Tunisia. Significantly, there is evidence for the continuation of this process in some regions well into the early Islamic phase.[23]

The second commercial sphere is the Persian Gulf and, by extension, the Indian Ocean and the maritime routes to China. Excavations of port sites in Oman, in the United Arab Emirates, and on the southern coast of Iran have given a better picture of the nature of trade in the centuries prior to the rise

of Islam (Fig. 2.8). It is apparent that there was a decline after the most prosperous phase, which occurred between the third century BCE and the first and
second century CE. On the Arabian coast, the phase from the second to the
fourth or fifth century is marked by a reduction in settlement size, the sedentary
population constructing small fortified enclosures. Although the excavated
ceramics indicate that trade continued along the established maritime routes in
the Persian Gulf and Indian Ocean, the near absence of coins suggests a move
to a non-monetarised economy. Recently it has been suggested that much of
the Arabian peninsula experienced an ecological disaster in the sixth century.
While this hypothesis cannot yet be proved, it is striking that all of the Arabian
fortified buildings were abandoned at this time. The sixth and early seventh
centuries were a period of significant economic and demographic decline; on
the Arabian coast only Suhar, Khatt, and Kush report ceramics of late Sasanian
date.[24]

From the third century on, the Sasanian Empire exerted a powerful influence
over the Arabian coast of the Gulf. It seems likely, however, that the evolution
of Sasanian commercial activity followed a somewhat different trajectory from
that of the Arabian ports surveyed above. Sasanian trade with the east did not
rely solely upon maritime traffic through the Persian Gulf. The Sasanians also
controlled a vital section of the 'silk route', which ran through western Asia.
Persian involvement in land trade is indicated both in texts and in finds of
Sasanian silver coins (drachms) and glassware in China. The Perso-Byzantine
wars of 502–6, 527–61, and 602–29 not only disrupted the passage of caravans
along this long road, but may have reinvigorated Persian maritime activity in
the Gulf just at the time of a major downturn in sedentary occupation on the
Arabian peninsula. Sasanian coins dating from the fifth to the early seventh
century have been located on coastal sites in China as well as in some eastern
entrepôts of the 'silk route'. Persian bullae, perhaps employed to seal packages
destined for transportation by land or sea, have been located around the Persian
Gulf and as far afield as Mantai in Sri Lanka.[25]

The Umayyad qusur of Greater Syria

From the time of their rediscovery at the end of the nineteenth century, the
early Islamic structures collectively known as the qusur – or, rather misleadingly,
as the 'desert castles' – have been the subject of extensive scholarly debate.[26]
The Arabic word qasr may be translated simply as 'castle', although it has a
wider semantic range, encompassing also the notion of a palatial residence.
This flexibility of meaning is appropriate to the present subject; for it is readily
apparent that the militarised appearance of these structures is, in fact, largely
illusory. A cursory examination of the extant monuments might lead to the

conclusion that, in terms of building technique, scale, architectural decoration, and surrounding environment, there is little that unites them into a single category. At one extreme is the magnificent palatial complex known as Khirbat al-Mafjar, near the town of Jericho, while at the other one could point to the *qasr* at Jabal Says, in the basalt desert east of Damascus.[27] The Spartan look of the buildings at Jabal Says may not be a wholly accurate guide as to their appearance in the eighth century (and this impression is also left by the decorative metalwork excavated at the site); but there is no doubt about the contrast, either in the ambition of the architecture or in the capacity of the surrounding land to support intensive cultivation. Khirbat al-Mafjar and Jabal Says were clearly not designed to perform the same range of functions, and we may also expect the other *qusur* to exhibit considerable variability in point of location, construction, and ornamentation.

Allowing for these considerations, there are factors that unify the *qusur* and permit one to ask larger questions relating to distribution, chronology, morphology, and utility. First, these buildings represent a phase of patronage by an Islamic elite during a relatively short period of time, from the late seventh to the mid-eighth century. This timespan means that the *qusur* may be considered largely the result of patronage by the ruling Umayyad family, although the recent discovery of the residence of the Abbasid family at Humayma illustrates that rural residences were employed by other powerful groups in Islamic society before 750.[28] Second, despite the wide range of climatic zones they occupy – the sub-tropical Jordan valley, the fertile plains of Jordan and northern Israel, and the arid eastern desert – the *qusur* are characterised by their non-urban setting and are largely confined to the area of Greater Syria (with some comparable structures in western Iraq: see chapter 8). The Umayyads also built urban palaces in cities such as Jerusalem and Damascus, and the official residences of governors were established in the Islamic Empire (chapters 3 and 5); but the *qusur* stand apart from these two types. While a desire for privacy may to some degree inform the phenomenon of building *qusur* in extra-urban locations, one should remain sensitive to the fact that such locations could still perform official functions. Indeed the positioning of many structures on or near well established trade routes means that many structures were less isolated than they might appear. Archaeological research has demonstrated the extent to which the early Islamic *qusur* were dependent upon the architectural heritage and wider infrastructure bequeathed to Greater Syria by the Roman and Byzantine empires, as well as by the Ghassanid tribal confederation.[29]

The early interpretations of the *qusur* stressed their remoteness from the major urban centres and suggested that the former were raised out of a desire to escape the confines of the cities.[30] Some support can be found for this assertion. The marginal lands of eastern Syria provided opportunities for recreational activities such as hunting; this is well illustrated in the fresco decoration of the audience hall of the early eighth-century bathhouse of Qusayr 'Amra. Textual sources dealing with the Umayyad period – most importantly the *Kitab al-Aghani* (*Book of Songs*) of Abu al-Faraj al-Isfahani (d. 973–74) – confirm that some members of the Umayyad clan, most notoriously Walid ibn al-Yazid (caliph Walid II, r. 743–4), led hedonistic private lives.[31] That this is more than simply a later fiction is indicated by the palatial complex of Khirbat al-Mafjar. The bathhouse is particularly opulent, its mosaic and stucco decoration being employed to communicate themes of royal iconography and sexuality. Similar preoccupations can be identified in the decorative programs of Qasr al-Hayr West and Qusayr 'Amra, while even the imposing palace of Mshatta included partially clothed male and female statuary.[32]

It would be a mistake to dismiss the complex iconographic programs, the frank eroticism of some of the ornamentation, and the acts of apparently willful eccentricity (such as the decorated façades of the palaces of Qasr al-Hayr West and Mshatta), but there are clearly other dynamics that need to be considered. Scholars have pointed to archaeological evidence for irrigation systems around various *qusur*, particularly those located in marginal agricultural zones of Jordan and Syria. This economic emphasis has also been taken up by those who have examined the relationship of the *qusur* to the major trade routes. Some of these structures probably functioned as caravanserais. Other interpretations have focussed on the use of these buildings in the mediation between the Umayyad elite and the tribes of the deserts of northern Arabia and eastern Syria. This possibility also leads to a comparison between the Umayyad *qusur* and Ghassanid monuments such as the sixth-century audience hall just outside the walls of Sergiopolis (Rusafa) in northern Syria. It is worth questioning the extent to which the strategic imperatives that led to the construction of the Umayyad *qusur* were derived from policies employed by ruling elites prior to the Islamic conquest.

The spatial distribution of the *qusur* of Jordan and Syria (excluding Umayyad rural palaces in Palestine such as Khirbat al-Mafjar and Khirbat al-Minya) suggests links between these structures in terms of function, and perhaps also of patronage (Fig. 2.9). Key factors would seem to be the locations of the principal routes running from the Hijaz into Syria and the different environments through which they pass. Given the arid conditions that prevail through much of the way from the Hijaz into the plains of Syria, the availability of water was a matter of primary concern. Written sources of the early Islamic period indicate that the most important route from the south passed through Tayma', leading north to the Wadi al-Sirhan, and then to the central Jordan plain known as Balqa'. The Wadi al-Sirhan has the advantage of being adequately supplied with wells. If one traces the continuation of this route, it leads to the oasis of Azraq.

Turning west from the northernmost extension of the Wadi al-Sirhan, one is led past Umayyad sites such as Qusayr 'Amra, Qasr al-Kharana (Fig. 2.10), and Qasr al-Muwaqqar on the way to the adminstrative capital of 'Amman. Other major routes into Jordan passed further to the west, one of them leading from Tayma', via a series of wells in the desert, to the Umayyad site of Qasr al-Tuba (which has several wells within a few kilometres from the site). From there, the northward route to Busra passed Qasr al-Kharana, Qasr al-Hallabat, and Umm al-Jimal, while to the north-west lay Jilat, Qasr al-Muwaqqar, and 'Amman. The final route into Jordan and Syria, the *Darb al-Sham*, came from Tabuk and passed through the plains of Jordan via Ma'an, the reservoir at Ziza', Qastal, and 'Amman. The unfinished Umayyad palace of Mshatta lies 6 km west of Qastal, on the margins of the cultivated land of the Balqa'.[33]

A further environmental consideration is posed by the basalt desert (*harra*) occupying the land north and east of Azraq. Camels are only able to traverse this area along narrow tracks where the rocks have been cleared, and the passage through some of the tracks is very difficult. One of the easier ways to reach southern Syria was to pass through the villages of the eastern Hawran, to Busra and then to Damascus. An alternative route involved skirting the eastern borders of the *harra* from Wadi al-Sirhan, through the Wadi al-Muqat and past Qasr al-Burqu' (which has a large rain-fed reservoir) and Jabal Says, to Damascus. Qasr al-Burqu' and Jabal Says had both been occupied in earlier periods, but were extensively reconstructed in the early eighth century.[34] Regarding the *qusur* of eastern Syria, it is possible to find similar relationships between them and the major routes. The road north from Jabal Says led through the desert to Bakhra', Tadmur (ancient Palmyra), Qasr al-Hayr East, Rusafa, and then to the bridge across the Euphrates which was probably constructed by Caliph Hisham (r. 724–43). The road from Damascus to Tadmur passed through the important Umayyad site of Qasr al-Hayr West, built during the rule of Caliph Hisham and supplied with water via a canal from the Roman (or possibly Umayyad) dam at Harbaqa.[35] It is worth noting the number of Syrian *qusur* located along the Roman road known as the *Strata Diocletiana* (constructed c.297), which linked Damascus to the Euphrates.[36]

While the evidence is far from conclusive, the distribution of the *qusur* in Jordan and eastern Syria suggests an attempt to create an infrastructure to support the key routes running north from the Hijaz. Important figures in the patronage of the *qusur* include the caliphs Walid I and Hisham; the latter was particularly active in establishing architectural complexes between Damascus and the Euphrates. The Umayyad *qusur* include palatial dwellings – such as those of Mshatta, Rusafa, Qasr al-Hayr East and Qasr al-Hayr West – but they might be associated with larger enclosures (sing. *khan*), probably designed for the accommodation of travellers or pilgrims making the journey (*hajj*) to Mecca and Medina. This function may tie together the reservoir at Ziza' and the *qusur* of Umm al-Walid, of Qastal, of Mshatta, and of the otherwise rather remote site of Qasr al-Tuba.

The existence of reliable water sources is a consistent factor in the location of the *qusur*, and it is noticeable that earlier engineering projects – the cistern at Qasr al-Burqu' or the Roman aqueduct near Khirbat al-Mafjar – were exploited by the Umayyads. The efficient provision of water to Khirbat al-Mafjar also supported the extravagant scale of the bathhouse on the site. The Umayyad *qasr* at Qastal has both a dam and a substantial reservoir in the vicinity of the site; similar structures have been located around Umm al-Walid.[37] The crucial importance of locating regular supplies of water along a desert road needs little further elaboration, but it is becoming increasingly clear that the hydraulic projects associated with some of the Umayyad *qusur* of Jordan and Syria were designed with the ambitious goal of promoting agriculture in otherwise marginal lands. For instance, reconnaissance at Ma'an in southern Jordan revealed a perimeter wall more than 11 km long, enclosing an irrigated area of more than 535 hectares. This major project has been persuasively dated to the Umayyad period, and Ma'an's important position as the first major stop in southern Jordan on the desert road from Tayma' is worth noting in this context. The giant enclosure wall and dam at Qasr al-Hayr East was probably also designed to control water for irrigation.[38]

One of the dominant characteristics of the Umayyad *qusur* is the employment of a plan comprising a square or rectangular enclosure wall with corner towers (usually circular in plan) and a single entrance in the middle of one side. The rooms are commonly arranged around a central courtyard. This obviously excludes building types where the plan is dictated by function – bathhouses and watchtowers being the obvious examples – but it is remarkable how many of the residential blocks follow this pattern. Interestingly, the ultimate source for this kind of plan is military: the Roman fortress (*castrum*) sometimes known as *quadriburgium* ('fortress with four towers'). The best preserved of these buildings is the Tetrarchate castle (293–305), known as Qasr al-Bashir, in the eastern desert of southern Jordan (Fig. 2.11). This structure was part of a defensive line known as the *limes Arabicus*. This was composed of small installations such as Qasr al-Bashir, as well as of much larger fortified compounds like Ayla, Humayma, and Lajjun, which housed Roman legions. Another aspect of this defensive system was the road, the *via nova Traiana*, constructed by Emperor Trajan (r. 98–117) to provide for the movement of troops and resources through southern Syria and Jordan. The chronological development and precise functions of the buildings which made up the *limes Arabicus* have been hotly debated, but there can be little doubt that the landscape of early Islamic Greater Syria was populated by many standing Roman fortresses and legionary camps.

The influence of the Roman *castrum* plan can be seen in the architecture of pre-Islamic Arabia. Best known is the trading settlement in the south-west of Saudi Arabia known as Qaryat al-Faw. The central compound is enclosed by a thick wall with four rectangular towers and a single entrance. Another fort has been located further north at Tayma', while two more, Dur and Mlayha, have been discovered in the Emirates. The site of Qal'at Bahrain includes a rectangular fort with circular corner towers, once thought to be Islamic and now reattributed to the third or early fourth century. A sixth-century fort later occupied during the Islamic period has also been excavated at Raya, at the southern end of the Sinai.[39] On the basis of this evidence it might appear straightforward that the Umayyads simply adopted the ubiquitous Roman design for plans of their *qusur*. In support of this idea, there are a few examples of existing Roman structures – most notably Bakhra' and Qasr al-Hallabat – that were extensively remodelled in the Umayyad period, but the accumulation of archaeological research suggests a more complex picture.[40]

A comparison between a late Roman *quadriburgium* like Qasr al-Bashir and the Umayyad *qusur* reveals two main points. First, the rectangular towers of the earlier building have in most cases been replaced by towers with a circular plan (Fig. 2.10). Second, these circular towers and other apparently defensive features of the Umayyad type serve in reality no defensive function. Frequently the towers are built of solid masonry or serve as latrines when there is an internal chamber; the exterior walls are thin and unable to withstand a serious attack; and the arrow slits in the walls are often too narrow or at the wrong height to function properly. In other words, there has been a clear shift in function, from a military to a residential one. This change is also seen in the interior, where the chambers around the courtyard are subdivided into compartments of four or five rooms, known as *bayts*. Even those Umayyad *qusur* which incorporate square or rectangular towers – for instance Khirbat al-Karak (probably one of the earliest Umayyad buildings) and Balis – exhibit no more defensive features than the other members of their group. It remains possible that the round towers of the Umayyad *qusur* derive from Sasanian models, but such features are also seen in partially fortified Roman encampments, which functioned as stations for both soldiers and civilians – like Zarqa' in Jordan, Abu Sayfi in the northern Sinai, and Dawwi in Egypt.[41]

More important than the specific plan of the corner towers, however, is that encampments such as Abu Sayfi or Dawwi represent aransitional model – partly military and partly residential – which can also be seen in late antique Greater Syria. Particularly significant are the fortified residential complexes of the mid-sixth century, a period when the defence of the eastern borders of Syria had been placed in the hands of the Arab Ghassanid dynasty. These complexes include two walled compounds – Istabl 'Antar and Andarin – of roughly the same dimensions

as those commonly encountered in the Umayyad *qusur* (c.70 x 70 m). The first
has square corner towers, while the second has towers with a hexagonal plan.
Built in 558–9, Andarin has trappings of luxury, including mosaic pavements
and a bathhouse constructed near the main residence. Another, larger, fortified
palatial structure of probable sixth-century date has been located at Dumayr.
The presence within the courtyard of Andarin of a church aligned with the
main entrance of the walled enclosure suggests interesting parallels with the
basilical audience hall within the *qasr* at Khirbat al-Karak and with the more
monumental eighth-century palace of Mshatta.[42] The opulent *villa rustica* exemplified by Andarin in Syria or by Ramat Hanadiv in Israel may have provided
another form of inspiration for the Umayyad patrons; these complexes might be
equipped with a bathhouse (a key feature of many of the *qusur*), as well as with
mosaics and other forms of architectural decoration.[43] Looking east, the site of
Tulul al-Ukhaydir, located close to the Abbasid palace of Ukhaydir in the desert
west of Karbala' in Iraq, was constructed in the mid-sixth century and refurbished in the Umayyad period. Originally known as Qasr Bani Muqatil, after
the Christian Arab family who occupied it, the *qasr* comprises, in the excavated
section, a basilical reception hall with six massive brick piers facing onto the
central courtyard. Reconnaissance in the western Iraqi desert suggests that the
plan of Tulul al-Ukhaydir was not unusual in this region while it was under the
control of the Lakhmids, an Arab client state of the Sasanians.[44]

   To conclude, the analysis offered above has stressed the points of continuity between the Umayyad *qusur* and the architectural fabric and transport
infrastructure of late antique Greater Syria (and Iraq). Given that routes across
an arid terrain and reliable water sources are likely to remain in use over the
long term, it should not be surprising that the Umayyad elite would wish to
follow the example of the Ghassanids and other architectural patrons of the
late antique period. Umayyad architectural decoration (particularly the frescos
and mosaics) exhibits strong links to the arts of late antique Syria. This feature
may be seen also in the artefacts recovered from the excavations of Jabal Says or
Mafraq/Fudayn.[45] That said, the Umayyad *qusur* also point towards new directions in Islamic culture: the famous brazier from Mafraq exhibits considerable
Coptic influence, though the synthesis with themes drawn from Sasanian Iran
and perhaps pre-Islamic Arabia is distinctively Umayyad. Similar observations
could be made about the hybrid façades of Qasr al-Hayr West and Mshatta,
or about the frescos of Qusayr 'Amra. An Arabian connection may also be
seen in the carved steatite artefacts in the Mafraq hoard. Persianate influence
(perhaps through the architecture of western Iraq) is apparent in the brick vaults
of Mshatta and Qasr al-Tuba, as well as in the squinches and stucco decoration
employed in Qasr al-Kharana.[46] With its increased scale and emphasis on
axiality, Mshatta is often seen as the precursor of the huge palatial complexes of

the Abbasid period, while the large compound at Qasr al-Hayr East (Fig. 5.3) and the less formal structures around it prompt questions regarding the early evolution of the 'Islamic city' (chapter 5).

Notes

1 On the internal organisation of the *amsar*, see Akbar (1989); Wheatley (2001), 40–50. See also Whitcomb (1994a).
2 Johns (1999), 59–69. For the traditional interpretation of the Prophet's Mosque, see Creswell (1969), 1:1, 6–15, 27–8; Creswell and Allan (1989), 4–6.
3 For different interpretations of the evidence on this issue, see Blair (1992); Johns (2003), 424–32.
4 See comments in Johns (2003), 412–14. The compilation of these sources does, however, have immense value in the reconstruction of early attitudes among non-Muslim communities to the rise of Islam. See Hoyland (1997).
5 For a discussion of Hijazi Qur'an fragments, see Déroche (1992), 27–33. On early developments in Arabic formal scripts, see Blair (2006), 77–100.
6 Johns (2003), 414–24; Hoyland (2006). For the coins of this period, see Album and Goodwin (2002), with extensive bibliography of earlier studies. Early rock inscriptions and papyri are also discussed and illustrated at www.islamic-awareness.org/History/Islam/Inscriptions.
7 For a discussion of this papyrus, see Jones (1998). On the evidence from the papyri of Nessana, Aphrodito, and elsewhere, see Hoyland (2006). Also Johns (2003), 418–24 and Magness (2003), 90–1, 177–82.
8 On the dating of these buildings, see Gaube (1974); Urice (1987), 6–7, fig. 79; Creswell and Allan (1989), 93, 104–5; Helms (1990), 55–9. The inscribed lintel stone at Qasr Burqu' was not found *in situ*, and its significance in dating the structures (which are probably of Ghassanid origin, with Umayyad reconstruction) cannot be determined conclusively.
9 Creswell (1969), 1:1, 48–58; Creswell and Allan (1989), 10–15; Whitcomb (2002); Genequand (2003 and 2006a, 10–12).
10 Bulliet (1979). See especially 78–9.
11 Sauvaget (1934), fig. 8. On the recovery of the classical street plan in Damascus, see Sauvaget (1949).
12 The transition from late antiquity to early Islam has been investigated on numerous urban sites in the Middle East. Those of Bet Shean (Scythopolis) and Pella have been well published. See Tsafrir and Foerster (1994) and (1997); McNicoll et al. (1992), 145–98.
13 Kennedy (1985a). On the changes experienced by cities, towns and villages in the Byzantine Empire, see also Foss (2002).
14 Kennedy (1985a), 26. On the disappearance of wheeled transport in the late antique North Africa, Middle East, and Central Asia, see Bulliet (1975).
15 Segal (1985); De Vries (1998), 91–127, 229–41; De Vries (2000). See also Hirschfeld (2001), 268–71; Magness (2003), 185–87; Walmsley (2007), 41–4.
16 On the architecture of these sites, see Peña (1996). For excavations, see Sodini et al. (1980); Tate (1992). There is increasing evidence that settlements in this

region continued into the early Islamic period. See Magness (2003), 196–206 and Walmsley (2007), 28–9.

17 Gelichi and Milanese (1998) and (2002); Leone (2003). On the 'manor houses' of late antique North Africa, see Hirschfeld (2001), 264–6.

18 On the *limes*, see Parker (1986). Ceramic evidence and reevaluation of stratigraphy is now indicating a later date for some of these forts. See Magness (2003), 112–29.

19 For a general survey of the archaeological evidence, see Kennet (2005). On specific sites, see al-Ansary (1982); Boucharlat et al. (1989); Boucharlat and Mouton (1994); Benoist, Mouton and Schiettecatte (2003).

20 Whitehouse and Williamson (1973), 33–42; Simpson (2000), 58–62; Daryaee (2003). On the fortifications of Merv, see Herrmann et al. (2001), 33–42 (and other International Merv Project preliminary reports published in the journal *Iran* since 1993); Brun (2005), 616–18.

21 Howard-Johnston (1995), 192–7.

22 Scholarship on this issue has its origins in the work of Henri Pirenne, particularly *Mahomet et Charlemagne* (1937). For an English translation, see Pirenne (1954). For a survey of the 'Pirenne thesis', its critics, and the role of archaeology, see Hodges and Whitehouse (1983), 1–19; Lopez (1943); Grierson (1959). On different aspects of early medieval trade in the Mediterranean, see Mango (1996); Lebecq (1997).

23 Vogt et al. (2002); Leone (2003), 21–4.

24 Benoist, Mouton and Schiettecatte (2003), 66–72; Kennet (2004), 68–85; Kennet (2005). See also Williamson (1972); Whitehouse and Williamson (1973).

25 Daryaee (2003), 11–15. On the appearance of Sasanian artefacts in Chinese tombs, see Dien (2004).

26 The bibliography on the Umayyad *qusur* is vast. For comprehensive surveys of the older scholarship on the monuments discussed in this section, see the notes for each building in Creswell (1969). For more recent works, see the bibliographies in: Urice (1987); Creswell and Allan (1989); Fowden (2004); Genequand (2006a); Walmsley (2007), 99–104. An up-to-date presentation of the monuments in Jordan is provided in Museum with no Frontiers (2000). For the architecture of the *qusur*, see also Hillenbrand (1994), 384–90.

27 Hamilton (1959); Brisch (1965); Creswell and Allan (1989), 118–22, 178–200.

28 Foote (1999). On the excavations of the Nabatean and Roman fort on the site, see Oleson et al. (1999).

29 On Ghassanid architecture, see Shahid (1992). Also Genequand (2006a), 20–4. Early Ghassanid building work is apparent on several 'Umayyad' *qusur*, including Qasr Burqu', Qasr al-Hallabat, and Qasr al-Hayr West. See Gaube (1974); Arce (2006); Genequand (2006b). For a brief review of the history of this phase, see Hoyland (2001), 78–82.

30 Helms (1990), 27–30. See also notes on earlier scholarship in: Urice (1987), 6–23; Fowden (2004), 1–30, 46–57.

31 Relevant Arabic sources are collected in Hillenbrand (1982). On the iconography of the painting, mosaic and sculptural ornamentation of these buildings, see Fowden (2004).

32 Hamilton (1959); Grabar (1973), 160–5, figs 65–89; Fowden (2004); Trümpelmann (1965).

33 King (1987) and (1989); also Sauvaget (1967). On the question of land ownership in Umayyad Greater Syria, see Bacharach (1996).

34 Brisch (1965), 155–6, figs 9a and b; Gaube (1974); Creswell and Allan (1989), 91–3, 118–22.

35 Schlumberger (1939), 200–9; Creswell and Allan (1989), 136. Recently, an Umayyad date has been proposed for the Harbaqa dam. See Genequand (2006b).

36 Genequand (2004b).

37 Carlier (1989); Bujard and Genequand (2001).

38 Grabar et al. (1978), 1: 98–109; Genequand (2003) and (2005). Also Creswell and Allan (1989), 149–64, 173–6.

39 Al-Ansary (1982), 31–9; Kawatoko (2005), 851–3; Kervran, Hiebert and Rouguelle (2005), 179–212, 415–16. See also Kennet (2005).

40 Genequand (2004a and b); Arce (2006). Qasr al-Hallabat was also renovated under the Ghassanids.

41 Genequand (2006a), 13–20.

42 Whitcomb (2002); Genequand (2006a), 20–4, figs 6.2, 7.2, 7.4.

43 Bisheh (1993); Hirschfeld (2001), 40.

44 Finster and Schmidt (1976); Finster and Schmidt (2005).

45 Museum with no Frontiers (2000), 51–2, 67–9.

46 Creswell and Allan (1989), 96–104, 203–5, 210; Urice (1987), 52–60, 71–80; also Hillenbrand (1981).

3

New directions in the early Islamic period

Artefacts such as bilingual papyri (Greek and Arabic) and 'Arab–Sasanian' coins provide persuasive evidence that the Arab elite relied heavily upon the pre-existing administrative practices and visual vocabulary of the newly conquered domains for most of the seventh century. The surviving epigraphic evidence shows how tentative the first employments of Muslim religious invocations and caliphal titulature were. Archaeology from regions such as Greater Syria indicates that the everyday lives of town and village dwellers experienced little radical change from the 630s to the end of the seventh century. Nevertheless, the Islamic conquests of the seventh and eighth centuries did represent a radical and irreversible break with the past that, over the course of decades and centuries, would transform the material culture of a vast area stretching from Spain to Central Asia. Changes can be detected in everything, from architecture, town planning, and portable artefacts to landscape, crops, and diet. Many of these issues will be revisited later in the book. This chapter will outline some of the key areas of interest by looking at the themes of synthesis, expansion, and innovation. The two case studies explore new aspects of the archaeological record of the eighth to the tenth century: first, the coin hoards of western Russia and Scandinavia; and, second, the two new building forms that transformed the early Islamic urban environment: the congregational mosque and the *dar al-imara*.

Before embarking on a brief survey of the archaeology of the eighth to the tenth century, some words are needed concerning the historical context. By the second quarter of the eighth century the pace of the conquests had slowed, and with the establishment of somewhat uneasy borders with existing states – such as Tang dynasty China, the Byzantine Empire, Merovingian/Carolingian France, and the northern Spanish kingdom of Asturias – the processes of consolidation become more evident. The vast new Islamic Empire was highly diverse in environment and culture, and the subjected populations heterogenous in terms of ethnicity, language, and confessional allegiance.

At the political level this period witnessed major changes, the first of which was the fall of the Umayyad dynasty and the establishment of the Abbasid caliphate in 749–50. While shifts from one dynasty to another often have little significant impact on material culture, this was not the case with what is sometimes termed the 'Abbasid revolution'. Most importantly, the Abbasids shifted their centre of power east (much of their support at the time of their coup had been located in Iraq and Khurasan). The rise of the Abbasids also marked the beginning of a process of political fragmentation in the Islamic world. The Iberian peninsula ('Andalus' in Arabic) came under the control of a surviving member of the Umayyad family in 756, while the Aghlabids ruled over Tunisia, Algeria, and Sicily from 800. In the east, the early part of the ninth century witnessed the rise of Persianate dynasties such as the Samanids (819–1005) and the Tahirids (821–91). These developments certainly compromised the political power and economic resources of the Abbasids, though all the new regional dynasties continued to accept the Abbasid claim to the caliphate (that is, the spiritual authority of the Abbasids over the Sunni Muslim community). The end of the ninth century marked a serious decline in the power of the Abbasids, which was due in part to an economic collapse precipitated by the diminishing agricultural base of Iraq and by the huge costs of maintaining a professional army. Further challenges came in the form of two rival claims to the title of caliph, first in 909 in Tunisia, from the founder of the Fatimid dynasty, 'Ubayd Allah, and second in 929, from the Umayyad ruler of Spain, 'Abd al-Rahman III. The political ascendancy of Shi'a dynasties, most notably the Buyids in Iraq and western Iran (932–1062) and the Fatimids in North Africa, Egypt, and Greater Syria, is a significant feature of the Islamic world in the tenth century.

The process of creating new towns (amsar) continued into the eighth and ninth centuries. Some, like 'Anjar in Lebanon, drew on the formal vocabulary of the classical polis, but new influences can also be detected. Abbasid foundations at Baghdad (also Madinat al-Salam, or the 'City of Peace') in 762–66, at Samarra in Iraq from 836, and at Rafiqa in north-eastern Syria from 771 owe their origins to concepts of urban planning and palatial architecture developed by the Sasanians, and earlier by the Persian dynasties. Other new cities and palatial complexes appear elsewhere in the Islamic world, including at Madinat al-Zahra' in Spain, at Mahdiyya and Sabra Mansuriyya in Tunisia, and at Cairo in Egypt. Seventh-century amsar such as Basra, Kufa, and Fustat evolved from rough-and-ready garrison towns into populous cities supported by markets and vibrant manufacturing sectors. In general terms, it also seems likely that there was a demographic shift over these centuries, marked by a steady increase in the urban population.

The relocation of the centre of political power following the Abbasid takeover had significant implications for many aspects of life, both in Iraq and in the formerly dominant region of Greater Syria. Jordan, Palestine, and southern Syria were further affected by a major earthquake in 749. Allowing for new archaeological evidence, which indicates the regeneration of urban centres in the later eighth and ninth centuries,[1] there can be little doubt that, from the second half of the eighth century on, Iraq outstripped its western neighbour in terms of economic productivity, scholarship, and artistic activity. Drawing on the earlier traditions of Sasanian learning at Gondeshapur in south-western Iran, the Abbasid elite promoted the translation of scientific, medical, and philosophical works from Greek, Persian and Sanskrit. Religious scholarship, poetry, history, and geography all flourished. A factor which contributed to the massive growth in intellectual activity was the introduction of the Chinese technology of paper making. This new writing material facilitated the large-scale production and transmission of books across the Islamic world.[2] Chronicles record numerous examples of diplomatic missions sent or received by Islamic rulers, though more significant in archaeological terms is the great expansion of international trade, particularly from the end of the eighth century.

While Caliph Mansur's (r. 754–75) magnificent circular city is probably irretrievably lost beneath the buildings of modern Baghdad and phenomena like the 'translation movement' are the domain of textual historians, archaeology provides important perspectives on this vibrant period of Islamic history. Chapter 5 addresses the transformation of existing towns and cities, as well as the establishment of new urban foundations; but evidence of extensive building programmes can be found in other locations too. The Umayyads and the Abbasids were also responsible for the renovation of urban citadels (for instance 'Amman and Samarqand), which combined administrative, military, residential, and religious functions. These fortified complexes, located in the vicinities of established towns and cities, are precursors to the great urban citadels which were to become a feature of the Islamic world from the eleventh century. As Iraq became the centre of political authority and economic activity, greater emphasis was placed on the main arteries of communication. Where many of the Umayyad *qusur* had been located on routes leading north from the Hijaz into Greater Syria, the late eighth and ninth centuries witnessed a greater concentration on the Darb Zubayda, leading from Medina to Kufa. The architectural patronage along this road ranges from small watchtowers to substantial fortified structures (chapter 8).

The diversity of the architecture and hydraulic systems along the Darb Zubayda suggests the interaction of skilled engineers and craftsmen from different regions of the Abbasid caliphate. This mixing of skilled workers from east and west can also be detected in earlier decades. Papyri of the early eighth century record the transfer of craftsmen from Egypt to work on projects in Jerusalem,[3] while the novel vaulting technologies and aspects of the decorative stone and stucco carving in some of the Umayyad *qusur* indicate the presence of Persian artisans in Greater Syria. It is as well to bear in mind that artisans did not always move away from their homes of their own free will; but the evidence from the archaeological record indicates greater fluidity of skilled labour. Particularly important was the establishment of 'industrial' zones, where craftsmen from different areas operated workshops in close proximity to one another. The great Iraqi industrial hub of Basra has been the subject of little archaeological investigation, although more is known of the early Islamic industrial sectors of Samarra, Raqqa-Rafiqa, Fustat, and eastern cities such as Nishapur and Samarqand (chapter 7).

The movement and interaction of people often resulted in innovation – for instance the advances in glass and glaze technology in Abbasid Iraq and Syria, or the later development of the stonepaste ceramic body. In other cases, the new patterns of the eighth century and later period can be better characterised as a creative synthesis of existing elements. This phenomenon is exemplified in the dispersal throughout the Islamic world of underground canals (qanats), reservoirs, water mills, and related technologies. Probably originating in ancient Iran, the qanat spread to other regions before the rise of Islam, though its widest distribution can be demonstrated from the eighth century onwards. In the case of Spain, the new technologies introduced in the aftermath of the Islamic conquest augmented the existing Roman and Visigothic infrastructure (chapter 4). The resulting synthesis allowed for the cultivation of new crops – most importantly sugar cane, rice, mulberry (required for the manufacture of silk), cotton, and orange – that were to have a profound impact on social and economic life in the Iberian peninsula.[4]

One of the key areas of expansion was trade. Some of the Umayyad caliphs, most notably Hisham, were enthusiastic about facilitating mercantile activity.[5] In the region of Greater Syria, this is seen in the erection of new market places and lines of shops along the streets of established towns and cities, including Scythopolis/Bet Shean, Apollonia/Arsuf, Tiberias/Tabariyya, Palmyra/Tadmur, and Gerasa/Jarash.[6] Perhaps the most impressive evidence for the expansion of trade comes after the fall of the Umayyad dynasty and the establishment of the Abbasid capital at Baghdad in Iraq. This move probably reduced the economic importance of the Mediterranean in the early Islamic economy and placed greater emphasis on maritime activity in the Persian Gulf, as well as on land routes – east via the 'silk road', south-west along the Darb Zubayda, and north (see below).

The archaeology of the Persian Gulf ports is discussed in greater detail in chapter 8, but some preliminary comments can be made about the changing nature of long-distance trade in the early Abbasid period. One aspect of this expansion of trade involved the export of raw and processed agricultural commodites such as dates and date syrup (dibs), as well as that of manufactured items from cities like Basra and Baghdad. Both the turquoise-glazed jars (Fig.

3.1) employed for storing liquids such as date syrup and the decorative tin-glazed bowls (Fig. 8.3) have a remarkably wide distribution along sea routes, being reported (together or separately) on sites in Egypt, Yemen, the coast of East Africa (and possibly also Kwa Gandaganda in South Africa), Sri Lanka, Thailand, and on coastal sites in south-east China. Ports involved in this long-distance export trade included Basra and the Persian settlement of Siraf. Land and riparian routes probably account for the presence of ceramics of this kind on Middle Eastern sites, including at Raqqa, Samarqand, Susa, and Rabadha in Saudi Arabia.[7] Another major item of export was glass; the distribution pattern is again striking. The recovery of Middle Eastern glass in Chinese royal tombs attests to the desirability of this commodity, though it is impossible to ascertain whether it travelled east via sea routes or along the 'silk road'.[8]

The other side of this mercantile activity was the import of raw materials and manufactured items from the regions surrounding the Indian Ocean, China and other parts of south-east Asia. The list of imports into Iraq compiled by Jahiz (d. 868 or 869) in *The Investigation of Commerce* (*al-Tabassar bi'l-Tijara*) makes it clear that cities such as Baghdad and Samarra represented huge markets for luxury goods, from silks to exotic animals and tropical hardwoods.[9] Recent archaeological work in the Persian Gulf has demonstrated that ceramics from India were finding their way to ports such as Kush in Ras al-Khaimah between the fourth and the ninth century. This represents the physical survival of a larger trade in spices, precious metals, woods, and printed textiles. At Kush, Chinese ceramics make their first appearance in excavated contexts dating to the eleventh century; but there is abundant evidence elsewhere for the influx of Chinese ware into the Islamic world three centuries earlier.[10] The well known account given by the eleventh-century historian Bayhaqi, of a gift of Chinese imperial porcelain (*sini faghfuri*) and other glazed wares sent by the governor of Khurasan to the Abbasid caliph, Harun al-Rashid (r. 786–809), demonstrates the high status enjoyed by Chinese glazed ware.[11] Stonewares and porcelains had an enduring influence on the evolution of fine Islamic pottery, from the eighth to the sixteenth century. An early example of this indebtedness is the imitation by Iraqi potters of the characteristic profiles and white glazes of Tang dynasty stoneware bowls.[12]

Chinese ceramics have been recovered from numerous early Islamic sites in the Middle East, and considerable concentrations occur in ports around the Persian Gulf as well as in inland towns and cities in southern Iraq and Iran. A striking feature of the archaeological evidence is the diversity of the imported ceramics, which range from stoneware storage jars (such as the 'Dusun ware') to high-quality table ware. Dusun ware has been reported from the *misr* of Banbhore in Pakistan, the island of Socotra, the East African coast, Siraf, and several other sites in Iran (as far north as Sirjan).[13] An example of the wide distribution of finer glazed ware is provided by Yüeh wares, produced in Yeu Zhou south of Shanghai between the ninth and the eleventh century. Reported finds in the Middle East are most frequent in Sind (the north-western part of the Indian subcontinent), southern Iraq, and the Persian Gulf, though a widespread distribution via land routes is suggested by the presence of Yüeh wares in Nishapur and Rayy in Iran.[14]

Early Islamic trade with the north

Islamic coins comprise three main metals: gold (dinar), silver (dirham), and copper (fals). The frequent presence of minting dates on gold and silver issues makes coins a crucial tool in fixing the chronological parameters of an excavated context. The epigraphic (or occasionally representational) content of Islamic coins was also a vehicle for the widespread propagation of ideology. A powerful demonstration of this fact is the series of experimental Umayyad coins of the 690s, leading up to the first fully epigraphic dinar in 696–97/77 (Fig. 2.1a–c). It has been plausibly argued that this radical departure was a final response to the minting, by the Byzantine Emperor Justinian II (r. 685–95), of a gold coin (solidus) carrying an image of Christ Pantokrator ('ruler of all'). Coin hoards provide some support for this idea. Seventh-century Syrian hoards contain groups of solidi minted by earlier emperors (but not those of Justinian II), and it may be surmised that these earlier Byzantine gold coins were able to circulate freely in Umayyad lands because they did not represent such an explicit doctrinal challenge to the Islamic state.[15] This last point raises another issue that can be examined through the analysis of Islamic coins, and particularly those buried in hoards: the wide circulation of coins allows for a consideration of long-distance trading networks and other modes of exchange. A remarkable feature of the geographical distribution of Islamic coin hoards dating from the eighth to the end of the tenth century is the number of them that have been found beyond the boundaries of the Islamic world (Fig. 3.2). Thomas Noonan records seventy-seven hoards of ninth-century dirhams in 'European Russia' (that is, between the Black Sea and the Baltic Sea), while reports from Scandinavia provide equally startling figures: around 80,000 dirhams from Sweden, 400 from Norway, 1,700 from Finland, and 5,000 from Denmark.[16] Even Viking hoards located in northern England (such as the Cuerdale hoard) contain small numbers of Islamic coins. Although these substantial numbers represent only a tiny fraction of the total output of the Islamic mints of this period, the phenomenon demands further explanation.

The overwhelming majority of Islamic coins in these northern hoards are silver dirhams, and most of these coins originate in mints operating in the east of the Islamic world, particularly in those of Madinat al-Salam (Baghdad), Muhammadiyya (Rayy), Balkh, and Samarqand. Coins from the Islamic west are rare; for instance, the mints of Umayyad Spain account for only four coins out of the 7,000 found in Denmark and for only 237 out of the 80,000 found in Sweden. The hoards from European Russia present a similar picture, North African and Spanish coins forming very small percentages.[17] With few exceptions, the coins were minted after 750 and before c.1000, most coins dating from after c.780. Coins may stay in circulation for centuries, and this longevity is often reflected in wide chronological ranges encountered in hoards (as a result, it is the coin with the latest mint date that provides the most reliable indication of the time when the hoard was buried). In the case of the northern hoards, however, very few Umayyad or Sasanian coins were detected. Taking into account both the geographical bias of the mints and the chronological evidence, it is apparent that the coins from the northern hoards can be closely associated with the output of the Abbasid caliphate and of the Samanid dynasty.

From the late eighth century, large quantities of *dirhams* were flowing out of the eastern Islamic lands, either through trade or through the payment of tribute. Rather than returning to circulation in the Islamic world as the result of reciprocal exchange, these *dirhams* were retained by the inhabitants of European Russia or transported further north, to the Baltic regions and Scandinavia. Luxury items also passed along the same routes; for instance, an Iranian or Iraqi ninth-century glass beaker with wheel-cut decoration was discovered during an excavation in Birka, Sweden.[18] Turning to the historical record, northern trade was facilitated by the cessation, in the mid-eighth century, of the long-standing conflict between the caliphate and the Turkic Khazar dynasty in the Caucasus. This political accommodation opened lines of mercantile activity between the eastern Islamic lands and the peoples to the north, particularly the Bulghars and the peoples known in the Arabic sources as the *rus'* (probably comprising Vikings and some Slavs and Finns). The famous journey of Ibn Fadlan in 922, through Khwarazm and north to the Bulghar capital on the Volga river, illustrates the extent to which the Abbasid caliphate sought to foster diplomatic communications.[19]

European Russia and Scandinavia possess no natural reserves of silver, and in the eighth and ninth centuries the peoples inhabiting these areas were not producing their own metallic currencies in any significant quantities. In this context, it is easy to see the attraction of Abbasid and Samanid *dirhams*; these Islamic coins may have functioned as the *de facto* currency in some regions. That hoards are often made up of coins (not infrequently clipped or fragmentary) with scrap silver may indicate, however, that exchanges were often negotiated by weight. In addition, the presence of groups of *dirhams* (including some refashioned into jewellery) in burials in Denmark is an important reminder that the value attributed to coinage is not always purely economic in character.[20] Thus a coin hoard is not in itself evidence of mercantile activity. Written sources describe the major commodities purchased with Abbasid and Samanid silver currency: slaves, furs, wax, and honey were the most important, while amber, walrus and narwhal ivory, dried fish, and birch bark were also mentioned. Transactions were not necessarily direct; goods from Viking lands could be transferred south, from transit points such as Old Ladoga (Staraja) in the north-east of modern Russia, but there is also textual evidence for Vikings venturing south, down the Volga river.[21]

The long-term impact of this steady flow of silver out of the economy of the Islamic east has been much debated. Although there is now scepticism about the existence of a 'silver famine' in the Islamic east during the eleventh and twelfth centuries, it is noteworthy that relatively few Islamic coins minted after the 970s appear in Scandinavian hoards.[22] This may indicate a reduced production of *dirhams* after this date, or a significant decline in levels of trade. Alternative explanations may also be found in the evolving economies of Scandinavia and in the increasing tendency for rulers to mint their own coins (perhaps melting down coins both from the Islamic east and from Frankish Europe). Lastly, the wide circulation of Islamic coins might have other, less predictable effects. Offa (r. 757–96), king of Mercia in England, even minted his own '*dinar*' (Fig. 3.3) imitating a coin struck for the Abbasid Caliph al-Mansur in 773–4/157.

New buildings: mosque and *dar al-imara*

Accounts of the Arab conquests of the seventh century include examples of the *ad hoc* employment of existing structures as places of Muslim prayer. For instance the great vaulted chamber (*iwan*) of the Sasanian palace of Ctesiphon was used for communal prayer by the conquering army of Sa'd ibn Abi Waqqas. In Damascus the Muslim authorities established a *musalla* in the south-east corner of a Hellenistic–Roman *temenos*. The central part of the *temenos* continued to be occupied by the Byzantine cathedral of St John the Baptist. Similar accommodations between Muslims and Christians seem to have occurred at Hama and Aleppo in Syria, and in several Visigothic churches during the early decades of Islamic rule in the Iberian peninsula.[23] Clearly, these opportunistic solutions could not be sustained long after the initial conquest of a region. Not only did the newly established *amsar* require mosques and other administrative institutions, but there was also a need to assert – in symbolic and practical terms – the authority of the Muslim state among the existing urban populations of the nascent empire. Major changes included the substitution of Arabic for Greek and Middle Persian in the bureaucracy and the employment of Muslim invocations onto coins, documents and inscriptions (chapter 2). Equally significant was the imposition of two institutions – the congregational mosque and the residence of the governor (*dar al-imara*) – into the towns and cities of the Islamic world.

According to written sources, rudimentary mosques in Basra (635) and Kufa (638) were replaced after a few decades by more monumental structures, whose plans share many of the characteristics of extant hypostyle mosques of the eighth century and later periods. Not all seventh-century mosques adopted the arrangement of a courtyard surrounded by arcades (*riwaqs*) on three sides and a prayer hall on the *qibla* side; for instance, both the first mosque established in the *misr* of Fustat after 641–42 and the Aqsa mosque in Jerusalem (chapter 6) comprised only a covered prayer hall with no courtyard.[24] From the early years of the eighth century, there is physical evidence for the form of the mosque. This evidence includes functioning buildings surviving with their groundplans and elevations, much as they were in the eighth century (for instance Walid I's mosque in Damascus, 705–16), as well as mosques that have been much altered through time but retain sufficient remnants of their original form – either below ground or in the existing architectural fabric – to be reconstructed with reasonable certainty. Examples of this second category include the mosques of San'a' (711–15) and Cordoba (786–87). A third category comprises abandoned or ruined congregational mosques and smaller *masjids*. Focussing on the congregational mosques, the archaeological record permits a consideration of their geographical distribution, chronology, and morphology, as well as of the topographical relationships between mosques and other structures within the urban environment.

Associated on historical grounds with the governor al-Hajjaj ibn Yusuf, the first phase of the mosque excavated in the Iraqi town of Wasit has been dated to 703 (Fig. 3.4).[25] The mosque is enclosed within a perimeter wall of approximately 100 m per side, with entrances on all sides except the *qibla* wall. A single colonnade runs around three sides of the courtyard, and the prayer hall is composed of five aisles. Although a shallow rectangular niche does appear in the centre of the *qibla* wall on the published plans of the earliest mosque, the excavator, Fuad Safar, explicitly states that there was no semi-circular *mihrab* (known as *mihrab mujawwaf*) – a feature first reported in Walid I's renovation of the Prophet's Mosque in Medina in 707–9 – in the earliest building phase at Wasit.[26] Some degree of architectural sophistication can be seen in the construction of the building. The walls were of baked brick, and the roofing of the covered areas was supported on carved sandstone columns. The prayer hall may have incorporated an enclosed area (*maqsura*) for the use of the governor, around the central part of the *qibla* wall. Surviving until the early years of the eleventh century, much of the original masonry was reused to create a courtyard mosque of similar plan, but with the *qibla* oriented, more correctly, to 34 degrees further to the south.

Excavations in other parts of the Islamic world have revealed numerous eighth-century congregational mosques which adopted the components seen in the first mosque of Wasit (Fig. 3.5). None is identical in plan, however. The early ninth-century mosque at Siraf (Fig. 6.3a) provides a relatively close parallel to the plan of the Wasit mosque, though the Persian example does not have a slightly widened axial nave in the prayer hall. Some mosques contained additional arcades around the courtyard. Double arcades may be seen at Banbhore (before 727), in the 'Amman citadel (c.709–30), at Susa (second phase: eighth century), at Samarqand (Afrasiyab, c.760–80), at Istakhr (late seventh or eighth century) and possibly at Harran (744–50), while the eighth-century mosque of San'a' had triple arcades.[27] The mosque of the lower town of 'Amman (before 750), Mansura in Pakistan (eighth century), and the earliest mosque at Cordoba (786–87) evidently dispensed with the arcades around the courtyard.[28] Excavations in the courtyard of Hisham's mosque at Rusafa revealed the foundations of a single arcade from the first phase (probably before 724), though the superstructure of the arcade was never built.[29] Other morphological variations may be seen in the presence or absence of an axial nave leading to the *mihrab*; in the orientation of the aisles in the prayer hall; and in the positioning of the minaret. A regional style that illustrates the influence of Byzantine architectural traditions is the employment in the prayer hall of a basilical plan with a central transverse nave. This is seen in Damascus (which offers the prototype); in Aleppo, Dar'a, and Diyarbakr; and in the larger compound at Qasr al-Hayr East (Fig. 5.3).[30]

This variability probably demonstrates that it was the *concept* of the mosque rather than a specific plan that was circulated around the growing Islamic Empire of the seventh and eighth centuries.[31] That the actual arrangement of the covered area, courtyard, arcades, *mihrab*, minaret, and other features varies so much is an indication of the role which local factors – craft traditions, available building materials, and pre-Islamic monumental architecture – had on the process of design and construction.

Turning to spatial analysis, an important issue is the relationship of the mosque to the market (*suq*), the commercial heart of the city or town. In Walid I's new city at 'Anjar, the mosque was placed in the south-east quadrant, directly south of the *decumanus*. The degree to which the mosque was meant to be integrated into the commercial activities of 'Anjar is illustrated by the fact that the north wall of the building functions as the back wall of five shops which face onto the arcaded main street (Fig. 5.1). A somewhat different arrangement can be seen in the example of the *misr* of Ayla on the coast of the Red Sea (Fig. 5.2); excavations revealed how the expansion of the eighth-century mosque led to the remodelling of the northern section of the north-east/south-west street. Mosques were also erected in the market areas of established towns and cities. In Jarash, one of the cities of the *decapolis* in northern Jordan, the mosque founded by Hisham sat directly behind the shops at the junction of two colonnaded streets.[32]

Like the previous examples, the congregational mosque in Siraf was also surrounded by markets, and in its second phase even incorporated a series of commercial units into the lower storey on the south-east side; but the placement of the building also raises another issue of interpretation (Fig. 6.3). The ruined structures of the earlier Sasanian fort, rather than being cleared to make way for the mosque, were simply encased within the two-metre-high platform of rubble and earth. While it might be tempting to suspect symbolic overtones in this appropriation of the Sasanian site by the Muslim religious structure, such an interpretation is explicitly rejected by the excavators.[33] The imposition of a mosque into an existing urban environment must have often required the clearing of other buildings, though it would appear that arrangements were often made by consent rather than through threat or the imposition of force. For instance, Walid I is reputed to have bought the area of the *temenos* in Damascus before demolishing the cathedral and erecting his mosque. That said, it is hard to imagine that the caliph would have been satisfied with any other location within the city. By contrast, the construction in the 740s of a mosque in the pagan city of Harran represented a bold statement of religious and political authority, regardless of the monument it may have replaced. The available evidence for the reuse of architectural elements from older structures in early mosques does not, however, provide a consistent pattern of appropriation as a symbol of the victory of Islam. A striking example of the rather opportunistic employment of older stonework can be seen in the *Siva-lingan* (Hindu phallic sculpture) incorporated in the masonry of the mosque of Banbhore.[34]

Archaeological research has led to the recovery of fewer palatial and administrative structures associated with the congregational mosques. The close association of the locus of political power – the governor's residence or a palatial complex employed by the caliph – with the mosque, the place of communal prayer and the delivery of the Friday sermon (*khutba*) was evidently established from an early stage in Islamic history. According to written sources, in 638 a *dar al-imara* was located south of the *qibla* wall of the mosque in Kufa by the governor, Sa'd ibn Abi Waqqas. In 665, Ziyad ibn Abihi moved his residence to the area directly south of the *qibla* wall of the mosque in Basra. The account of the event given by the historian al-Baladhuri (d. c.892) states that the governor did this so that he could enter the mosque discreetly, without having to pass through the Muslim congregation. Given the very real danger of assassination during communal prayer, practical considerations of security may have motivated this decision in some part. The potent political symbolism of establishing an intimate connection between palace and mosque should be acknowledged, however.[35]

The earliest extant remains of a *dar al-imara* were located during excavations directly south of the congregational mosque in Kufa (Fig. 2.3). This
impressive brick-built complex was found to have been constructed in three
separate phases, from the seventh century to the second half of the eighth. The
earliest layer – of which only sections of the fortified wall and the main (north)
gate survived – revealed a square-planned enclosure with four rectangular corner
towers and additional salients on each side. The groundplan of the first building
was retained in the second stage, though the new wall employed round towers.
The whole was enclosed within a second fortified wall, separated from the inner
one by over twenty metres. The inner palace had a tripartite arrangement, the
central zone providing a ceremonial axis from the outer and inner gates through
to a courtyard, a three-aisled hall and, finally, a square domed chamber. The
changes of the third phase were less radical, though they included the reconstruction of the gateway on the north side of the outer wall and the addition
of an underground pool (*sirdab*) in the north-west corner of the palace. The
mosque was evidently enclosed within a wall of just over 100 metres per side.[36]

Although the written sources, the excavated coins and the architecture
provide somewhat contradictory data, it is possible that the excavations
recovered some seventh-century building work (perhaps associated with the
governorship of Ziyad ibn Abihi). Whatever the precise chronology, features
such as the rectangular salients of the first phase are reminiscent of pre-Islamic
Persian building practices. The round towers of the subsequent phase are similar
to those found on most of the Umayyad *qusur*. The tripartite arrangement and
ceremonial axis of the palace perhaps derives from pre-Islamic Persian prototypes (Sasanian and Lakhmid), but also marks an important stage towards the
more sophisticated Islamic palaces of the mid to the late eighth century, like
Mshatta and Ukhaydir. For the present purposes, however, the most important
point is that the excavations at Kufa provide physical confirmation of the close
spatial relationship between mosque and *dar al-imara*.

The fragmentary remains of a governor's palace were also located directly
south of the mosque in Wasit. In this case, the palace was the larger structure
of the two, probably measuring about 200 metres per side.[37] The early eighth-
century urban foundation of 'Anjar illustrates the integration of the congregational mosque and of the *dar al-imara* within the city plan. The mosque contains
two principal entrances, to the north and west, and two additional doorways
in the *qibla* wall. The doorway west of the *mihrab* gives direct access from the
dar al-imara into the *maqsura*. It is also possible to detect the same arrangement
of mosque and *dar al-imara* at the *misr* of Istakhr in Iran (possibly a seventh-
century one) and in the eighth-century foundation of Mansura in Pakistan.
While eighth-century structures were recovered around the perimeter of the
mosque in Banbhore, the excavators do not identify any of them as a governor's

residence. In later periods there appears to be a downgrading (in architectural terms) of the *dar al-imara*.[38] For instance the complexes located south of the *qibla* walls of the congregational mosque and mosque of Abu Dulaf in Samarra are constructed on a relatively modest scale and were probably designed for the caliph's personal use before prayer. A similar arrangement appears to have existed at the mosque of Ibn Tulun in Cairo (876–9).[39]

A greater degree of spatial complexity could also be introduced into this relationship between mosque and palace. Excavations beyond the southern and eastern walls of the Haram al-Sharif in Jerusalem revealed an elaborate palatial/residential complex dating to the Umayyad period (Fig. 3.6). Noteworthy is the relationship with the Aqsa mosque immediately to the north. In its second form, the mosque (known as Aqsa II) was accessed from the south in two ways, one more public and the other private. The first led through the Double Gate via a tunnel to the courtyard of the Haram, immediately north of the mosque. The gate was evidently refurbished in the Umayyad period, and the ancient Herodian tunnel was also lengthened, to allow for the expansion of the prayer hall. The second access ran from the upper part of the central palace through a door in the eastern section of the *qibla* wall.[40]

The physical separation between the mosque and the governor's or the caliph's residence is also encountered elsewhere. A monumental arcade on the south side of the Great Mosque of Damascus is believed to have connected the caliph's palace (known as the *Khadra'*) to two entrances on the east and west sides of the *qibla* wall. This increased complexity is also seen slightly later, in the mosque constructed by Caliph Hisham in Rusafa (Sergiopolis). In this case the caliph's palaces were located outside the walls of the late antique city, while the mosque – containing two *mihrab*s with the gate of the caliph between them – cut into the space of the northern courtyard of the Church of St Sergius. Another example can be seen in 'Amman, where the excavation of an eighth-century mosque at the south end of the citadel changes our appreciation of the functioning of the site (chapter 5).[41] In common with the inhabitants of later urban citadels such as Aleppo and Cairo, those of the 'Amman citadel had their own congregrational mosque, another one being located in the town below (Fig. 5.4).[42] It is apparent from the plan of the citadel, however, that the positioning of the mosque does not follow the models outlined above. As all of the palatial complexes are to the north of the mosque, the governor could have entered the mosque, like the rest of the congregation, from the entrance on the north side. That said, the plan of the mosque does reveal an entrance through the *qibla* wall just to the west of the monumental *mihrab* that may have been reserved for the governor. A later combination of palace and mosque in the tenth-century town of Mahdiyya in Tunisia certainly precluded the provision of an entrance through the *qibla* wall, as this part of the mosque abutted the sea wall. Nevertheless, the reconstruction of this early Fatimid capital indicates the existence of a ceremonial connection between the congregational mosque and the palaces of 'Ubayd Allah and Abu al-Qasim. Just like the later eastern and western palaces in Fatimid Cairo, the palaces of Mahdiyya faced one another on either side of a large parade ground (*maydan*).[43]

Notes

1   Walmsley (2007), 118–20.
2   Bloom (2001).
3   Küchler (1991).
4   Watson (1983), 90–8; Glick (2002).
5   Khamis (2001), 173–6.
6   Roll and Ayalon (1987); Tsafrir and Foerster (1994), 111–15; Al-As'ad and Stepniowski (1989); Walmsley and Damgaard (2005); also Foote (2000); Rosen-Ayalon (2006), 58; Walmsley (2007), 84–7.
7   Mason (2004), 23. On the glazed pottery from Rabadha, see al-Rashid (1986), 54–62.
8   Laing (1991); Jiayao (1991). See also Dien (2004).
9   Translated in Lopez and Raymond (2001), 28–9.
10 Kennet (2005), 68–85, 114–16.
11 Translated in Lane (1957), 10–11.
12 On Chinese ceramics and their influence on early Islamic glazed wares, see Lane (1957), 10–16; Rawson, Tite and Hughes (1989); Northedge and Kennet (1994), 34; Northedge (1996) and (2001); Mason (2004), 29–32, 43–4.
13 Whitehouse (1973a), 244–6. For criticisms of the ceramic chronology at Siraf, see Kennet (2004), 83–4.
14 Williamson (1987), 11–14.
15 Blair (1992), 81–5; Walmsley (2007), 59–64. For a detailed discussion of 'pre-Reform' Islamic gold, silver and bronze coinage, see Album and Goodwin (2002).
16 Noonan (1981). See also Jansson (1988).
17 Kromann and Roesdahl (1996), 16, fig. 6; Hovén (1981), 119; Noonan (1981), 64–6, table C.
18 Kröger (1995), 152, fig. 13. Among the other unusual imported items was a Kashmiri cast metal Budda found at Helgö, Sweden. See Hodges and Whitehouse (1983), 118, fig. 49.
19 Frye (2005).
20 Kromann and Roesdahl (1996), figs 2, 3.
21 Noonan (1986); Frye (2005), 103–9.
22 Kromann and Roesdahl (1996), 12; Hovén (1981). See also Hodges and Whitehouse (1983), 111–22.
23 Creswell (1969), 1:1, 17–22, 187–96; Creswell and Allan (1989), 6–8, 63–8; Flood (2001), 2, 123; Zozaya (1998), 245–7.
24 Evidence summarised in Johns (1999), 59–69. See also Creswell and Allan (1989); Hillenbrand (1994), 66–78.
25 Safar (1945); Creswell and Allan (1989), 40–41; Johns (1999), 59–64; Johns (2003), 414–15.

26 Safar (1945), 20, 24–7, fig. 11.
27 Khan (1976), 24–30; Whitcomb (1979), 363–6, fig. at 365; Kervran and Rouguelle (1984), 13–31; Grenet and Rapin (1998), fig. 2; Karev (2004), 56–7, fig. 3.3; Almagro and Jiménez (2000). Also Creswell and Allan (1989), 83–8, 217–25.
28 Anon. (1968); Ashfaque (1969); Farooq (1974–86), 11–15; Khan (1990); Northedge (1992), 63–9; Dodds, ed. (1992), 11–16, fig. 1. On the mosques of Pakistan, see also Khan (1991).
29 Sack (1996), 63–7, pls 70, 74.
30 Sauvaget (1947), 122–57; Creswell (1969), 1:1, 197–8; Creswell and Allan (1989), 72–3. The origins of this arrangement are palatial – the *chalke* (vestibule) of the imperial palace in Constantinople. The most detailed treatment of this question appears in Flood (2001).
31 Johns (1999), 109–10.
32 Whitcomb (1994b); Hillenbrand (1999), 62–4, fig. 1; Walmsley and Damgaard (2005). Also Creswell and Allan (1989), 122–4; Walmsley (2007), 84–7.
33 Whitehouse (1980), 4.
34 Khan (1976), 27.
35 Creswell and Allan (1989), 7–10; Johns (1999), 86–8.
36 Creswell (1969), 1:1, 48–58; Creswell and Allan (1989), 10–15; Johns (2003), 417–18.
37 Safar (1945), 20–3, 27–8.
38 Whitcomb (1979), 363–6; Farooq (1974–86), 16–35; Khan (1990), 33–9.
39 Creswell and Allan (1989), 370–3, 392; Northedge (2005a), 122–5, 216, figs 50, 97.
40 Ben-Dov (1985), 293–321. Also Rosen-Ayalon (1989), 8–11.
41 Flood (2001), 139–59; Sack (1996), 63–7, pl. 71; Almagro and Jiménez (2000). Also Walmsley (2007), 81–90.
42 Northedge (1992), 60–9. For a detailed study of Aleppo citadel and the monumental architecture of the city, see Tabbaa (1997).
43 Lézine (1965), fig. 3; Lézine (1967), 82–101.

4

The countryside

The study of life in rural areas is an important aspect of Islamic archaeology. Allowing for the importance of trade and industry, the production of agricultural commodities represented the economic foundation of most pre-modern Islamic polities. Clearly this is a vast topic, and a single chapter is insufficient to do justice to the range of environmental and cultural factors that have shaped every aspect of rural life, from demographic patterns and strategies of land exploitation to the internal arrangement of structures within a settlement and to the nature of the material record. Settlements themselves can vary from villages and small market towns to more transient modes of occupation, while some groups may shift on a seasonal basis between sedentary and nomadic lifestyles.[1]

To take just one example, the issue of diversity is well illustrated through the consideration of rural settlements. As discussed in chapter 2, late antique provincial towns such as Umm al-Jimal in northern Jordan (Fig. 2.7) and Shivta in the Negev adopt an 'organic' plan, composed of an agglomeration of clusters of buildings that probably reflect familial and clan ties. Irregular arrangements of buildings can also be seen in the vicinities of some Umayyad *qusur* (chapter 5), while at a smaller level the late antique/early Islamic village of Risha in the east Jordanian steppe is composed of a loose configuration of varied courtyard houses. Numerous excavations have illuminated the evolution of villages in Jordan and Palestine throughout the Islamic period.[2] Looking elsewhere in the Middle East, however, it is evident that village plans could be conditioned by such factors as ecology and considerations of security. An example of the former kind may be seen in the ribbon-like settlements stretching along the levees of the Diyala plain and other heavily irrigated zones.[3] By contrast, Anatolian rural communities in the contested borderlands (*thughur*) between the Byzantine Empire and Islam were often closely packed on top of a hill and enclosed within a fortified perimeter wall. This strategy can be seen in Turkish sites such as Taşkun Kale and Gritille, and in the settlement of Ilkhanid period (1256–1353) at Hasanlu Tepe in Iranian Azerbaijan (Fig. 4.1).[4] Built in one phase and occupied for a relatively short period, Hasanlu Tepe probably functioned as a fort administering the surrounding agricultural region. Despite its rural location, its inhabitants evidently enjoyed access to some relatively luxurious imported items, including lustre-painted glass and a type of gilded glazed pottery known as Lajvardina ware.

Muslim states were also involved in the construction of fortified buildings in rural areas; these ranged from caravanserais (Fig. 8.1) and watchtowers along pilgrimage routes to castles and other military installations. Often designed to accommodate substantial populations of soldiers and members of the bureaucratic elite, castles evidently performed defensive and administrative functions, as well as representing the major economic centre for the surrounding region. The complex relationship between castle and rural hinterland has been examined in studies conducted in different regions of the Islamic world.[5]

Many techniques are employed in the archaeological examination of rural life. Most obvious are field surveys and the excavation of rural sites. Archaeobotanical studies of carbonised seeds and pollen have helped to establish aspects of crops and diet. Notable too is the analysis of weed flora as a means to study the employment of irrigation technology.[6] The analysis of faunal remains also contributes to our understanding of animal rearing, butchering practices, diet, and potentially the trade in meat and other animal products.[7] For instance the presence of pig bones on a site is often the sign of the presence of a Christian community (though the possibility of pork consumption by Muslims or other religious groups should not be discounted). The first section of the present chapter reviews the methods utilised in regional surveys and the ways in which the data collected in these projects have been interpreted. The second section concentrates upon complex water transport and collection systems. The last part of the chapter looks at one specialised commodity – sugar – and considers the role of archaeology in reconstructing the spread and the eventual decline of this lucrative industry in the Middle East.

Rural settlement patterns: methods and interpretation

Much of the archaeological study of rural areas in the Middle East has been directed toward the analysis of settlement and land exploitation strategies that occur over the long term. Importantly, changes in agricultural practices or rural settlement patterns usually occur relatively slowly, often over the course of centuries. These are phenomena that frequently exhibit little observable correlation with wars, dynastic changes, or other major events in the historical record. The study of settlement patterns over larger areas can only be achieved through survey techniques. Regional surveys usually aim to record the visible evidence of occupation prior to the modern period – standing structures, ruins, walls demarcating fields, or hydraulic features – and collect the artefacts left on the surface. Leaving aside such ancient items as worked flints, pottery is the most ubiquitous artefact type gathered on multi-period surveys. Generally collection procedures tend to focus attention on the more easily datable 'diagnostics': that is, potsherds that retain parts of the rim, base, handle, or surface decoration (including the use of glazes).

Before considering the results from selected field surveys in the Middle East, it is worth noting some of the methodological problems inherent in this archaeological technique. The criteria for defining what constitutes a settlement are significant in the assessment of the nature and extent of the population in a given period. This point has particular resonance in many regions of North Africa, the Middle East and Central Asia because of the coexistence of sedentary, partially nomadic, and fully nomadic populations. Cultivated areas often border semi-arid steppe lands, and settled and bedouin groups may interact in the same spaces on a seasonal basis. Naturally, the traces of temporary encampments and of transient types of occupation such as cave dwelling are more difficult to identify than standing or ruined villages. Furthermore, nomadic groups may make little or no use of ceramics, thus leaving much less trace in the archaeological record. The failure to incorporate such settlement strategies into the design of a survey will often result in an underestimation of population levels.

The study of the ceramics also presents some serious interpretive issues, which can determine the results of the survey. The chronological parameters for ceramic wares rely largely upon data collected from excavated contexts. If the excavated sites are, for instance, located within towns and cities, then one needs to account for the possibility that some wares or vessel shapes may persist longer (sometimes much longer) in rural areas than in urban environments. If this possibility of persistence is ignored, it often leads to apparent lacunae in the ceramic sequences for particular areas. Sometimes re-examination of survey ceramics will suggest quite different dating for key types of ware, leading to a radical reassessment of the settlement patterns. Thus such gaps can be due to a sudden decline in sedentary occupation, but may also be explained through insufficiently accurate dating for certain ceramic wares. Lastly, rural areas may present rather different ceramic traditions from those of towns, as is seen in the remarkable emergence of handmade ware all over the Middle East from the eleventh century (chapter 7).

Recent re-examination by Jodi Magness of ceramics gathered from surveys in semi-arid regions of Nahal Yattir, Darom, and the Negev in the south of Israel has suggested a picture of settlement patterns that diverges from previously held views. Initial research in Nahal Yattir indicated a slow decline in settlement in the last phase of Byzantine rule (sixth and early seventh centuries), which continued into the early centuries of Islam. The revision of the ceramic chronology creates a more positive picture, there being a continuity of settlement from the Byzantine period until as late as the eighth or the ninth century. Thus

the Islamic conquest probably had little impact on the extent of the rural population in these marginal lands. Interestingly, Jodi Magness did find evidence for
the abandonment of some military installations, churches, and monasteries in
the seventh century. Elsewhere in these regions there are signs of relative prosperity during the sixth century, as well as possible evidence of state investment.
In towns of Negev such as Nessana and Shivta there was continued occupation
into the Abbasid and even into the Fatimid period (that is, after 969). In the
case of Nessana, the papyri from the site also support this picture of prosperity
in the late seventh and early eighth centuries.[8]

These results are significant because they conflict with the view that the
economy of Greater Syria suffered a severe downturn in the sixth century.[9] At
present, the patchy geographical coverage of archaeological work, particularly
in Syria, does not allow for the formulation of a coherent picture, but there
are some interesting examples suggesting continuity of occupation through
the sixth century and into the Islamic period. For instance, the so-called 'dead
cities' of the Jabal Ansariyya have been interpreted as part of an expansion into
somewhat marginal agricultural land in the period c.350–550. The widespread
abandonment of these settlements prior to the Islamic conquest is now questioned by results from Dehes/Dayhis, where excavations show probable evidence
of occupation through to the eighth or ninth century. It is also possible that the
foundation dates of this and some of the other villages of the region could be
pushed into the sixth century (the period of supposed decline).[10] By contrast,
abandonment of settlements in the seventh century seems likely in the case
of the hinterland above Pella, on the east side of the Jordan valley.[11] Further
to the west, surveys in Tunisia indicate that the countryside remained relatively prosperous and populous in the fifth century, though abandonment of
settlements does appear to have occurred some time in the sixth. The period
of Vandal rule (c.429–533) may actually have benefited the rural economy, as
the annual surplus remained in the region rather than being sent via Carthage
to Constantinople. The tendency of published surveys and excavations to end
their analysis with the seventh century makes it difficult to assess the nature of
rural settlement in North Africa between the Islamic conquest and the apparent
revival of the agricultural sector in the tenth to eleventh centuries.[12]

The Karak Plateau in Jordan has been subjected to relatively intense
field surveys in recent decades and provides interesting data about long-term
settlement patterns and rural material culture from the late antique to the early
Ottoman period (Fig. 4.2). Bounded to the north by the Wadi al-Mujib, to
the south by the Wadi al-Hasa, and to the west by the Dead Sea depression,
modern settlement is concentrated on the central zone, which combines fertile
soils with a rainfall of c.350 mm per annum. The more arid lands to the east
contain fewer villages and are populated by pastoral nomads (bedouin), who

often bring their flocks west in the summer to graze the stubble left in the fields. This general pattern of settlement can be identified in earlier centuries, though the evidence from the architecture, and particularly from the ceramic record, indicates fluctuations in the sedentary population over time. Like the rural areas of Palestine to the west, the Karak Plateau appears to have been densely settled in the last phase of Byzantine rule. The initial interpretation of the ceramic evidence suggested a drop during the Umayyad period, followed by a precipitous decline in the settled population between the late eighth and the late eleventh century. The revival of this region occurred during the period from the twelfth to the fourteenth century (which correlates with crusader, Ayyubid and early Mamluk rule); a second phase of decline started in the fifteenth century and lasted until the end of the nineteenth.

How much credence should be given to the pronounced peaks and troughs registered in the surveys of the plateau? Did this region become largely depopulated in the early Islamic centuries, and again during the late Mamluk and Ottoman periods, or did the occupants reject village life in favour of pastoral nomadism? In the absence of the more precise dating now available for the ceramics circulating to the west in Palestine, considerable caution should be exercised in the reconstruction of settlement in this region during the early Islamic centuries. It seems probable, however, that the persistence of some late antique ceramic types would permit both a reduction in the late Byzantine peak and a less steep decline in settlement from the eighth century. Likewise, the difficulty in dating later handmade pottery and plain-glazed earthenware means that a larger proportion of this extensive corpus could be placed into the first centuries of Ottoman rule. This would certainly accord well with the rather more positive picture of agricultural life in sixteenth-century Ottoman cadastral records.[13]

Turning to the character of the material culture, the period from the twelfth to the fourteenth century is most varied. Significant is the dominating presence of handmade pottery – comprising 90–100 per cent of the total assemblage per site – in other places than the administrative and economic centre of Karak (Fig. 7.7a and b). This finding suggests that rural communities were largely self-reliant in the matter of craft production, though it should be balanced against the rather richer finds – including marvered glass, copper finger rings, and glazed ceramics – recovered from the excavation of the village of Khirbat Faris.[14] The distribution of glazed pottery on the plateau, an indicator of greater wealth on a site, is concentrated among sites in the immediate vicinity of Karak and on either side of the major road through the region, the 'King's Highway' (Darb al-Malik). Proximity to the major economic centre of Karak (and, to a lesser extent, to the smaller market towns of Rabba and Mu'ta) and to the main artery employed by merchants and by the annual hajj caravan from Damascus helped to stimulate economic activity in the villages of the plateau, probably through the sale of agricultural produce. The importance of trade routes is also indicated by the relative abundance of glazed ware in settlements at the southern end of the Dead Sea (it was via this route that most of the manufactured goods from Jerusalem and Hebron found their way to the Karak Plateau). The more remote rural communities south of the Wadi al-Hasa appear to have enjoyed little access to glazed wares, however, and ceramic assemblages from villages are composed almost exclusively of handmade pottery.[15]

The archaeology of water transport and conservation

The lands of Central Asia, the Middle East, North Africa, and the Iberian peninsula are notable for their environmental diversity. In general, however, these lands are dominated by semi-arid and arid climates. Precipitation is concentrated in the winter months (November–March), and summers are hot and dry. In such environments it is vital to find ways either of capturing winter rainfall for use during the summer months or of locating other reliable perennial sources (rivers and streams, natural springs, and underground aquifers). Another challenge is presented by the uneven distribution of the areas of fertile soil, which is such that it becomes necessary to transport the water from its source to the area destined for cultivation.

The simplest modes of agriculture – dry farming techniques – do not employ irrigation systems, relying instead on annual rainfall for the cultivation of wheat, barley, and legumes, often supplemented by olive, almond and fruit trees. In Jordan as in many other parts of the Middle East, the additional water was provided by springs or deep plaster-lined cisterns cut into the limestone bedrock. Positioned where they could capture the maximum quantity of winter rain, Jordanian cisterns are between 5 and 25 m deep and can store water for as long as two or three years.[16] Dry farming techniques require limited capital investment, but they result in lower crop yields. Relatively simple water conservation techniques such as the construction of retaining walls can help to conserve the available moisture within the cultivated areas. Examples of large enclosures of this type exist at the eighth-century settlements at Ma'an and Qasr al-Hayr East (chapter 2). Walled terraces in mountainous regions such as Oman, Yemen, and Iran operate on a similar principle. These artificial steps also impede the erosion of the fertile soil during the winter rains. The damming of wadis collects water and controls the destructive flash floods generated after periods of sustained rainfall. These simple dams could be connected to pools for storing the overflow. Structures like the 'great dam' at Ma'rib in Yemen require much more sophisticated engineering skills. Supporting the ancient irrigated agriculture of the Ma'rib region, the dam was composed of a giant earth barrier with two monumental masonry sluices, to the south and to the north. The north sluice reached its present form as the result of construction phases in the mid-fifth and mid-sixth centuries.[17]

Other hydraulic systems were designed to transport water and distribute it over large areas of cultivated land. This could be achieved by two means: open canals or underground channels, commonly known as *qanats*. An individual system might employ both types, while other features such as aqueducts were built where the terrain demanded. Open canals were suitable where it was necessary to tap directly into the waters of a river. They could also run directly from a source such as a natural spring and follow the contours of the landscape in a manner similar to that of terracing on hillsides. In order to prevent the erosion of the canal itself, the gradient had to be kept shallow, though rapid drops in altitude could be achieved through the inclusion of a vertical plaster-lined shaft. The energy created by the swift passage of water was often exploited through the construction of an undershot mill (known as an Arubah-penstock).[18]

While the digging of open canal channels and the building-up of levees certainly required technical skill and a considerable expenditure of labour, the construction of a *qanat* represents a challenge of a greater magnitude. Believed to be of Iranian origin, the *qanat* comprises an underground channel set at a shallow gradient and connected to the surface by a series of vertical shafts (Fig. 4.3). The shafts provide air for the diggers of the *qanat* as well as access points for subsequent maintenance work. The underground tunnels collect their water as it percolates through the soil (for instance at the base of a mountain range or alongside a river), and then direct it towards the cultivated land. The length of the tunnels varies, but it may reach up to 50–60 km. The initial depth of the channel is dependent upon the location of the water source and upon the horizontal extension of the *qanat*. The depth of the vertical shafts of those at Gonabad in Iran measures up to 300 m, though this is exceptional.[19] The great skill of the *qanat* builder was in maintaining the shallow gradient of the tunnel such that it emerged from the ground just above the area destined for cultivation. At this point the water may be collected in a large cistern, from which it can be transferred to the fields via a system of open channels. While the costs involved in the initial construction phase are very high and regular maintenance is essential, a *qanat* can have an active life spanning centuries. Even where they have collapsed it is still possible to trace their course through the regular lines of sink holes.

Retaining walls, terracing, cisterns, mills, open canals, *qanats*, water wheels (*norias*) and *shadufs* (a simple lever) have all left their mark on the landscapes of the Islamic world. Ceramic vessels associated with water-lifting devices also appear on excavations.[20] These features provide invaluable evidence concerning the exploitation of agricultural land before the intervention of modern farming practices, but their interpretation is often problematic. The key issue is the difficulty of establishing relative or absolute chronologies for water control systems encountered in excavations and surveys. With rare exceptions these constructions are not provided with monumental inscriptions. Furthermore, long phases of active use – sometimes stretching across several centuries – and of successive repairs can obliterate the evidence for the initial date of construction.

The ancient canal systems of the Diyala plain in Iraq were studied by Robert Adams. Confronted by the problem of dating individual channels within this complex network of canals, Adams correlated textual and archaeological data. In particular, he relied upon the ceramics gathered from the abandoned villages and towns established along the courses of canals. His reasoning was that the ceramic assemblages from these sites could provide the dating both for the settlements and for the phases of canal construction and use. In order to refine the chronological parameters of the glazed and unglazed ceramics of the late Sasanian and Islamic periods, Adams also conducted a stratigraphic excavation in one site of the region, Tal Abu Sarifa.[21] The larger conclusions concerning the expansion or contraction of the canal system over time depend upon the reliability of pottery sherds (and especially those from the coarse unglazed wares, which make up the bulk of the finds) as chronological indicators. This aspect of Adams' work has been the subject of extensive criticism. Apart from the obvious possibility of assigning the wrong date to a group of sherds, there is also the problem of how to interpret negative evidence such as the absence from a survey site of 'diagnostic' pottery from a given period. Adams sometimes inferred settlement size from the area covered by the surface ceramics, though this may have led him to overestimate the density of the population on the plain.[22]

Although Adams' survey of the Diyala plain should be read in the light of these caveats, his work remains of great value for the insights it provides into the rural landscape of central Iraq from c.4000 BCE to the sixteenth century CE (Fig. 4.4). The earliest phases of the irrigation system are not directly relevant, though it should be noted that the techniques involved in raising and diverting water and in cutting watercourses bounded by levees were not innovations of the Islamic period, or even of the Sasanian dynasty. Several features of fundamental importance can be detected, however, in the Sasanian period. First, ceramics collected in surface reconnaissance indicate that the largest number of settlements occurred under Sasanian rule. The eastern bank of the Tigris was also the locus of significant urban activity, with the foundation of Veh Ardashir in the third century and the continued development of its northern neighbour, Ctesiphon. Second, such information as we have concerning tax revenues from agriculture indicates that the sixth century marked the *floruit* of the Sawad – an area which encompassed the Diyala plain and the remainder of central and southern Mesopotamia – in terms of rural population and area of land under cultivation. The strain placed on the Diyala river by the massive extraction of water into irrigation systems was ameliorated during this period by the construction of a major waterway, known as the Nahrawan/Katul al-Kisrawi and probably commissioned by Khusraw I Anushirvan (r. 531–79), which drew water from two points on the Tigris and directed it south-east to the Diyala plain.[23]

The expansion of the total area of irrigated land in the fifth and sixth centuries may be attributed to the capital investment and administrative practices of the Sasanian state. Although the turbulence of the late Sasanian period doubt-lessly resulted in some reduction of this irrigation system, the new Islamic rulers inherited a very productive agricultural sector in the Diyala plain and elsewhere in Iraq. Adams established three broad divisions in the Islamic ceramic assem-blages: the first one would go from the conquest to the end of the ninth century; the second would start around the time of the abandonment of Samarra by the Abbasid caliphs in 892 and finish with the Mongol conquest of Baghdad in 1258; and the third would encompass the Ilkhanid and later dynasties. The second and third phases may both be characterised as centuries of decline in which over-taxation, under-investment, attacks by nomads and periodic political instability resulted in a steady reduction of the total area of irrigated land. Some sectors of the Diyala plain fared better than others over the long-term, but this process of rural decay eventually led to the virtual collapse of the entire irrigation system by the sixteenth century. More interesting in archaeological terms, however, is the evidence for the first phase, from the conquest of Iraq in the 630s to the end of the ninth century. This was also the period that witnessed the foundation of two cities on the borders of the Diyala plain, Baghdad (762–66) and Samarra (from 836), conceived on a scale unparalleled in the earlier history of the region. The imposition of these massive urban centres leads to questions concerning the ability of the rural hinterland to supply the city dwellers.

The records for the Sawad show a significant decline in annual revenue from the heights of the Sasanian period to the early decades of Islamic rule, with further falls during the ninth and tenth centuries. Against this negative picture, archaeological surveys suggest a relatively healthy situation, with considerable continuity of settlement from the late Sasanian to the early Islamic period. Adams was also able to identify 160 villages and provincial towns founded in the seventh and eighth centuries, though this creation of new settlements appears to have tailed off in the ninth century. In other words, the Diyala plain continued to be relatively prosperous and populous following the Islamic conquest. The eighth and ninth centuries are marked by a reduction in the area under culti-vation (in relation to the sixth century), which coincided with the creation of the great Abbasid capitals on the Tigris. This disparity between the urban centres and the hinterland could be supported in periods of prosperity, but the tendency of states to place an excessive tax burden upon rural areas seems to have started an inexorable cycle of decay.

Results from the Diyala plain can be compared with surveys of other areas formerly encompassed by the Sasanian Empire. Reconnaisance work in the Deh Luran region in Khuzistan (western Iran) has found evidence of rural settlement and complex water systems making use of the springs and natural contours of the landscape. Qanats were constructed to bring water from the Mehmeh and Dawairij rivers to the fertile plain. While the dating of the ceramics allowed only for rather broad chronological categorisation, it would appear that it was during the Sasanian and early Islamic period (up to c.800) that the region witnessed its greatest population density. The majority of the qanats, open canals, dams, and mills can be associated with this phase. It remains unclear whether this burst of construction work can be attributed to local initiative or to the intervention of Shapur II (r. 309–79), of Khusraw I, or even of the Umayyad Caliph Hisham.[24] Recent re-examination of ceramic evidence from northern Mesopotamia also suggests that the rural areas were relatively populous during the Sasanian period. Studies of canalisation and settlement patterns in the Balikh valley in north-eastern Syria also present a picture of rural prosperity from the seventh to the eleventh centuries.[25]

The Susiana plain further to the south, in Khuzistan, presents a different picture: the period of greatest rural population density and investment in the irrigation infrastructure occurs under Parthian rule, particularly between c.25 BCE and 125 CE. Significant changes did occur, however, under the Sasanians; smaller irrigation canals were replaced by larger channels and massive stone weirs were built along the major rivers. The plain also supported three large Sasanian cities – Shushtar, Ivan-i Karkhah and Gondeshapur – the latter two requiring the construction of networks of canals and qanats to supply the inhabitants with water. Survey work indicates that it was during the Parthian period that the rural population reached its greatest extent, though parts of the region evidently continued in later times with the intensive cultivation of such irrigation-dependent crops as rice and sugar-cane. Despite having to supply three cities, the Susiana plain does not appear to have suffered the collapse experienced in the Diyala plain during the early Islamic period, and evidence of continued specialised agriculture is demonstrated by the existence of sugar manufacture through to the eleventh or twelfth century.[26]

Complex irrigation systems known as falaj (plural aflaj) have been located in surveys in Oman. These systems usually combine qanats with open canals and rely upon the springs and abundant ground water which are a feature of the geology of this region. The aflaj sustained agriculture in the mountainous areas, but they also fed water onto the arid coastal plain (supplementing the animal-powered hoist wells) where it was collected in large pools before being diverted into the field system. The presence of numerous wadis also allowed for the collection of surface water, but the preference for *qanats* probably indicates an Iranian influence – perhaps as early as the eighth century BC – in the initial establishment of the irrigation systems of Oman.

The port of Suhar enjoyed its most active period of commercial activity during the ninth and the tenth centuries. During this time copper was mined in the nearby mountains[27] and an area of 6,100 hectares of land around Suhar was subjected to intense cultivation. Surveys of the Wadi Jizzi and the hills behind Suhar revealed a network of open channels, *qanats*, and associated structures that were designed to supply the irrigated coastal zone.[28] The natural ravines can have destructive flash floods in winter, and it is necessary for *aflaj* to pass over (via aqueducts) or under them. The latter solution may be seen in the Wadi Jizzi, where channels made of rubble and waterproof mortar (*saruj*) were constructed beneath the bed of the ravine. The vertical drop required by these subterranean channels provided the opportunity to create water powered mills (often constructed underground). Ceramics collected around these structures confirm that the mills were in operation during the ninth and tenth centuries, correlating well with the evidence of trade at Suhar during the 'golden age' of the First Imamate in Oman. While some parts of the irrigated area around Suhar reported glazed potsherds of the twelfth and thirteenth centuries, the ceramic evidence pointed to a cessation in the maintenance of the *aflaj* until the seventeenth century. This latter phase of activity can probably be correlated with the rise of the Ya'ariba Imamate (1625–1743).[29]

Different technological traditions left their mark on practices of cultivation in the regions bordering the Mediterranean. In Spain there is still abundant evidence of Roman hydraulic engineering, including the impressive aqueduct of Segovia, though much of it appears to have been designed to supply water for urban populations rather than for irrigated fields (chapter 5). Islamic rule brought with it crops – sugar cane, rice, cotton, apricot, mulberry, and orange – that were unknown in Roman and Visigothic times.[30] What is less clear from the historical and archaeological evidence is the extent to which the irrigation technology was imported from the Middle East and North Africa to the south of the Iberian peninsula by the eighth-century Arab and Berber conquerors. One fairly clear Islamic innovation was the use of the *qanat* – though this does not appear to have found common application – but other aspects of the water-control systems were probably already widely known in late antique Iberia and North Africa.[31]

Analysis of the irrigation system (*huerta* in Spanish) in the region inland from Valencia revealed the presence of networks on various scales, exhibiting different degrees of complexity.[32] Macro-scale systems comprise the irrigation networks within the floodplains of rivers such as the Mijares. The south side of the Mijares river supported an irrigated zone of 6,700 hectares in the nineteenth century; similar figures have been calcultated for the systems associated with other rivers in the region. Archaeological research has provided evidence for the existence of Roman canals within this network, while other canals can be associated with the *Reconquista* foundation of Vilareal in 1274.[33] The presence of numerous Arabic toponyms (coupled with evidence from Arabic geographical sources) indicates, however, a substantial contribution during the Islamic period. An intermediate irrigation system ('mesosystem') consists of terraced fields fed by springs and making use of cisterns and waterlifting mechanisms such as *shadufs* and *norias*. Thomas Glick identifies intermediate networks in Mallorca that employ *qanats*. The smallest scale ('microsystems') could be sustained by a single farmstead comprising either a cistern or a *noria* (possibly animal-powered) feeding water into a set of fields.[34] The Spanish term for such spring-fed cisterns, *alberca*, is clearly derived from the Arabic *birka* (pool), while another loan word, *aljibe* (or *algibe*, from the Arabic *al-jubb*), is used to describe the cisterns excavated within palaces, large houses, and castles.[35]

Thus the Islamic period did not witness substantial technological innovations, though the example of Spain does illustrate what has been aptly described as the 'creative synthesis' of different irrigation technologies. In other words, the new rulers maintained the existing Roman–Visigothic irrigation infrastructure, but also introduced technologies such as *qanats* and spring-fed cisterns, which had long been in use in the Middle East. The introduction of new crops necessitated the intensification of the irrigation networks around the rivers of southern Spain. In Oman surveys revealed extensive water distribution networks (*aflaj*) and sophisticated mills dating from two Islamic phases, though earlier systems evidently existed. There is also evidence of Islamic intervention into the massive system of canals in the Diyala plain from the seventh to the ninth century, but the total number of waterways was probably smaller than it had been during the late Sasanian period.

Sugar production

Sugar cane was one of the most lucrative crops in the Islamic world. Its cultivation is restricted by the requirements for a sub-tropical climate with abundant water, while the cutting and processing of the cane – designed to produce crystallised sugar and molasses – are labour intensive, not infrequently involving the use of slaves. Given the problems caused by increasing salination in heavily irrigated areas, it is worth noting that sugar cane can withstand relatively high concentrations of salt. The transfer of the plant from Bengal, where it originates, to Iran may have occurred in the fifth century. Sugar cane (*qasab al-sukkar*) appears to be one of the crops of the Sawad in Caliph 'Umar's cadastral survey of the former Sasanian territories. From its initial foothold in Iraq and Khuzistan, sugar was later transferred to Greater Syria, the Nile valley and delta regions of Egypt, and as far west as Spain.[36]

Physical evidence for sugar production takes two forms: first, the structures that were associated with the crushing of the cane, the boiling of the syrup, and the crystallisation of the liquid; and, second, the ceramic vessels – conical sugar pots and bag-shaped molasses jars – in which the crystallised and liquid fractions were captured and stored (Fig. 4.5). Numerous sugar manufacturing sites have been recorded in the Islamic world, including installations at Tall Nimrin on the east side of the Jordan valley, at Tawahin al-Sukkar on the shores of the Dead Sea, and others, probably built during the crusader period (1098–1291) along the Syrian littoral between Acre and Beirut.[37] Fourteen sugar mills have been identified in Morocco, with one substantial example (dating from the sixteenth or early seventeenth century) at Chichaoua retaining its plan and sections of its superstructure. Many of the Moroccan plants were supplied with water by extensive networks of canals and aqueducts.[38] Perhaps the earliest Islamic sugar mill to be excavated is one located in the vicinity of the ancient Achaemenid palace at Susa, in Khuzistan. As noted above, this region benefited from an extensive irrigation system established during the Parthian and Sasanian dynasties. Constructed largely of *pisé* (rammed earth), with baked brick employed in the areas of the ovens, excavators detected three distinct construction phases, probably spanning the eleventh and twelfth centuries. The different components of the site correspond well to the descriptions of sugar making provided by the Arab author al-Nuwayri (d. *c.*1332). The copper boiling vats no longer survive, though many sugar pots and molasses jars were recovered. A surprising aspect of the excavation was the relative richness of the portable artefacts, including metalwork, steatite, glass, and glazed ceramics.[39]

The Jordan valley and the shores around the Dead Sea produced large quantities of sugar and molasses that were traded all over the Mediterranean. The production centres of these regions have been extensively studied. Surveys in the Jordan valley and around the south and east banks of the Dead Sea have identified over thirty installations for the production of sugar.[40] The distribution of sugar mills provides a good indication of the intensity of the industry in the thirteenth and fourteenth centuries. The steep wadis running from the plains of Jordan into the Jordan valley, Dead Sea and Wadi 'Araba are dotted with small water-powered mills, and it might be thought that sugar processing sites could have been located near to these convenient sources of mechanical power.[41] The need to process cane within three hours of its being cut made this unfeasible, however. Some mills probably employed animal power to crush the cane, but at Tawahin al-Sukkar the milling chamber was fed by water channels (Fig. 4.6). The mills also required fuel (for boiling the cane juice) and clarifying agents such as lime (CaO). Timber and brushwood are not abundant in these regions, and other fuels like dried animal dung or crushed fibres from the sugar cane may have been utilised (potters in Upper Egypt in the late twentieth century certainly made use of this material on account of its high burning temperature).

Excavators of the Frankish sugar mill at Kouklia (Palaeopaphos) in Cyprus identified significant variability in the internal volumes of conical sugar pots found on the site. The pots were grouped into three main categories: type 1, containing c.1–2 litres, type 2, containing c.4–6 litres, and type 3, containing c.7–9 litres. Of these, the smallest vessels (type 1) proved to be the rarest and type 3 vessels the most common. The finds from Kouklia find broad confirmation in the Middle East; for instance at Karak castle, where nearly 500 diagnostic fragments of sugar pots and syrup jars were located, the largest conical pot was found to have a volume of c.9 litres and the smallest of c.2.4 litres, but the great majority had a capacity of 5–6 litres. This variation of internal volume may be related to the production of different grades of sugar. The fourteenth-century Italian merchant Francesco Balducci Pegolotti records three different grades of sugar listed according to price, the most expensive being *bambillonia* or *caffetino* (the former term probably refers to Babylon, the Roman name for the area of Fustat), the second grade being *musciatto*, and the cheapest being *polvere di zucchero*. Similar distinctions can be found in Arabic sources of this period, and it would appear that the cost of the sugar depended upon the number of boilings – one, two or three – which the sugar received before it was left to crystallise.[42]

At Kouklia the smallest pots were probably used for the three times boiled sugar, and the largest for the single-boiled variety. If this interpretive model is applied to the sugar pots from Greater Syria, then one can build some hypotheses concerning the nature of the industry. Starting with the assemblage at Karak, it would appear that the occupants of the castle primarily consumed twice-boiled (*musciatto*) sugar. Petrographic analysis of finds from Karak and from the mill at Safi provides persuasive evidence that most of the sugar consumed in Karak originated around the Dead Sea. Analysis of the pots from the excavated sugar mills of the Jordan valley would also suggest that the bulk of the production concentrated on the middle-priced *musciatto* sugar for sale in Middle Eastern and Mediterranean markets. The jars designed for collecting the molasses are more scarce than the sugar pots from sites in Jordan and Palestine – often by a factor of eight or ten. This would suggest that a single jar would collect the molasses that gathered in the bases of numerous sugar pots.[43]

Historical sources suggest a period of greatest productivity in the thirteenth and fourteenth centuries (a time when the sugar from the Nile Delta and from Greater Syria was extensively traded in the Mediterranean), with a slow decline in the fifteenth century. In an influential study of Arabic and European written sources, the economic historian Eliyahu Ashtor suggested that the demise of the sugar industry in Egypt and Syria resulted from the failure of the elite of the Mamluk sultanate to invest in new technology, particularly in the late fourteenth and early fifteenth centuries. Responding to lower agricultural revenues – likely attributable in part to depopulation in rural areas caused by the waves of plague after 1348 – the Mamluk elite adopted the counterproductive strategy of raising taxes in order to maintain state revenues. By the end of the fifteenth century the Mediterranean market was dominated by sugar produced in Cyprus and elsewhere in southern Europe.[44] If one turns to the sixteenth-century cadastral records (*daftars*) for Jordan and Palestine, no reference is made there to sugar among the agricultural products of the Jordan valley. That said, recent archaeological studies are providing persuasive evidence that some installations continued to function into the early sixteenth century, while the inclusion of villages in the *waqfs* of religious foundations in Cairo is perhaps another indication of some economic vitality.[45] These signs of persistence have implications beyond the study of sugar production; the model of economic and technological decline in the Islamic Middle East and the contemporaneous rise of late medieval and early modern Europe have dominated historical discourse, but regionally focused studies of Islamic industries and mercantile activity are now creating a more varied picture (chapter 9).

Notes

1 For archaeological perspectives on pastoralism in the Middle East (ranging from prehistory to the present), see contributions in Bar-Yosef and Khazanov (1992).

2 Helms (1990), 71–131. The transition of Pella (known in Arabic sources as Fihl) from late antique town to Islamic village has been the subject of considerable archaeological research. See McNicoll et al. (1992), 145–98; Walmsley (1997–8). For a comparable study from Tunisia, see Gelichi and Milanese (1998) and (2002).

3 Adams (1965).

4 McNicoll (1983), 7–21; Redford (1998), 31–76; Danti (2004). Similar questions arise in the analysis of Byzantine rural settlements. See Dunn (1999); Foss (2002).

5 For instance Zozaya (1996); Cressier (1999); Milwright (2008a).

6 Charles et al. (2003). For archaeobotanical studies focused on carbonised plant remains, see Naomi Miller in Redford (1998), 211–52; McQuitty et al. (1997–8), 194–8. Cf. Adams (1996), 100–6.

7 For instance, see Gil Stein in Redford (1998), 183–209; Michael Toplyn in De Vries (1998), 221–8; Stevens, Kalinkowski and van der Leest, eds (2005), 528–33.

8 Magness (2003); also summarised in Walmsley (2007), 107–11. On possible changes in the climate of late antique Negev, see Rubin (1989).

9 Kennedy (1985b).

10 Sodini et al. (1980); Tate (1992). Magness (2003), 196–206.

11 Walmsley (2007), 110.

12 Ørsted et al. (1992). See also Leone (2003).

13 Johns (1995a). See also Brown (2000); Milwright (2008a), 109–13, 244–55.

14 McQuitty et al. (1997–8), 185–93.
15 Milwright (2008a), 113–17, 248–9.
16 Pace (1996). See also Oleson (2001), 604–8.
17 Wade (1979); Vogt (2005).
18 Mills of this type are well known in Iran and around the eastern Mediterranean. See Neely (2002); McQuitty (1995); Given (2000); Milwright and Baboula (forthcoming).
19 Watson (1983), 103–11; Ward (2002); Wilkinson (2002), 178.
20 For a study of *saqiya* pots used in water-lifting devices, see Stevens, Kalinkowski and van der Leest, eds (2005), 524–8.
21 Adams (1970).
22 For the Sasanian and Islamic periods, see: Adams (1965), 69–111; (1985), 200–28. For criticisms of his methodology and conclusions, see Morony (1994).
23 On the canal systems of this area, see also Northedge (2005a), 62–80.
24 Neely (2002); Wenke (1987), 256–9.
25 Simpson (1997), 89–101; Wilkinson (1998), 83.
26 Wenke (1987), 254–6; Boucharlat, Labrousse and Kervran (1979).
27 Weisgerber (1980).
28 On these systems, see Wilkinson (2002); Wilkinson (1975) and (1980); also Costa (2002).
29 Wilkinson (2002), 182–5.
30 Watson (1983), 9–73, 103–11; Glick (2002).
31 On the agriculture and irrigation technology of late antique and Islamic North Africa, see Solignac (1964) and Jalloul (1998).
32 Glick (1970), 11–145; Butzer et al. (1985), 486–99.
33 Guichard (1999).
34 Glick (2002), 332–3. Other studies of medieval Spanish irrigation systems include Cressier (1999) and Lemeunier (1999).
35 Cressier (1996); Bazzana (1999).
36 Miles (1951), 34–35, no. 41; Watson (1983), 24–30.
37 On the mills of Jordan, see Flanagan, McCreery and Yassine (1994); Jones et al. (2000). On the Islamic and crusader period mills of Palestine, see Benvenisti (1970), 253–6; Boas (1999), 81; Rosen-Ayalon (2006), 86.
38 Berthier (1966). On the two mills (north and south) at Chichaoua, see his vol. 1: 163–71, 174–9; vol. 2: figs ii.1–12 and pls B.i–xlviii. The plan of the north mill is reproduced in Boucharlat, Labrousse and Kervran (1979), fig. 46.
39 Boucharlat, Labrousse and Kervran (1979). On the processes involved in producing sugar and molasses, see Berthier (1966), 1: 233–45.
40 Hamarneh (1977–8); Kareem (2000), 12–13, 66–80.
41 McQuitty (1995).
42 Maier and Wartburg (1983), 314. See also Ashtor (1981), 97. Cf. Berthier (1966), 1: 194–5. For a detailed typology of sugar pots from the Jordan valley, see LaGro and de Haas (1989–90).
43 Milwright (2008a), 158–64.
44 Ashtor (1981).
45 Jones et al. (2000); Walker (2004), 134–5.

5

Towns, cities and palaces

Originating in the writings of French scholars who worked in North Africa in the first decades of the twentieth century, the study of the 'Islamic city' has attempted to establish the fundamental characteristics that distinguish the traditional urban environments of the Islamic world from towns and cities in Europe and elsewhere. In the realm of architecture and town planning, researchers have pointed to such factors as the centrality of the mosque and market area (*suq* or *bazar*), the general absence of large open spaces, and a street plan consisting of narrow, twisting streets and alleys. As Jean Sauvaget has demonstrated in his analysis of the centres of Damascus and Latakia in Syria, those straight passageways remaining in the urban fabric were vestiges of classical street plans.[1] The emphasis on privacy is seen in the inward focussing of domestic architecture on the courtyard. Houses often lack a distinctive façade to the street, having only a doorway and walls punctuated on upper storeys by wooden grille windows (*mashrabiyya*). Indeed this internalised focus can also be detected in the design of some mosques; for instance the drab exterior walls of the monumental Masjid-i Jami' in Isfahan look much the same as those of other buildings around it.

There is much of value to be taken from pioneering studies of the early and mid-twentieth century, but this body of scholarship should not be read uncritically.[2] The attempt to isolate certain essential features making up an 'Islamic city' has been extensively criticised. Two methodological problems are particularly relevant in the present context. First, many scholars based their analysis upon towns and cities in a specific region of the Islamic world, and then assumed that patterns identified there would necessarily apply in different regions. This approach tends to downplay the action of environmental, cultural, and historical factors on the evolution of urban spaces in a given locality. Second, many of the characteristics of the 'traditional' Islamic urban space were based on observations of functioning contemporary cities, from which was inferred that the features in question represented long-term patterns tracing back centuries. Implicit in such approaches is the notion that stasis, and even stagnation, were deemed to have manifested themselves following the formative phase of Islamic urban development between the seventh and the eleventh century.

Archaeology is well placed to apprehend the dynamic nature of Islamic urban life. The close focus on the physical evidence – construction phases, changes of function within buildings or open spaces, evidence for commercial or industrial activity (chapters 7 and 8), consumption of food, and the objects used in everyday life – allows for reconstructions of urban life as it has evolved over decades and centuries.

The remainder of the present chapter is divided into three sections. The first gives a summary of the archaeology of towns and cities from the eighth to the tenth century. A further consideration in this context is the role of the palace in the formation of the urban environment. The second section addresses the question of urban life in later centuries by looking at results of excavations conducted in different regions of the Islamic world. The final section is devoted to the provision of water and sanitation for the inhabitants of towns, cities, and palaces.

Archaeology and the early Islamic city

The regions encompassed by the new Islamic Empire comprised a wide variety of existing settlement types (chapter 2). In the territories which formerly belonged to Byzantium, one finds the orthogonal plans of the 'classical' city (many of which had undergone considerable changes during late antiquity) and the more organic arrangement of smaller towns. That the Umayyad elite admired 'classical' urban planning may be seen in its imposition of ordered market areas onto the existing towns of Greater Syria (chapter 3). To the east, the Islamic conquerors were confronted by the great Sasanian cities of Mesopotamia and other fortified citadels, like Merv in Turkmenistan. Unsurprisingly, Islamic urbanism elaborated upon these and other themes. Even the early evolution of the *amsar* may be traced in part to the types of pre-Islamic Arab encampments (*hadirs*) located outside established towns like Qinnasrin in Palestine. Recent archaeological work on this site suggests an occupation phase running from the late Byzantine into the early Islamic period.[3]

The early eighth-century site of 'Anjar in Lebanon is a startling illustration of the tenacity of Roman–Hellenistic principles of urban planning (Fig. 5.1). At first sight this site appears to accord well with the notion of a 'classical city': the enclosure wall (measuring 370 x 310 m) is punctured by four monumental gates, and the internal area is broken into quadrants by the *cardo* and *decumanus*. In accordance with classical models, the two major arteries meet at a tetrapylon and are colonnaded with lines of cubicles on either side. Evidently left with parts of the four quadrants unconstructed, the more fully developed zones were located in the south-western sector and immediately north and south of the eastern half of the *decumanus*. The most important structures, the mosque and the *dar al-imara*, were placed in the south-east quadrant.[4] This last point is significant for an assessment of the urban character of Umayyad 'Anjar; as Diocletian's palace at Split demonstrates, not all sites with orthogonal planning and a fortified rectangular enclosure wall need to be considered, first and foremost, as cities. Another Diocletianic fortress, Nag al-Hagar in Egypt, devotes the south-east quadrant to a palatial complex.[5] Ultimately the intentions of the patron of 'Anjar remain an enigma, and the fact of its remarkable preservation is telling evidence of its failure as an urban, palatial, and perhaps military project.

Similar ideas were followed elsewhere in the Islamic world; for instance it has been conjectured that the slightly later Umayyad *misr* of Ramla was conceived along the same lines as 'Anjar, though the subsequent development of this town has eradicated much of the eighth-century plan.[6] The Islamic *misr* at Istakhr in Iran was located directly to the east of the Sasanian city, and, like 'Anjar, was designed with a rectangular plan divided into four quadrants (in this case the mosque and the *dar al-imara* were placed in the south-western sector of the city).[7] On a smaller scale, the walled compound of Ayla on Jordan's Red Sea coast comprises, again, a rectangular enclosure wall (167 x 134 m) and an internal plan organised around the intersection of a *cardo* and a *decumanus* so as to create four roughly equal quadrants (Fig. 5.2). A *misr* was established at Ayla as early as c.650, although archaeological examination of the site has not provided definitive evidence for the form of the settlement in the seventh century. It may be that the rectangular, fortified outer wall and the orthogonal plan were established in mid-seventh century, though recently an early eighth-century date has been proposed. This problem aside, the archaeology of Ayla presents a fascinating example of the evolution of a small but thriving port from the Umayyad period down to c.1100. The expansion of the mosque in the early Abbasid period (c. 750–850) necessitated a disruption in the straight path of the *cardo*, and other changes also reflect processes of urban growth and transformation. In the Fatimid period city, the central crossing was taken up with a rectangular structure which functioned as a residence, though excavation of the lower levels indicated that it had probably been established as a pavilion, perhaps with some administrative function. The growth of Ayla led to the creation of an extra-mural suburb along the road that extended beyond the Egypt (north-west) gate. This suburb comprised commercial and domestic buildings, and possibly also a mosque. The Hijaz (south-east) gate was closed at an early stage in the history of the site, the area outside of it becoming a cemetery. In the Abbasid period the exterior wall next to the Sea gate (south-west) was given over to shops.[8]

The Umayyad *qusur* of Greater Syria present another facet of early Islamic urbanism. In many cases the fortified compounds do not stand alone, but, like the pre-Islamic Arabian entrepôt of Qaryat al-Faw, were the central focus of a larger settlement of less imposing structures, apparently laid out with little consideration for the overall planning. Good examples of this wider pattern of settlement are to be found around the late seventh-century *qasr* of Bakhra' near Palmyra (Fig. 2.4) and Caliph Walid I's foundation at Jabal Says in the basalt desert in south-eastern Syria (in both cases, some of the associated buildings probably predate the Umayyad period).[9] That the settlements around the Umayyad *qusur* might be thought of in explicitly urban terms is suggested by an inscription dated 110/728–29, found at Qasr al-Hayr East, which contains the Arabic word for town: *madina*.

What is the *madina* in this case? Uncertainties surrounding the original location of the (now lost) inscription make it impossible to answer this question definitively, but two solutions have been suggested. First, it would refer to the larger enclosure facing the *qasr* (Fig. 5.3). This interpretation is supported by the fact that the built area around the central, porticoed courtyard is actually composed of a small hypostyle mosque in the south-east corner and of seven self-contained structures, each one being made up of modules of rooms (*bayts*) arranged around an internal courtyard. The courtyard building immediately to the west of the mosque has been tentatively identified as a *dar al-imara* on the strength of its unusual plan. Directly north of the mosque was an area given over to olive presses, a large cistern, and perhaps a bathhouse (an extra-mural bathhouse is located to the north). In other words, despite its relatively small dimensions (168 x 166 m), this enclosure comprises the basic components of an Islamic urban foundation. The second solution adopts the view that the *madina* represented in fact a much larger settlement area, encompassing the mud-brick houses located beyond the *qasr* and a large enclosure to the north, east and south, as well as two square buildings (65 x 65 m), also of mud-brick, 2 km further to the south. The chronology of the mud-brick buildings making up the larger settlement at Qasr al-Hayr East will need to be established through excavation; certainly the larger enclosure was reoccupied between the twelfth and fourteenth century. It is conceivable that the mud brick dwellings and other structures were erected some time after the Umayyad foundation and represent the gradual transition from a state-sponsored project to a more organic phase of urban evolution.[10]

The combination of utilities – official, religious, agricultural/industrial, and residential – in the larger enclosure of Qasr al-Hayr East can be compared to the multiple functions performed by some Roman frontier fortresses in Egypt. For instance, in its second construction phase *c.*150, Mons Claudianus in Upper Egypt was occupied by soldiers and workers at the nearby imperial quarry. The third/fourth-century fort at Qal'at Bahrain in the Persian Gulf is also notable for the presence of self-contained units, each centred on a small central courtyard.[11] It might be the case therefore that some blurring of categories should be conceived between the *madina* as a functioning town and the *qasr* as a solely princely residence. The trend toward larger palaces – a process that culminates in palace cities like Samarra, Madinat al-Zahra', the Qal'a of the Bani Hammad, and Lashkari Bazar – can be detected in Mshatta (144 x 144 m) and Ukhaydir (175 x 169 m) later in the eighth century. Subdivided into largely self-contained sectors, each containing complexes of rooms that probably performed multiple functions, these palatial compounds take on urban characteristics. Notably both Mshatta and Ukhaydir include an intra-mural mosque integrated into the overall plan and orientation of the *qasr*.[12]

Following a different trajectory, the concept of the palatial/administrative complex as a self-contained urban entity can also be applied to citadels such as 'Amman and Samarqand. In both cases Islamic patrons commissioned new buildings, but they incorporated them into a densely built architectural fabric and a pre-established street plan (Fig. 5.4). The 'Amman citadel occupies a roughly l-shaped plateau, oriented approximately east (the lower citadel) and north-west (the upper citadel). Analysis of the palatial zone revealed that the outer walls defining the inner and the outer compounds belonged to the Roman period *temenos* of the northern temple complex. Little else was retained, however, when the citadel was transformed into an Islamic administrative centre; the south gate to the *temenos* was replaced by an impressive reception hall leading into the outer compound. This ceremonial way comprised a courtyard leading to a colonnaded street (at a slightly different alignment to that of the Roman road) running towards the entrance to the inner compound, the *dar al-imara*. Like the palace of Mshatta, the domed throne chamber of the *dar al-imara* is cruciform in plan. Surviving in more fragmentary form, the residential units east and west of the colonnaded street in the outer compound have *bayts* arranged around small courtyards in a manner reminiscent of the houses in the large enclosure at Qasr al-Hayr East. To the south of the reception hall, the Muslim presence was emphasised through the erection of a congregational mosque (chapter 3). While the 'Amman citadel was occupied in later centuries, its status was much reduced following the fall of the Umayyads in 750.[13]

By the time of the Arab conquest in 712 CE, the 220-hectare site of Afrasiyab comprised a citadel to the east made up of a central fortified donjon, or *keshk*, and of a lower terrace, and a western zone, known in published reports as the 'sacred area', which may have contained the Soghdian temple. This 'sacred area' witnessed some of the earliest changes with the construction of what appears to be a palace, tentatively dated to the governorship of Nasr b. Sayyar (738–48). The mode of construction and the asymmetry of the surviving parts of the plan largely reflect the designs of the Soghdian palaces at Panjikent and elsewhere. In the period c.760–80, a new, more assertively Muslim presence is evident in the construction of a courtyard mosque over this part of the site (the mosque was enlarged *c*.820). The mosque, with its orientation to the *qibla* (south-west), necessitated the obliteration of surrounding buildings (including the first palace) and changes to the street plan. The other significant change at this time was the erection of a *dar al-imara* in the lower terrace of the citadel. Dating from the 740s but with later phases of construction through the eighth to the ninth century, the design of this major administrative centre follows Umayyad models developed in the *qusur* of Greater Syria and Iraq and in the *dar al-imara* in Kufa. Like the mosque to the west, the construction of this symbol of Muslim authority required the demolition of earlier structures. Afrasiyab continued to be occupied in later centuries, benefiting from some lavish architectural patronage – including a palace constructed by the Ghazanavid sultans.[14]

Of the new urban foundations constructed by the Abbasid caliphs, two – Rafiqa and Samarra – retain enough of their original form to permit an archaeological evaluation of their plans. The first, Rafiqa (meaning 'Companion'), is located about 600 metres west of the existing town of Kallinikos (renamed Raqqa after the Arab conquest in 639–40), at the confluence of the Euphrates and Balikh rivers in north-east Syria. This area had received some state patronage earlier, in the eighth century; the Umayyad Caliph Hisham had established a new market in Raqqa which was probably designed to supply goods to his palace south of the Euphrates, at Rusafa. Hisham also commissioned the building of a bridge over the river and the digging of a canal to supply water to Raqqa. The scale of the Umayyad interventions was, however, dwarfed by the Abbasid project of Rafiqa, started in 771–2. Planned with a horseshoe-shaped fortified wall of mud-brick pierced by a series of monumental and lesser gateways, Rafiqa was surrounded by a second line of walls, which created an *intervallum* similar to that employed around Caliph Mansur's round city of Baghdad. Like the garrison towns of Madinat al-Far (Hisn Maslama) and at Kharab Sayyar, in the borderlands between the Abbasid caliphate and the Byzantine Empire,[15] Rafiqa was designed to house troops. A further expansion of the urban agglomeration occurred with the construction of a complex of palaces to the north; this complex was occupied by Caliph Harun al-Rashid and his court between 786 and 808 (Fig. 5.5). About 5 km west, at Hiraqla, there is an unfinished rectangular masonry platform surrounded by a circular wall: it may have been intended as a monument to an Abbasid military triumph in Anatolia. An extensive system of canals has been located to the east and north of Raqqa–Rafiqa, and the paths of open waterways and *qanats* are also apparent in early aerial photographs of the urban areas.[16]

The establishment of Rafiqa fits into an earlier pattern of locating a *misr* in the immediate vicinity of an existing settlement (such as Fustat near Roman Babylon in the seventh and Ramla near Ludd in the early eighth century). That Rafiqa and Raqqa were considered to be distinct urban entities is indicated by the fact that both were furnished with congregational mosques and other amenities for a functioning Islamic city (on the later creation of a third *madina* in the industrial district between the two, see chapter 7). Where Rafiqa differs from surviving *amsar*, however, is in the scale of the undertaking, as well as in aspects of design. The walled city was never fully developed, but reconstruction of the street plan (still visible in early aerial photographs) indicates a rigid grid, similar to the 'cantonments' surrounding the palaces of Samarra.[17]

The palatial dwellings and ancillary buildings to the north lack a congregational mosque and the other urban characteristics of their southern neighbours, Rafiqa and Raqqa/Kallinikos. The palaces do not adhere to the square *castrum* design adopted by the Umayyad *qusur*. In common with the large enclosure at Qasr al-Hayr East and at the citadel of 'Amman, several of the walled palatial compounds (such as palaces B, C, and G, excavated in the 1950s) allocate much of the interior space to self-contained courtyard houses. These developments north of Rafiqa anticipate aspects of the next great Abbasid urban foundation, Samarra. Constructed mainly of mud brick, the palaces retain aspects of their original stucco decoration, carved or painted (Fig. 5.6), as well as other more lavish ornamental features such as glass tiles. The apparently informal arrangement of clusters of buildings on either side of the north and east canal clearly marks a departure from the relative rigidity of the 'classical' urban model of employed at 'Anjar. Another interesting parallel with Samarra is the space allocated to the hippodrome.[18]

North of Baghdad on the Tigris river, Samarra was occupied by Abbasid caliphs between 836 and 892. While it continued to function as a city after 892, its most important phases of development can be traced to the caliphates of Mu'tasim (r. 833–42) and Mutawakkil (r. 847–61). In sheer scale, Samarra exceeds all Islamic cities before it; mainly located on the east bank of the river, its built area covers about fifty-seven square kilometers, stretching over 50 km from end to end (Fig. 5.7). Archaeological reconnaissance work has revealed a Sasanian presence on the east bank of the Tigris in the form of some small towns and, most relevantly in the present context, the construction of the Qatul al-Kisrawi, the canal connecting to the river at the northern extension of Samarra and feeding the Nahr al-Rasasi through a sluice. This watercourse ran into the Nahrawan canal that irrigated the Diyala plain (chapter 4). Two pre-Islamic canals pass along both sides of the palace of Istablat on the western side of the river. The Sasanians also constructed palaces and hunting reserves in the area encompassed by Abbasid Samarra. Thus the development of Samarra relied in considerable part on this earlier phase of hydraulic engineering, though the Abbasid caliphs also instigated further building of canals and *qanats*. That the Abbasid elite enjoyed the same activities as their Sasanian predecessors is indicated by the large walled game reserves (*hayrs*) located beyond the settled areas of the city. Horse racing was evidently popular, three tracks being located east of the principal caliphal palace (Dar al-Khilafa) and others elsewhere in the city. Pavilions were placed at high points, for the use of the court during such sporting events.[19]

Samarra cannot be considered an 'Islamic city' in conventional terms, since its urban growth does not radiate from a single zone containing a mosque, market, and *dar al-imara*. First, there are two congregational mosques, one south of the Dar al-Khilafa and the other, the so-called mosque of Abu Dulaf, in the northern urban entity of Mutawakkiliyya (founded in 859 and also known as Ja'fariyya). Taking this point further, it is apparent that the palaces form the foci of urban development from Qadisiyya and Balkuwara in the south (Fig. 5.8), the Dar al-Khilafa in the central zone, and al-Ja'fari palace in the north. An important clue concerning the urban character of Samarra is provided by the extensive pattern 'cantonments' (a term used to describe blocks composed of simple repeated building units based around courtyards). Either contained within palaces (such as Istablat) or situated in the vicinity of major palaces, these cantonments probably functioned principally for the garrisoning of Turkish troops (the professional army of the Abbasid caliphate) and of their families. The large military compounds were also furnished with markets and other facilities needed by the inhabitants. The geographical extent of these cantonments and their close association with the palaces fit in well with the historical evidence concerning both the number of slave soldiers (*mamluks*) employed by the caliphs during the Samarran period and the increasingly powerful role of the Turkish military in the political life of the Abbasid court. Wide highways were constructed to facilitate the movement of troops between different sectors of the city.[20]

Like at Rafiqa, the low cost of the building materials (baked brick and expensive ornamental media being reserved for the two mosques and for the most important zones of the caliphal palaces) and the probable utilisation of seasonal supplies of unskilled labour from the agricultural hinterland favoured horizontal expansion and scale over verticality and structural sophistication. While there certainly was formal experimentation in the architecture of the Samarran period, the abiding impression is one of repetition within a limited vocabulary of structural elements and decorative modes (the latter are epitomised by the moulding of stucco in the so-called 'bevelled style').[21] While the palaces may not have risen more than two or three storeys, their placement often betrays a keen interest in the creation of elevated viewpoints over formal terraces, race tracks, or other parts of the city. Except for such features as cruciform audience halls and monumental gateways, which have clearly defined functions, it is often difficult to guess the range of utilities performed by different rooms and complexes within individual palaces. The extensive employment of hydraulic engineering, Sasanian and Islamic, was required both for the everyday needs of the city's inhabitants and for the more lavish aspects of courtly entertainment. Considerable water supplies would have been required for palatial fountains, pools, baths, and the irrigation of the gardens and orchards on the west bank of the Tigris.[22] In common with the situation at the Umayyad *qusur* of Syria and at the *munyas* of Umayyad Spain, the diversion of water into ponds and irrigation systems could perhaps have performed an economic role (the cultivation of fruit and other crops for sale) as well as providing an elegant backdrop to courtly entertainments.

Although the scale of the Samarran palaces was never surpassed, architectural themes found in this Abbasid city recur in royal projects elsewhere in the Islamic world. Located west of Cordoba, the Spanish Umayyad palatial complex of Madinat al-Zahra' (founded in 958) has, as its name suggests, characteristics that lend it an urban quality. The palace proper is located in the central sector of the northern part of the great walled compound (it runs more than 1,300 m along its longest side). Its placement on a slope offers the main rooms of the palace commanding views over the formal terraced gardens and pools and over the wider landscape. In common with Samarran prototypes, the central zone also contains areas given over to administrative and military functions, while the sectors to the east and west were occupied by housing.[23] The royal architecture of the sultans of Kilwa Island (Tanzania) comprised palatial structures within the town and the larger late thirteenth-century extra-urban foundation of Husuni Kubwa, 1.5 km to the east.[24] In the Islamic east, the continued use of mud brick and stucco allowed for the construction of massive palatial complexes such as Lashkari Bazar near Bust in Afghanistan. Covering an area of approximately 7 x 2 km along the Helmand river, this complex of palaces was erected and occupied between the tenth and twelfth centuries. The 'southern palace' is another example of a palace located within a larger compound (in this case, one also containing a congregational mosque). Built around a large central courtyard with four *iwans*, the 'southern palace' is broken down into largely self-contained units performing a range of functions.[25]

Urban life in medieval Islam

There seems to be little reason for archaeologists to pursue the debate concerning the supposedly essential characteristics of the traditional 'Islamic city'. The archaeology of the first three centuries of Islam is instructive in this regard; simply to locate the key elements of congregational mosque, palace or *dar al-imara*, and markets hardly suffices in the face of the sheer diversity of the urban environments. Archaeology is better equipped to explain such heterogeneity across the Islamic world by looking at the interaction of environmental, demographic, cultural, and economic factors underlying the various processes of urbanism. Excavations are also an excellent means to analyse the adaptation of small sectors of towns or cities over time.

The synthesis of data from towns in Muslim Spain suggests that population growth manifested itself in changes to the buildings, open spaces, and activities conducted within and beyond the city walls. The abandoned twelfth and thirteenth-century town of Cieza (Siyasa) illustrates that the area encompassed within the walls incorporated open spaces which often functioned as orchards prior to their encroachment by domestic, religious, or commercial architecture. In other words, the initial placement of the defensive wall allowed for later urban expansion. Another feature of this initial stage was the presence of cemeteries and places for 'industrial' activity such as pottery workshops, which are conventionally considered to be extra-mural features (chapters 6 and 7). Cemeteries formed part of the central open spaces in the districts (*khitta*) of the seventh-century *amsar* of Basra and Kufa; and, by reviewing the evidence from Spain, it becomes apparent that in the period prior to Christian reconquest intra-mural burial grounds tended to resist encroachment by urban buildings. Indeed, at Murcia cemeteries were established on the sites of abandoned houses or workshops, while at Denia graves spread even onto the main street. Lacking the legal protection accorded to cemeteries, orchards and industrial installations disappeared from intra-mural areas as the population grew. As the walled city (or, at least, the central area) reached a point of saturation, new processes can be detected; streets narrowed or disappeared completely, houses were subdivided to make smaller dwellings, and buildings increased in height through the addition of extra storeys. Lastly one sees the creation of extra-mural suburbs, which further displaced the workshops and the specialised agriculture.[26]

While it is difficult to use published archaeological evidence from other Islamic regions to illustrate such a complete process of evolution from an initial settlement to the stage of extra-mural overflow, interesting examples exist of transformations and adaptations (see Ayla above). In the following paragraphs the examples of Fustat and Nishapur are employed to illustrate aspects of urban domestic architecture. The final part of the chapter considers the information that can be gathered about urban life through the analysis of excavated artefacts.

Established as the administrative capital of Egypt after the Arab conquest in 641–2, Fustat developed from a garrison camp into a sprawling city, made up of different districts, in an area defined on the west by the Nile and on the east by the Muqattam hills. Our understanding of the earliest decades of urban development comes from written sources, but physical traces of domestic architecture and occupational debris existed from the late seventh century. In several excavated sectors the lowest stratum – located just above the sandstone shelf (*gabal*), on which Fustat was erected – consisted of remnants of simple dwellings constructed of mud brick. The crude building materials would have limited the height of these houses to one or two storeys. Excavations in the district of Istabl 'Antar revealed a complex of such buildings, made up of interconnected small rooms divided by narrow alleys, and an aqueduct (dated to c.680–90) connecting the district to the water source of Birkat al-Habash. Other state investment in this zone came in the form of a mosque dating to the mid-eighth century. A substantial mausoleum from the Abbasid period was further renovated during the Fatimid caliphate.[27]

Low quality domestic architecture from later periods was also revealed at the site known as 'Fustat-C'. This area consisted of a series of simple houses arranged along a street. Lacking in courtyards, which were *de rigueur* for larger dwellings, these simple houses consisted of a two or three-room module. Each house was equipped, however, with a latrine. In the first phase, between the mid-ninth and the mid-tenth century, the houses probably rose to a second storey, though analysis of the walls indicated that the structures needed continual repair to offset the poor construction techniques. Later occupation, between c.990 and 1090, was restricted to single-storey rooms, roofed with matting or basketry.[28] The rather rudimentary quality of the late seventh-century dwellings at Istabl 'Antar and the Fatimid period houses of 'Fustat-C' contrast with the grandiose tenth and eleventh-century houses and domestic complexes (akin to Roman *insulae*) excavated in other parts of Fustat (Fig. 5.9). A common arrangement involved a central courtyard, sometimes equipped with a pool, and, on one or two sides of the courtyard, porticos leading to a larger central room (*majlis*) with two smaller rooms on either side. The other rooms vary considerably in plan and dimensions as a result of the irregular path of the outer wall (a path partly dictated by the winding alleyways of this congested urban environment). From the testimony of al-Muqaddasi (d. 990) and Nasir-i Khusraw (d. 1088) and from references in the Geniza archive, it becomes apparent that a domestic structure might rise to four or five storeys; the robust construction techniques of the houses supports this picture of multi-storey dwellings, while features such as decorative stonework and tiled floors all speak of considerable affluence.[29]

The Iranian city of Nishapur was one of the great urban centres of Khurasan, along with Merv in modern Turkmenistan and with Herat and Balkh in Afghanistan. Originally founded in the third or fourth century, the Sasanian city was occupied by the Arab General 'Abd Allah ibn Amir in 656–7, and again in 661. The site of Sasanian and Umayyad period Nishapur remains unknown, however, and the coins and ceramics from the excavated sites at Nishapur (located south-east of the modern town) indicate an occupational sequence from the late eighth century through to the time of the Mongol conquest of the city in 1221. Fed with water by a system of *qanat* constructed by 'Abd Allah ibn Tahir (r. 828–45), and benefiting economically from its position on the eastern trade routes, Nishapur developed into a major centre for commerce, industry, and learning. Written sources indicated that the city contained some thirty-nine *madrasas*, although these have not been recovered archaeologically – including one founded by the Saljuq vizier Nizam al-Mulk. Several sections of old Nishapur were exposed during the excavations conducted by the Metropolitan Museum in the 1930s. While the final publication of the architecture (the areas are known as Tepe Madrasa, Vineyard Tepe, Sabz Pushan, and Qanat Tepe) lacks the precise stratigraphic information that would be expected in a more recent excavation report, the results provide important insights into urban life in the Islamic east.[30]

In common with other settlements in Khurasan, Nishapur used mud brick as the principal building material and kiln-fired bricks only occasionally, for the footings of walls, flooring, and ornamental purposes. At Tepe Madrasa, wooden beams were sometimes set into the walls for reinforcement. The palatial complex and mosque identified at Tepe Madrasa was constructed in three distinct phases. That this area had been subjected to a more consistent plan throughout its history was indicated by the rectilinear walls and by the fact that all the rooms were oriented, like the *qibla* of the mosque, so that one wall would face southwest. Although the central zone was not fully excavated, it would appear that the focus of the complex was a large courtyard with porticos and *iwan* chambers on two sides (or perhaps four). Elsewhere the excavators recovered evidence of continuous renovations and modifications to the domestic architecture (perhaps partly to be explained by the regular repairs needed to keep mud-brick walls structurally sound). The reliance upon mud brick also seems to have dictated a greater horizontal expansion in comparison to the multi-storey houses of Fustat; for instance at Sabz Pushan the buildings either side of the narrow alleyway comprised a maze of interconnected rooms of varying dimensions. A central feature of many rooms was a charcoal brazier consisting of a sunken ceramic vessel, punctured at the base and connected to ceramic flues leading back up to floor level; thus it provided a steady flow of air to the burning charcoal. It may be that the distribution of braziers, which were employed both for heating and cooking, gives some clue concerning the number of family units living within such large complexes. Apart from the neighbourhood mosques located during the excavations, the presence of Islam is also indicated by the *mihrabs* encountered within the domestic architecture.

The predominant use of mud brick limited the structural inventiveness of the dwellings and mosques of Nishapur, but the inhabitants compensated for this deficiency through the addition of carved and painted stucco. Sabz Pushan, most actively occupied between the late eighth and the tenth century, produced a series of carved stucco dados reminiscent of styles found at Samarra. The recovery from this site of a group of painted plaster panels from a *muqarnas* vault does suggest, however, the introduction of new decorative modes in the eleventh century. The styles of stucco carving were most varied at Tepe Madrasa, and this was complemented by other ornamental media – including cut brick, carved terracotta, glazed brick plugs, and glazed tiles with relief inscriptions. The painted panels exhibited both eastern and western influences; the symmetrical abstract designs are perhaps a last vestige of the bookmatched coloured marble dados and *opus sectile* designs of the late antique Mediterranean; while the figural panels may be compared to painting from Samarra, from the Ghaznavid palaces of Lashkari Bazar in Afghanistan and Samarqand in Uzbekistan, and, more distantly, with the ancient Buddhist murals of sites along the 'silk road' in western China.[31]

The character of urban life across the Islamic world is also revealed in the portable artefacts recovered from excavations. The fifteenth-century Egyptian author al-Maqrizi remarks in his topographic history, the *Khitat*, that 'the rubbish that was thrown into the waste heaps of Cairo each day was worth a thousand gold *dinars*'.[32] Referring to the glazed and unglazed pottery employed by tradesmen and for the serving of food in the cookshops frequented by the poor, Maqrizi's account speaks of a massive level of manufacture of cheap, disposable vessels. Surveying the published ceramics from the waste heaps of Fustat, it is difficult to disagree with his assessment. The upper deposits from the site, being above the last occupation levels, have produced countless sherds of pottery and glass dating largely from the twelfth to the fifteenth century.

The practice of digging this upper material for fertiliser (*sibakh*), coupled with the numerous illicit excavations, has destroyed any stratigraphic distinctions that might have permitted a more accurate dating to be made within these mounds; but the sheer scope of the published material is worthy of further comment. The huge market in the Egyptian capital stimulated skilled craftsmen from diverse regions to set up workshops in Fustat, and it clearly represented an equal draw for merchants bringing exotic merchandise from distant lands. To judge by the extant pottery and glass, active economic contacts existed with China, Iran, Syria, Upper Egypt and Nubia, North Africa, Italy, Spain, Cyprus, and the coastal regions of the Aegean (Egypt's Mediterranean relations are also illustrated by finds from the port of Alexandria).[33] Printed cotton was imported via the Red Sea ports for sale in Cairo and Fustat (chapter 8). Local ceramic industries also catered for the inhabitants producing everything, from unglazed water jars (often equipped with elaborate pierced filters) to glazed bowls imitating the expensive porcelains and stonewares imported from China. Plain and decorated lead-glazed earthenware was produced in vast quantities, from the Fatimid through to the Mamluk periods (Fig. 5.10).[34] Many other industries thrived, including the production of textiles and leather, glass-making, and carving.[35]

The houses of 'Fustat-C' provide an intriguing insight into the consumption patterns of the less wealthy inhabitants of the city from the mid-ninth to the late eleventh century. While it is certainly the case that the material record from these houses was not as lavish as that of larger dwellings in other parts of Fustat, the finds are more diverse than might be expected. Although the proportion of unglazed pottery at 'Fustat-C' was higher than excavated assemblages elsewhere in the city, significant numbers were in fact 'Nubian wares' imported from Aswan and other sites further south on the Nile. Locally produced glazed earthenware included lamps and chamber pots, sgraffito bowls, and imitations of Tang dynasty *sancai* ('three colour') vessels. Luxury ware comprised examples of eleventh-century Egyptian lustre-painted ware and three pieces of Chinese glazed pottery dating to the tenth or early eleventh century. Other signs of affluence were glass, textiles, carved wood, bone, ivory, and stucco, and a single piece of gilded and tooled leather (perhaps from a pouch). The numerous textiles from 'Fustat-C' included fragments of knotted carpets (probably imported from Spain, Iran, and Armenia) and decorated linens, two of which carried finely embroidered *tiraz* bands naming the Abbasid Caliph al-Muqtadir (r. 908–32) (cf. Fig. 7.1). The scraps of paper and parchment include a marriage contract and the acknowledgement of a debt. A block-printed amulet reflects the importance of forms of magical protection among the urban and rural populations of the Middle East.[36]

The wealth of Nishapur between the late eighth and the twelfth century was founded on its participation in international trade and on its native industries. The recovery of pottery kilns, ceramic wasters, and decorative moulds (made of baked ceramic or carved wood) confirmed the existence of an extensive local industry, though clearly much else was imported. In the absence of a full catalogue of the ceramic finds, it is impossible to reconstruct the distribution of the different unglazed and glazed wares at each excavated site. Unglazed ceramics must have formed a significant part of the output of the Nishapur kilns. Until the eleventh century, the only decoration comprises incised lines and repeated stamps; the use of moulds provided a wider range of ornamental possibilities in later periods. Nishapur is also notable for its lively tradition of decorated glazed wares – which included a sgraffito with splashed glazes; some slip-painted wares; and the famous 'egg and spinach' wares, with their engagingly cluttered figural compositions. Potters also sought to imitate the sober designs and restricted palette of the so-called Samanid epigraphic wares produced in Samarqand/ Afrasiyab. From the late eleventh century, alkaline-glazed ware with elaborate relief-moulded decoration became an important feature of the ceramic assemblage. In the ninth and tenth centuries tin-glazed pottery (with splashed decoration, cobalt painting, or lustre) was imported from Iraq. The most expensive imported pottery came from China and included Tang *sancai*, Yüeh green-glazed stoneware, and Ch'ing pai porcelain. Long-distance trade with China appears to have been most active during the ninth and tenth centuries.[37]

The glass and metalwork confirm the overall picture gained from the ceramic record. Most of the glass objects were vessels (ewers, jugs, beakers, and molar flasks). Glass was also employed for lamps, alembics, inkwells, beads, decorative settings in finger rings, and as insets in plaster window grilles and lanterns. The most common decorative techniques were mould-blowing, incising, stamping, wheel-cutting, and threading. Significantly, only one piece of lustre glass (a technique associated with Egypt and Iraq) was recovered; marvered glass and enamelled glass (both of which were much employed in Egypt and Syria from the twelfth century onwards) were absent from Nishapur. Whether glass was exported from Nishapur remains unclear. Correlations drawn between pieces from the Iranian city and material from sites as dispersed as Fustat and tombs in China do at least contribute to the understanding of the wide circulation of early Islamic glass.[38] Less well preserved, the corpus of metalwork comprised a spectrum from simple tools and weights to more elaborate items like decorated belt fittings, jewellery and cosmetic items, lamps, bowls, and an elegant eleventh-century copper alloy ewer. The corroded sword found at Nishapur may have been imported from Merv or from one of the other major steelworking centres of the Islamic east (chapter 7). This coexistence of local craft activities and imported goods can also be seen in excavations of Samarqand/Afrasiyab, Merv, Rayy, Sirjan, and Susa.[39]

Greater Syria provides numerous examples of well excavated towns and cities. The citadel of Hama provided rich finds of ceramics, glass, and metalwork from the centuries prior to the sacking of the city by Timur in 1401. Evidently, the occupants of the citadel could rely upon the fertile hinterland and upon the local industries for much of their everyday needs, though the glazed pottery and decorated glassware point to the presence of active markets, dealing in imported luxuries from manufacturing centres in the eastern Mediterranean and as far away as China.[40] Similar consumption patterns are apparent, albeit on a reduced scale, in smaller fortified sites such as Karak in Jordan.[41] Full publication of the portable artefacts from the citadels of Damascus and Aleppo will doubtlessly expand our knowledge of everyday life among the urban elites of the region.[42] The extensive archaeological investigation of Jerusalem allows for some consideration of the material culture of non-elite groups in Palestine, particularly during the Ayyubid and Mamluk phases. The recovery of kilns either inside the city or in the surrounding area confirms the existence of an active industry producing a range of unglazed, relief-moulded, and lead-glazed pottery. Khalil (Hebron) to the south was famous for its glassware. Finds excavated from sites such as the Damascus Gate and the Armenian Garden suggest that Jerusalem remained well connected to wider trading networks in Greater Syria. The regular influx of Jewish, Christian, and Muslim pilgrims also contributed to the diversity of the material culture.[43]

The material culture of the urban centres of Islamic North Africa is more difficult to assess, due to the uneven coverage of excavations and the dominant scholarly focus on monumental architecture and urban planning. With exceptions such as the new Islamic foundation of Qayrawan, urban life in North Africa seems to have gone into serious decline in the early Islamic period, only starting to revive in the tenth and eleventh centuries. The arrival of the Fatimids in Tunisia in 909 led to the creation of new capitals as Mahdiyya and Sabra-Mansuriyya, and the later dynasties, the Zirids and Hammadids (972–1152), were also responsible for further construction in Tunisia and Algeria. Among the ceramics – the most extensively published portable artefacts – there appears to be consistent reliance upon local production in both glazed and unglazed wares. Particularly prevalent are the types of sgraffito ware and of painted tin-glazed earthenware that are also found adorning the façades of churches in Italy (chapter 8). Some tenth-century glazed pottery from Raqqada exhibits stylistic affinities with bowls produced in Abbasid Iraq – and the tiles of the *mihrab* in the congregational mosque of Qayrawan demonstrate the transport of Iraqi ceramics to North Africa. Lustre-painted ceramics, possibly from Spain, have also been recovered from excavations in the port of Bougie and in the Qal'a of the Bani Hammad, both located in Algeria.[44] Stretching the definition of urban culture, the finds from Islamic occupation levels at Carthage (best considered at this time to be an agrarian settlement in the shadow of its more populous neighbour, Tunis) reflect the features noted above. Despite the reduced status of Carthage by the eleventh century – many of the churches and other buildings of the late antique city had been given over to squatter occupation – some degree of wealth was indicated by the considerable variety of the decorated glazed ware and the finely carved marble cenotaphs recovered from a small cemetery dating from the eleventh to the thirteenth century.[45]

Fresh water and sanitation

The provision of water is a vital aspect of urban life. Clearly, the means by which water was delivered to town and city dwellers were dependent upon a range of factors, including the size of the population, the altitude and topography of the settlement, and the proximity and quality of the principal water sources. These factors largely dictated the approaches taken by the engineers responsible for the hydraulic systems (many of which were constructed below ground) and for the buildings served by them, though regional and historical variations are also evident. The following paragraphs address different solutions to the challenge of water provision and sanitation which were adopted in the Islamic world.

The Greek port of Nafpaktos (known in Italian sources as Lepanto and in Turkish as İnebahtı), on the northern coast of the Gulf of Corinth (the region of Aetolia), retains much of the water system developed in the centuries before the advent of the independent Greek state in the 1820s. The massive defensive walls and upper citadel of Nafpaktos were first constructed by the Venetian Republic in the fifteenth century, though this system of fortification was augmented by the Ottoman sultanate after its capture of the site in 1499. Home of the Ottoman fleet in the Aegean, this strategic possession was retained even after the defeat suffered by the Turks at the naval battle of Lepanto in 1571. Nafpaktos was only lost to the Venetians, and briefly – between 1687 and 1699. The importance of Nafpaktos to the Turkish sultanate is demonstrated by the surviving monuments of the town, including four mosques, bathhouses, and a large fortified compound in the lower town. Less conspicuous but equally important for understanding the urban development of Ottoman Nafpaktos are the structures designed for the transport, storage, and supply of water. In the citadel, the water supplies were ensured through the cutting of large rain-fed cisterns (probably constructed during the Venetian occupation). The presence of a spring on the eastern side of the upper town meant that the two lower intra-mural sectors of the town could be supplied through a series of fountains (çeşme in Turkish). The seventeenth-century traveller Evliya Çelebi reports that there were more than forty fountains; and fourteen have survived to the present day. The extant fountains range from complete structures still flowing with water to others that are defunct, ruined, or renovated with modern masonry. In some places, the open channels connecting the fountains still survive, running along the margins of small alleyways.

If one tracks the spatial distribution, it becomes evident that the system has its origins in the vicinity of a Muslim religious foundation (Külliye) commissioned by the Ottoman Vizier Amcazade Hüseyin Pasha Köprülü after 1699. A line of fountains starts to the north of the Külliye and follows past the monumental Ottoman bathhouse to the main gate separating the upper and the lower town. From here, two branches of fountains descend into the lower town towards the coast. Beyond the fortified wall, a line of fountains and cisterns went east from the Külliye, past a large mosque (only the platform now remains), supplying water for an area of agricultural land and for the principal extra-mural suburb (Fig. 5.11). The extant water system at Nafpaktos corresponds closely to the information recorded on an Ottoman topographic drawing in the Topkapı library. In this drawing there are representations of numerous water mills and associated aqueducts along the nearby Scala and Mornos rivers; structures of this type have been identified in archaeological reconnaissance along these water courses and in the valleys to the north of Nafpaktos, illustrating extensive investment, during the Ottoman phase, both in the urban system and in the wider hydraulic infrastructure of the surrounding lands of Aetolia.[46]

For those settlements lacking in springs or other natural sources of potable water, other solutions were required. The Umayyad dynasty in Spain was faced with the challenge of bringing water to the city of Cordoba, the palace–city of Madinat al-Zahra' (constructed from 936), and the agricultural estates (*munyas*) of the area between the Guadalquivir river and the Sierra Morena. The ingenuity of the engineers of Umayyad Spain is illustrated by the elaborate drainage system constructed on the huge roof covering the congregational mosque that drained water into underground cisterns and fed the orchard of orange trees in the courtyard. More extensive systems were required, however, for the needs of the urban population. These relied upon the Fontis Aureae, a Roman aqueduct renovated in 967 by Caliph Hakam II. A necessary component in the construction of Madinat al-Zahra' to the east was the refurbishment of the Aqua Augusta, a first-century aqueduct. The placement of the *munyas* may also have been dictated by the paths of the Roman aqueduct system running south and east from the foothills of the Sierra Morena. Certainly these agricultural estates appear to have incorporated large water features; the monumental pool at Rummaniyya had a capacity of more than 1,300 cubic metres, being fed by a subterranean reservoir and aqueduct to the north. Like in the case of the Umayyad *qusur* of Greater Syria (chapter 2), part of the motivation behind this hydraulic engineering may have been economic – here, the rearing of fish and the cultivation of the surrounding agricultural lands – though the evidence for what may have been a suspended walkway at the pool of Rummaniyya suggests that the monumental pools were also a venue for courtly entertainment. The pool in the *dar al-bahr* within the eleventh-century palatial complex of Qal'a Bani Hammad in Algeria is perhaps a later example of this confluence of practical concerns and elitist pleasure.[47]

The extensive excavation of the palatial sector of Madinat al-Zahra' permits an insight into the role of subterranean hydraulic engineering in the evolution of the site. Although the Aqua Augusta ran through the central part of the palace, its depth below ground in this area necessitated the construction of a branch line about 300 metres north of the perimeter wall, to provide water for the buildings on the upper terraces. Once it entered the walled city, the water was taken down the slope through a complex system of channels, which supplied buildings and the large garden pools in the lower terraces (Fig. 5.12). The absence of cisterns and rain-fed underground tanks in the buildings (a feature commonly encountered elsewhere in medieval Spain) indicates that the water from the branch of the Aqua Augusta was sufficient for the needs of the inhabitants. The sanitary infrastructure is particularly impressive, comprising some 1,800 metres of subterranean channels of different dimensions that took water and waste from the courtyards, latrines, bathhouses, and roofs of buildings. These drainage routes must have been established prior to the erection of the buildings; new phases of building are often in evidence below ground, in the form of doubled lines of drains where an old section remained in place even when it was rendered redundant. The section of the Aqua Augusta running beneath the palace lost its initial function and was transformed into the main sewer. The presence of considerable volumes of broken pottery and other refuse in this and in the smaller drainage channels suggests that the subterranean system also served as a site for the dumping of domestic refuse.[48] For the same reason, the underground sanitation systems of Fustat and the palatial complex in the citadel of Damascus also proved to be rich sources of archaeological material.

The rapid growth of many of the *amsar* of the early Islamic world necessitated considerable investment in the provision of fresh water and in the construction of sanitation systems. This is best seen at Fustat, where excavations have illuminated different phases of the hydraulic engineering projects. Sections of aqueducts constructed during the Umayyad, Abbasid, and Fatimid periods have been located around the districts of Fustat, indicating a continued concern for the wellbeing of the urban population. The foundation of Fustat on a sloping shelf of sandstone allowed for the cutting of large water cisterns, which were constantly supplied with water by means of pack animals carrying skins of water (the means by which the fountains of Cairo were supplied in later times). In the finest houses of Fustat water was supplied through pipes into fountains and basins, often with distinctions being made between drinking water and the kind used for washing and cooking. Cesspits might also be dug into the bedrock; in the simplest houses (as seen in 'Fustat-C') the latrines were usually located directly above the pit, though in multi-storey blocks latrines were placed on each floor, with flues constructed within the walls. In the most elaborate sanitation systems, flues from the domestic complexes were connected with underground canals which ran into communal cesspits. Bringing to mind the achievements of Roman urban design, the sanitation systems at Fustat suggest some forethought and subsequent management by municipal authorities, particularly in the placement of drainage channels and cesspits beyond the confines of private property.[49]

Different approaches were taken by the engineers of water systems in two Islamic citadels: the Isma'ili stronghold of Alamut, south of the Caspian Sea in Iran, and the ancient settlement of Hama, in central Syria. Constructed largely during the twelfth century, Alamut makes impressive use of the typically Persian technology of *qanats* as well as of deep rock-cut cisterns that collected rain or water from underground springs.[50] Islamic engineers at Hama elaborated upon an existing Byzantine infrastructure. Lifting devices were used to bring water from the Orontes to the citadel, and from there it was fed, through networks of underground ceramic pipes, to cisterns, elegant fountains, and the bathhouse.[51] Baked ceramic drainpipes are much in evidence, both at Hama and at Fustat (and also at other sites in the Middle East), and must have represented a vital industry in Islamic cities: the production of drainpipes certainly comprised a significant proportion of the output of the pottery workshops of Tal Aswad, north of Raqqa, along with other practical vessels like water jugs and chamber pots (chapter 7).[52]

Notes

1 Sauvaget (1934) and (1949).
2 For a thorough critique (with extensive bibliography) of traditional scholarship on the 'Islamic city', see Abu-Lughod (1987). Among the older works on this issue, the contributions in Hourani and Stern, eds (1970) remain useful and are notable for the introduction of archaeological and art-historical perspectives. For a detailed assessment of regional variability in the planning of the *amsar*, see Wheatley (2001), 227–326.
3 Whitcomb (2000); Walmsley (2007), 79–80.
4 Hillenbrand (1999). See also Creswell and Allan (1989), 122–4.
5 Genequand (2006a), 18–20, fig. 5a.
6 Luz (1997); Rosen-Ayalon (2006), 52–8.
7 Whitcomb (1979), 363–6.
8 On this site, see Whitcomb (1989), (1994a), (1994c), (2006). For the suggested revision of the date of the earliest excavated strata, see Walmsley (2007), 94–5.
9 Al-Ansary (1982), 50–8; Creswell and Allan (1989), 118–22; Genequand (2004a).
10 The initial excavation of the site was conducted by Oleg Grabar. See Grabar et al. (1978). For other interpretations of the site, and for results from recent archaeological work, see Northedge (1994), 235–7; Genequand (2005).
11 Genequand (2006a), 16–17, fig. 4.5; Kervran, Hiebert and Rouguelle (2005), 179–201.
12 Northedge (1994); Hillenbrand (1981); Hillenbrand (1994), 388–98; Arce (2004).
13 Northedge (1992), 71–88, 151–65; Almagro, Jiménez and Navarro (2000).
14 Grenet and Rapin (1998); Karev (2004).
15 On these sites, see contributions by Haase and Meyer in Kennedy, ed. (2006), 45–60.
16 On the excavations of the walls and gates of Rafiqa and of the monument of Hiraqla, see contributions in Daiber and Becker, eds (2004), 3–55, 137–56, and plates. On the canal system, see Challis et al. (2004).
17 On the reconstructed street plan within the walls of Rafiqa, see Udo Becker in Heideman and Becker, eds (2003), 199–212, and pls 3 and 5.
18 For the archaeology of the palaces, see contributions in Daiber and Becker, eds (2004), 59–134 and plates. On the stucco decoration, see also Meinecke (1992). For summaries of the architecture of Rafiqa and the palaces, see Creswell and Allan (1989), 243–7, 270–8.
19 On the architecture of Samarra (with a comprehensive bibliography of earlier literature), see Northedge (2005a); also Leisten (2003). For a short summary of the major palaces and mosques, see Creswell and Allan (1989), 279–80, 331–44, 359–76; Hillenbrand (1994), 74–5, 398–408.
20 On the cantonments and the estimation of the size of the army during the Samarran period, see Kennet (2001); Kennedy (2001), 205–8; Northedge (2005a), 167–92.

21 Milwright (2001b). On decorative stucco and the transmission of the 'bevelled style' around the early Islamic world, see Ettinghausen (1952); Creswell and Allan (1989), 374–6; Meinecke (1992).

22 Northedge (2005a), 227–30. See also Ruggles (2000), 94–100.

23 Hillenbrand (1994), 443–6; Ruggles (2000), 51–109; Vallejo (2007).

24 Chittick (1974), I: 100–95. For the chronology of the site, see 13–21.

25 Schlumberger (1978). For the southern palace, see his Ia: 19–73, pls 3–22, 52–91. Summarised in Hillenbrand (1994), 413.

26 Navarro and Jiménez (2007). On the seventh-century amsar, see Akbar (1989).

27 On the archaeology of the earliest phases at Fustat, see Bianquis, Scanlon and Watson (1974); Gayraud (1998).

28 Kubiak and Scanlon, eds (1989), 4–31.

29 Evidence from Aly Bahgat's excavations is summarised in Creswell (1952), I: 119–30. For a revised dating of the houses, see Kubiak and Scanlon (1973). For evidence in the Geniza archive concerning the houses of Fustat, see Goitein (1967–88), 4: 49–82.

30 Wilkinson (1986).

31 Ibid., 92–184, 192–218, 229–58, 264–309. See also Sims (2002), 7–30, 127–31, 211, 218. For the painted decoration of Lashkari Bazar, see Schlumberger (1978), Ia: 101–8, pls 120–4.

32 Translated in Milwright (1999), 505.

33 On the imported pottery found at Fustat, see Kubiak and Scanlon, eds (1989), 38–9, 46–9; Kubiak (1998); Carswell (2000), 65–7. The largest assemblage of published ceramics from the site appears in Bahgat and Massoul (1930).

34 Locally produced ceramics are discussed in Scanlon (1984) and (1986).

35 On these different media, see Kubiak and Scanlon, eds (1989), 49–99; Barnes (1997), I: 33–42; Scanlon and Pinder-Wilson (2001); also Atil (1981).

36 Kubiak and Scanlon, eds (1989), 32–99.

37 Wilkinson (1973). Bulliet's (1992) attempt to link the different styles of Nishapur glazed ware to socio-cultural groups in the town should be read in the light of criticisms voiced by Whitcomb in Bierman, ed. (1995), 58–60.

38 Kröger (1995).

39 Allan (1982); Allan and Gilmour (2000), 50–5.

40 For the pottery and glass from Hama, see Riis, Poulsen and Hammershaimb (1957).

41 Milwright (2008a), 244–55.

42 On the ceramics from Damascus, see François (2002).

43 For the excavations at the Armenian garden and Damascus Gate, see Tushingham (1985), 108–55; Wightman (1989).

44 Marçais (1928); Golvin (1957), 206–11; Jenkins (1975); Benco (1987), 134–42. On the Islamic glazed ceramics of Spain, see Dodds, ed. (1992), cat. no. 33; Jenkins in Anon. (1993), cat. nos. 52, 53.

45 Vitelli (1981). Also Stevens, Kalinkowski and van der Leest, eds (2005), 505–23.

46 Milwright and Baboula (2009).

47 Anderson (2007); Ruggles (2000), 111–23. For the Qal'a of the Bani Hammad, see also Golvin (1957), 188–91.

48 Vallejo (2007), 8–12. Similar finds have been recorded in the Umayyad phases at the 'Amman citadel; see Arce (2004).

49 Scanlon (1970); Kubiak and Scanlon, eds (1989), 21–31. For references to drainage and sanitation in the Cairo *Geniza*, see Goitein (1967–88), 4: 36, 54.

50 Willey (2004), 109–14.

51 Pentz (1997), 1: 37–75.

52 Miglus, ed. (1999), pls 17, 61. Water pipes might also be fashioned out of stone, as is seen in the early Islamic town of Rabadha in Saudia Arabia. See al-Rashid (1986), 48.

Figure 1.1 Gilded bronze plate with enamel decoration, Anatolia or Georgia. Twelfth century. Tiroler Landesmuseum Ferdinandeum, Innsbruck (K 1036). Photo: Frischauf Bild.

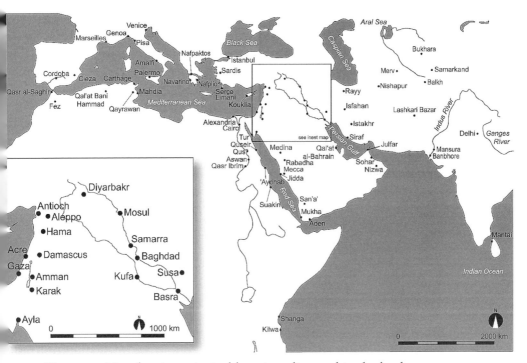

Figure 1.2 Map showing principal locations discussed in the book.

(a)

(b)

(c)

Figure 2.1 (a) 'Orans' type *dirham* (692–95/73–75), SICA no. 107;
(b) 'Standing caliph' *dinar* (696–97/77), SICA no. 705;
(c) Epigraphic *dinar* (697–98/78), Shamma no. 11.
By permission of the Visitors of the Ashmolean Museum.

(a)

(b)

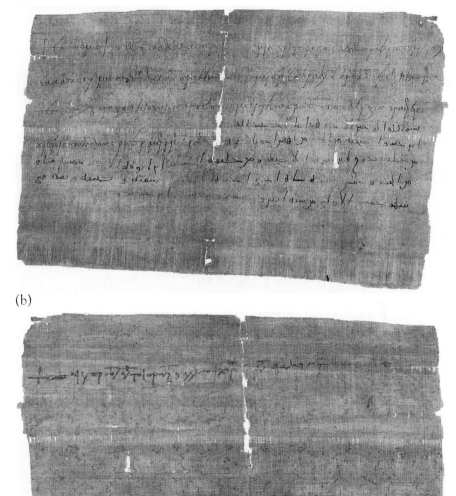

Figure 2.2 Recto (a) and verso (b) of a bilingual (Greek and Arabic) papyrus dated 642/20, Egypt. Pap. G39726, Österreichische Nationalbibliothek, Vienna.

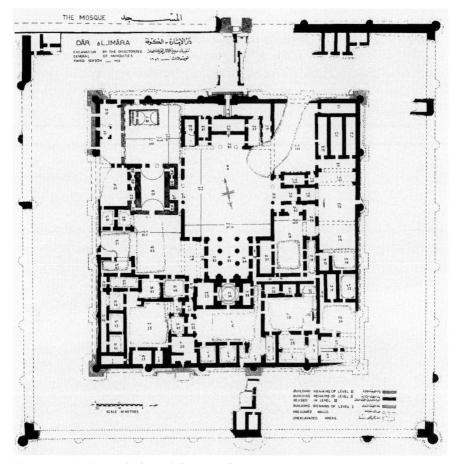

Figure 2.3 Excavated plan of the *Dar al-Imara* at Kufa, Iraq, seventh century and later. After Creswell (1969). Courtesy of Oxford University Press.

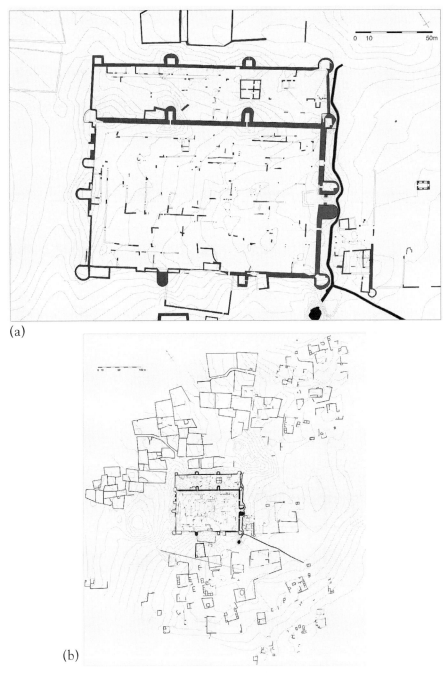

(a)

(b)

Figure 2.4 (a) Plan of the *qasr* of Bakhra', Syria (293–305 and late seventh century); (b) *Qasr* and surrounding buildings. Survey and drawings by Sophie Reynard, Christian de Reynier and Denis Genequand.

Figure 2.5 View along the main colonnaded street towards the Temple of Bel, Palmyra (Tadmur), Syria. Photograph: Marcus Milwright.

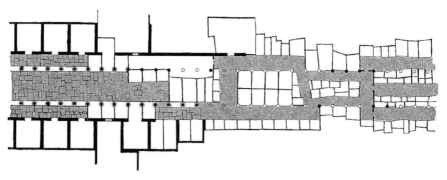

Figure 2.6 Diagram showing the encroachment of building onto a colonnaded street. Generalised from examples in Syria. After Sauvaget (1934).

Figure 2.7 Plan of the Byzantine–Umayyad town of Umm al-Jimal. Drawn by Bert de Vries, Umm el-Jimal Project.

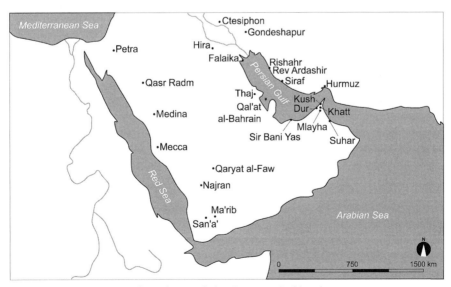

Figure 2.8 Main sites of Arabia and the Persian Gulf in late antiquity.

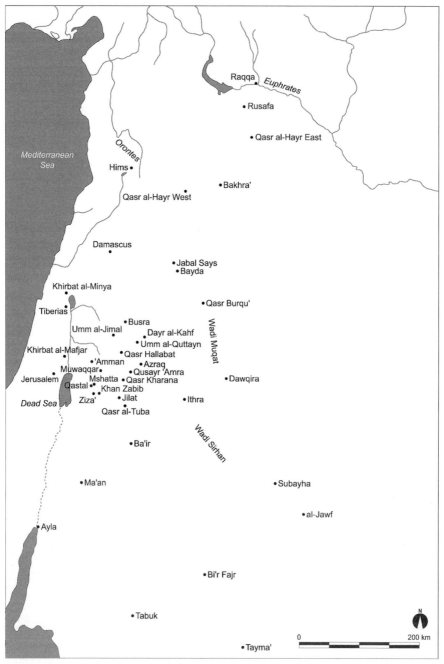

Figure 2.9 The distribution of the Umayyad *qusur* and related towns and cities in Greater Syria. Adapted from maps in King (1987) and Bacharach (1996).

Figure 2.10 Exterior of Qasr al-Kharana, Jordan (before 92/710).
Photograph: Marcus Milwright.

Figure 2.11 Late Roman *castrum* known as Qasr al-Bashir, Jordan (293–305).
Photograph: Marcus Milwright.

Figure 3.1 Turquoise-glazed storage jar, sixth/seventh century, Iran or Iraq. 1978.2242. Courtesy of the Ashmolean Museum, University of Oxford. Photograph: Marcus Milwright.

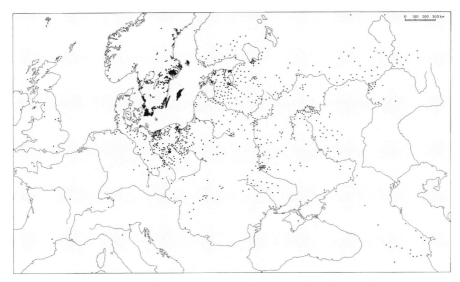

Figure 3.2 Distribution of Islamic coins in Europe. After Ingmar Jansson (1988), Fig. 2 (adapted from map by Bàlint).

Figure 3.3 'Dinar' minted by Offa, king of Mercia, 773–96. CM 1913-12-13-1. Copyright Trustees of the British Museum.

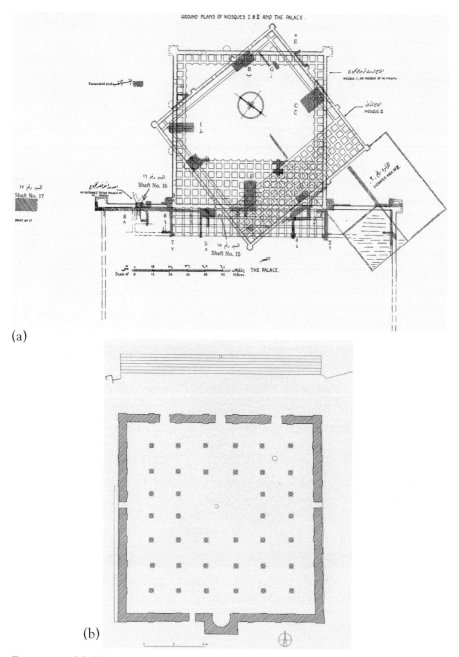

(a)

(b)

Figure 3.4 (a) Two construction phases of the mosque at Wasit (the eighth-century mosque is marked in black and the thirteenth-century building in grey). After Safar (1945). (b) Early eighth-century mosque excavated at the citadel of 'Amman. Courtesy of Antonio Almagro.

108

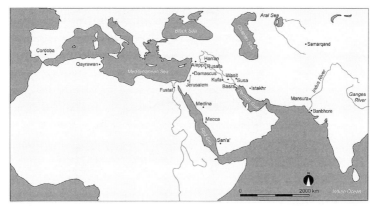

Figure 3.5 Distribution of the principal congregational mosques constructed during the seventh and eighth centuries.

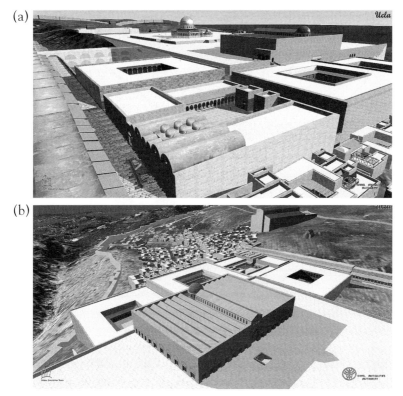

Figure 3.6 Computer reconstructions of the Haram al-Sharif (Temple Mount) and the Umayyad buildings to the south and west before 749: (a) view from the south-west; (b) view from the north-east. Based on the reconstruction of Yuval Baruch. © The Urban Simulation Project at UCLA/UC Regents and the Israel Antiquities Authority.

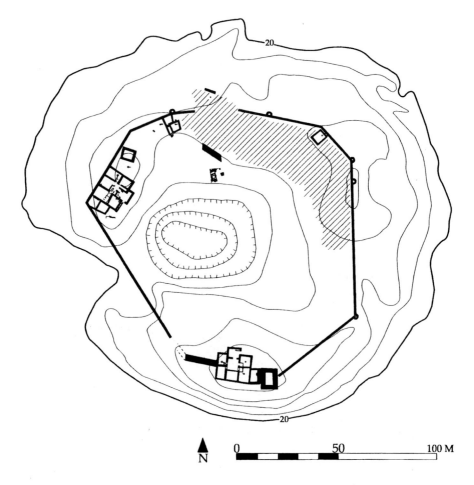

N

0   50   100 M

Probable location of
unexcavated Period I architecture

Figure 4.1 Plan of the last occupation phase of Hasanlu Tepe, north-west Iran. Thirteenth/fourteenth century. Initial mapping by Sir Aurel Stein. Plan by Michael Danti.

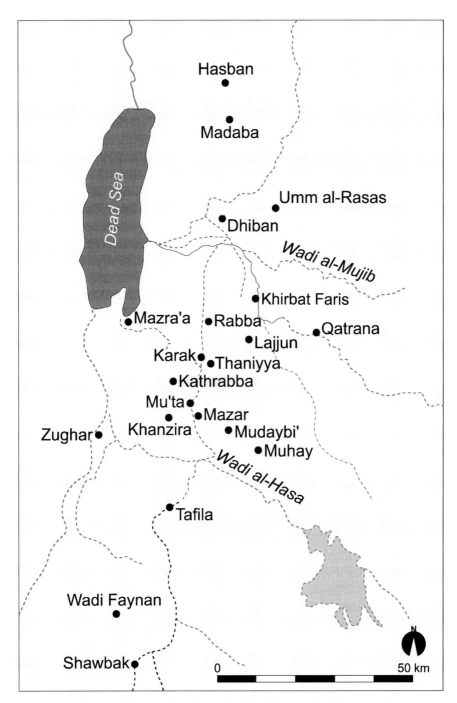

Figure 4.2 Principal sites of southern Jordan during the Islamic and crusader periods.

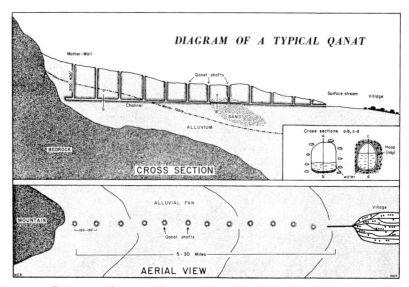

Figure 4.3 Diagram of a typical *qanat*. From Paul Ward English, *City and Village in Iran* (University of Wisconsin Press; Copyright 1966 by the Regents of the University of Wisconsin, p. 31).

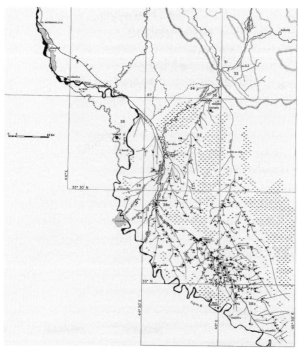

Figure 4.4 Settlements and canals in the Diyala plain, Iraq, during the Islamic period. After Adams (1965). Copyright University of Chicago Press.

112

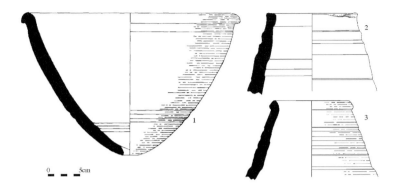

Figure 4.5 Sugar pot (1) and molasses jars (2 and 3) found in Karak Castle, Jordan. Probably from sugar mills at the south end of the Dead Sea. Thirteenth/fourteenth century. Drawings by Marcus Milwright.

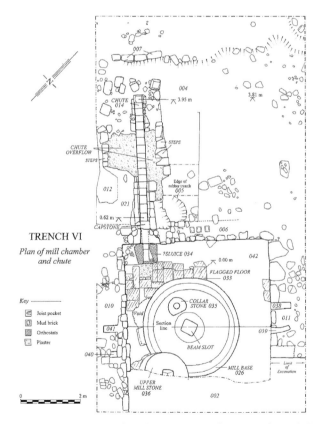

Figure 4.6 Plan of the milling chamber excavated at Tawahin al-Sukkar, Ghur al-Safi, Jordan. Constructed in the thirteenth century. Courtesy of Konstantinos Politis and Richard Jones.

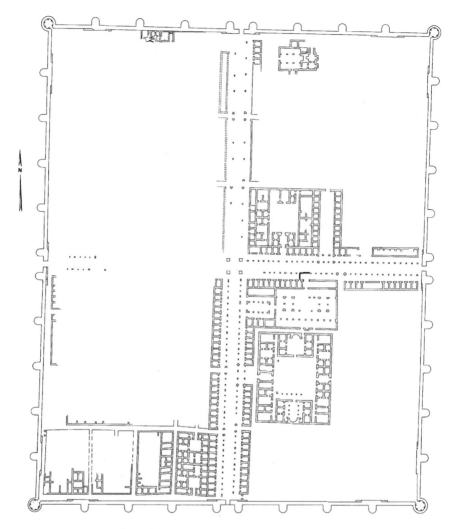

Figure 5.1 Plan of 'Anjar, Lebanon. Early eighth century. After Creswell (1969). Courtesy of Oxford University Press.

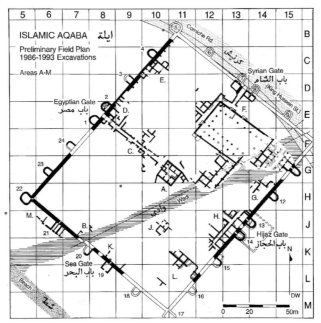

Figure 5.2 Plan of Ayla, Jordan. Seventh/eleventh century. Courtesy of Donald Whitcomb.

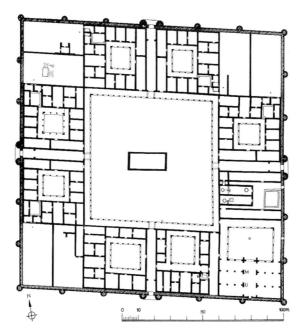

Figure 5.3 Plan of the larger compound at Qasr al-Hayr East, Syria. Early eighth century. After Grabar et al. (1978). Courtesy of Oleg Grabar.

115

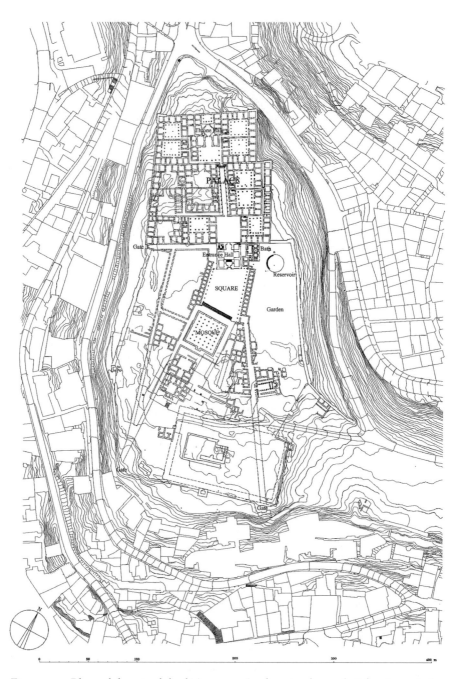

Figure 5.4 Plan of the citadel of 'Amman, Jordan, in the early Islamic period. Courtesy of Antonio Almagro.

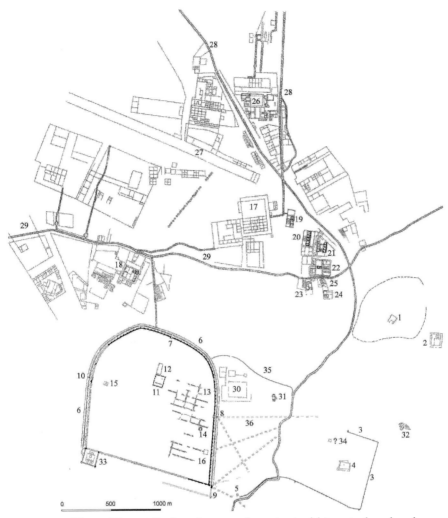

Figure 5.5 Plan of Raqqa-Rafiqa showing the principal historical and archaeological sites. (1) Dair al-Zakka; (2) Roman–Byzantine square building;
(3) Walls of Kallinikos/Raqqa; (4) Congregational mosque; (5) and (34)
Mausoleums; (6) Walls of Rafiqa; (7) North Gate; (8) East Gate or Bab
Sibal; (9) Baghdad Gate; (10) West Gate; (11) Congregational mosque;
(12) Cistern; (13) Street grid; (14) Qasr al-Banat; (15) So-called 'church';
(16) Square complex; (17) Main palace of Harun al-Rashid; (18)–(26) and
(30) Palaces and associated complexes; (27) Hippodrome; (28 and (29)
Canals; (31) Tal Zujaj; (32) Tal Aswad; (33) Ayyubid Citadel; (35) Wall of
Tahir ibn al-Husayn; (36) Main street of al-Raqqa al-Muhtariqa. Copyright:
Orient-Abteilung, Deutsches Archäologische Institut. Courtesy of Stefan
Heidemann.

117

Figure 5.6 Carved stucco panel from the Abbasid period palaces of Raqqa-Rafiqa. Late eighth or early ninth century. Raqqa Archaeological Museum. Photograph: Marcus Milwright.

Figure 5.7 Plan of Samarra, Iraq, showing the principal monuments of the Abbasid phase (836–92). Courtesy of Alastair Northedge.

119

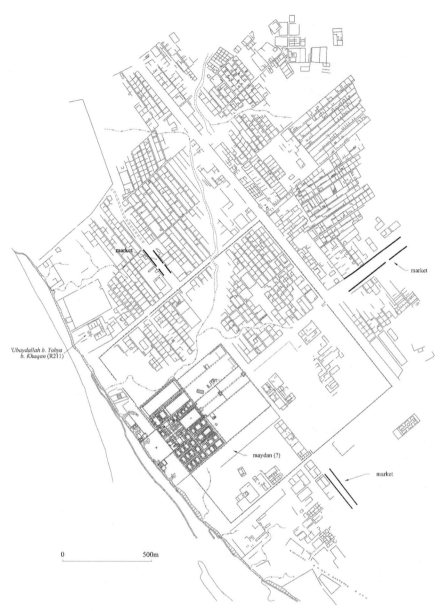

market

market

'Ubaydallah b. Yahya
b. Khaqan (R211)

maydan (?)

market

0   500m

Figure 5.8 Balkuwara and surrounding cantonments, Samarra, Iraq. Courtesy
of Alastair Northedge.

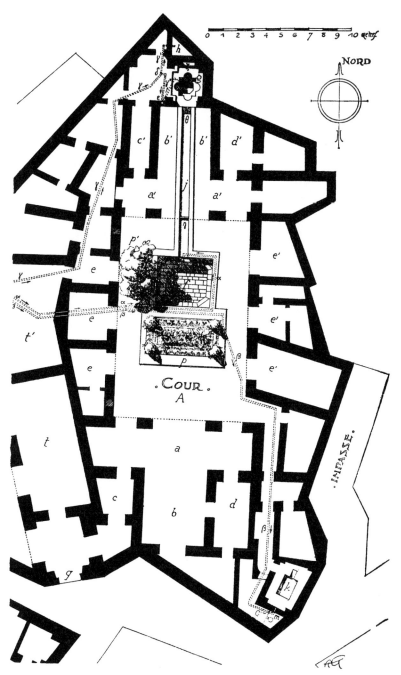

Figure 5.9 Fatimid period house excavated at Fustat. After Creswell (1952). Reproduced from A. Bahgat and A. Gabriel, *Fouilles d'al-Foustat* (Paris, 1921). Courtesy of Oxford University Press.

121

Figure 5.10 Pottery gathered by Erica Dodd from surface collection in Barqiya, Cairo, by permission of the Egyptian Directorate of Antiquities. (1) Chinese blue and white porcelain, fifteenth century; (2) Chinese celadon (greenware), fourteenth century; (3) Tin-glazed, lustre-painted earthenware bowl, Spain, fifteenth century; (4) Underglaze-painted blue and black stonepaste, Syria, early fourteenth century; (5) Underglaze-painted blue and white stonepaste jar, Egypt (?), fifteenth century; (6) Turquoise glazed stonepaste bowl, Egypt or Syria, twelfth century; (7) Underglaze-painted blue and black stonepaste, Syria, thirteenth century; (8) Slip-painted glazed earthenware, Egypt, fifteenth century; (9)–(11) Lead-glazed sgraffito ware, Egypt, late thirteenth/early fourteenth century; (12) Lead-glazed earthenware jug, Egypt, fourteenth century (?); (13) Unglazed wheelthrown jug, Egypt, thirteenth/fifteenth century. Photograph: Caitlin Cuthbert. Reproduced courtesy of the Maltwood Museum, University of Victoria.

Figure 5.11 Satellite map with the distribution of Ottoman period fountains and mosques in Nafpaktos, Greece. Base map courtesy of Google Earth.

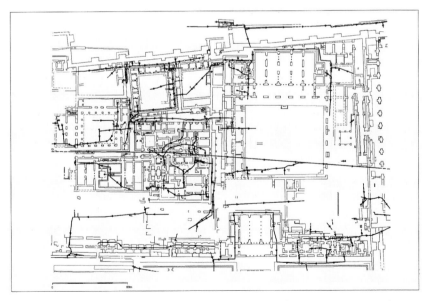

Figure 5.12 Detail of the sanitary infrastructure on the upper terrace of Madinat al-Zahra'. The central rectilinear channel is the Roman channel. Image courtesy of Antonio Vallejo Triano.

6

Religious practice in the Islamic world

Belief and ritual practice have had a profound impact upon the material culture of the Islamic world. Muslim religious invocations and sections taken from the *Qur'an* appear on documents, monumental inscriptions and coins during the seventh century (chapter 2). The placement of Qur'anic passages on coins ensured their wide circulation among Muslims and non-Muslims alike. While the precise content of such epigraphic coins would have eluded the illiterate user, it is conceivable that the more general significance of the text would have been appreciated by the wider populace. Certainly the fascination with script (both as a carrier of information and as an object of aesthetic appreciation) becomes a defining characteristic of Islamic visual culture, and is evident also in artefacts recovered during excavations and surveys. Confronted by the conspicuous place of religious architecture in the urban landscape of late antiquity, Islamic authorities devoted great energy to the construction of congregational mosques (chapter 3). Other religious monuments – schools (*madrasas*), sufi convents (*khanqahs*), hospitals (*maristans*), and tomb complexes – transformed the towns and cities of the Islamic world from the tenth century onwards. The countryside, too, was populated with Muslim structures, including mosques, tombs, buildings associated with the *hajj*, and even free-standing minarets. Rural mosques ranged from substantial stone buildings to the diminutive open-air (hypaethral) structures of the early Islamic period located in the Negev desert.[1]

Some aspects of Muslim ritual practice – the orientation of a corpse, or the plan of a courtyard mosque – leave a distinct trace in the archaeological record, but the interactions among different religious communities inevitably blur confessional distinctions between other aspects of the material culture. For instance the pilgrimages (*ziyaras*) made to the tombs of holy men and women might well be attended by all the community members who shared a given region, regardless of their confessional allegiance. Often harking back to pre-Islamic practices, a belief survived in the blessings (*baraka*) gained through the visitation of a shrine. As a result, dedicatory artefacts left within such spaces cannot be associated solely with the activities of one religious community. Coexisting with orthodox religious beliefs, most cultures of the Islamic world also appear to have shared a fascination for astrology and forms of magical protection. Finally, just as Islamic culture assimilated the visual traditions of late antiquity, so 'Islamic' artistic modes later became an integral component of Christian and Jewish religious art. The art of the Copts in Egypt abounds in examples of Islamic acculturation, from the Fatimid period altar screen of Sitt Barbara in Cairo to the carpet pages of fourteenth and fifteenth-century Gospels that emulate the ornamentation of contemporary Mamluk Qur'ans.[2]

The examples discussed in the previous paragraph have important implications for archaeology. While there can be little doubt that Islam permeated aspects of everyday life (diet, the arrangement of domestic space, the decoration of personal possessions, and so on), the nuances of localised cultural norms, cross-confessional interaction, personal choices, and short-term historical factors are difficult to reconstruct by using archaeological data. In other words, considerable caution must be exercised when attempting to assign a specific religious 'identity' (including distinctions between different branches of Islam) to material recovered in excavations and surveys.

With this in mind, the remainder of the present chapter considers the archaeology of religious practice from three perspectives. The first section deals with the mosque and the ways in which this locus for communal prayer might adapt over time. The second section considers the variations in the practice of Muslim burials, concentrating particularly upon the excavations of non-elite cemeteries in the Middle East. The last section addresses the status of non-Muslim communities under Islam, especially in relation to the churches of southern Greater Syria, in the centuries before and after the Islamic conquests.

Interpretations of the evolution of the mosque

A significant characteristic of the hypostyle mosque is its ability to expand horizontally, either by adding further bays into the prayer hall or through changes to the courtyard and surrounding arcades. Such changes to the fabric of an existing mosque were often driven by rather practical concerns; as the Muslim community of a region grew, so congregational mosques had to expand in order to accommodate the faithful for the Friday prayer. Other factors might also contribute to the adaptation of a monument; importantly, the renovation of a congregational mosque was a means by which a ruler or a state official could both make a public expression of piety and express the ideological concerns of the ruling dynasty.

The evolution of mosques over the centuries is an area of considerable interest both for archaeology and architectural history. If one concentrates upon structural history, there is much that can be achieved through the combination of a systematic analysis of the standing elements and, where possible, a selective excavation. These techniques have brought impressive results with the congregational mosques of Isfahan, San'a', Qayrawan, and Cordoba, as well as with many other, less prestigious, mosques elsewhere in the Islamic world.[3] The Masjid-i Jami at Isfahan illustrates the transformation of an eighth-century hypostyle mosque into a Saljuq imperial mosque through the addition of four *iwans* around the courtyard, and of a massive domed chamber in the prayer hall (and yet another to the north of the mosque). Although the four *iwans* and the prayer hall dome were to become standard in later Iranian mosques, these features were not the result of a single building campaign at Isfahan. Likewise, the complex structural history of the mosque of Cordoba prior to the *Reconquista* can be attributed to the activities of numerous rulers and viziers. Radical changes might also occur over shorter time periods, as is demonstrated in the addition of the salients covering the towers flanking the entrance of the Fatimid mosque of al-Hakim in Cairo.[4] The remainder of this section assesses the archaeology of three mosques – the Aqsa mosque and the congregational mosques of Shanga and Siraf – and considers the evidence concerning the evolution of these places of worship. The last part broadens the focus so as to look at the establishment of smaller neighbourhood mosques within the urban environment.

The Aqsa mosque stands at the southernmost extent of the Haram al-Sharif (Temple Mount) in Jerusalem. The Haram al-Sharif is dominated by the Dome of the Rock, built by the Umayyad Caliph 'Abd al-Malik (chapter 2). While the Dome of the Rock has, to a great extent, retained its late seventh-century plan and elevation (and even much of its internal decoration), the Aqsa mosque has been transformed through destruction, rebuilding, and renovation. It has even endured changes of function, being employed as the palace of the crusading King Baldwin I (r. 1100–16), and later as the headquarters of the Templar Order (until 1187). Evidence for the construction of the Aqsa mosque can be gathered from written sources and inscriptions. Written descriptions vary both in detail and in reliability, however. Even the eye-witness accounts of Arculf (before 680) and Muqaddasi (c.985) are difficult to reconcile with the physical evidence recovered in excavations and surveys. Monumental inscriptions – valuable though they undoubtedly are for providing dates and identifying patrons – cannot always be taken at face value. Statements concerning the 'renewal' (*jaddada*) of an existing structure do not necessarily indicate that the patron instigated major changes to the architectural fabric.

Between 1938 and 1942 the authorities of the Haram al-Sharif undertook a project of substantial demolition and replacement of the structural fabric of the existing Aqsa. The systematic description of the building and the limited excavations conducted by Robert Hamilton at that time allowed for a much more complete picture of the building's early history (Fig. 6.1 a–c).[5] On the basis of his observations, Hamilton proposed three major construction phases (known as Aqsa I–III) in the period prior to the crusades. Importantly, in all of these phases the building was wider than its present form, probably comprising, at its greatest extent, fifteen aisles perpendicular to the *qibla* wall. Hamilton's analysis indicated that the third phase had involved the replacement of the structural elements of the nave. The substantial round limestone piers in the nave of Aqsa III supported larger spans than their predecessors in Aqsa II. In effect this change allowed for a wider central nave and for a reduction in the number of bays from fifteen to eleven. That the earlier buildings did not follow the pattern of supports in Aqsa III was confirmed through the excavation; trenches dug beneath the floor of the prayer hall and to the east of the present building revealed the foundations of columns in the nave and the bedding and marble flags of an earlier floor (in some places laid directly over the masonry making up the vault of the Herodian period tunnel which ran from the Double Gate in the south wall through into the Haram al-Sharif). This floor terminated nineteen metres to the south of the present north wall, and also extended beyond the present east wall. A tentative reconstruction of this first mosque, Hamilton's Aqsa I, has been proposed by combining this evidence with the textual accounts and the locations of the earliest columns (most of which lie east of the main dome).[6]

The dating of the three major construction phases of the Aqsa in this early period continues to be debated, and Hamilton himself offered different interpretations. In his later pronouncements on the subject, he concluded that the mosque described by Muqaddasi was in fact Aqsa III and not Aqsa II, as both himself and Creswell had formerly assumed. The implications of this conclusion are, first, that the work of the Fatimid Caliph al-Zahir was confined to the mosaic ornament and did not involve major structural changes and, second, that the rebuilding of the nave was undertaken earlier (namely before 985). Turning to written sources, it would appear that this phase of demolition and reconstruction occurred after the great earthquake of 749 and was ordered by the Abbasid Caliph Mansur and completed by Mahdi (r. 775–85). Papyri recovered from the Egyptian site of Aphrodito record the provision of workers for the 'mosque and palace' of Jerusalem in 715–16/97, and Hamilton concludes that this refers to work on the construction of Aqsa II. Aqsa I is attributed to Walid's father, 'Abd al-Malik, the caliph responsible for the Dome of the Rock. Hamilton reasons that the rapid expansion of the mosque in Aqsa II happened simply because 'Abd al-Malik's building was too small for the Muslim inhabitants of Jerusalem and for the many pilgrims coming to the Haram al-Sharif in the early eighth century.

Hamilton's conclusions concerning the revised date of Aqsa III have been widely accepted. There are, however, alternatives to his chronology of Aqsa I and II, and these are suggested by a consideration of two remaining problems.

First, what happened to the mosque on the Temple Mount described by the Christian pilgrim Arculf? While it may well have been constructed largely out of spolia from the vicinity and it is described by Arculf as 'rudely built', it was able to hold, by his estimate, 3,000 men. Second, what remains of Aqsa I hardly compares, in terms of architectural sophistication, with the Dome of the Rock. This is clearly problematic if 'Abd al-Malik is proposed as the patron of Aqsa I (as is the fact that his design so quickly proved too small to perform its primary function). An alternative hypothesis places Aqsa I before the visit of Arculf and, possibly, during the reign of Caliph Mu'awiya in the 660s. The implication of this shift in the dating is that Aqsa II, the grandest of all the phases, would have been planned during the reign of 'Abd al-Malik but completed during, or just after, the reign of Walid I.

While the ruined congregational mosque in the port of Shanga, on Pate Island off the Kenyan coast, possesses nothing of the imperial grandeur of the Aqsa, it can boast solid construction materials and an impressive *mihrab*. Like the rest of the town, the mosque was abandoned in the fifteenth century. As it stands now, the building is the result of construction carried between the eleventh and the fourteenth century. The first phase, dating to *c.*1000, comprised a prayer hall with a roof supported on four pillars; a southern room abutting the prayer hall; and an eastern veranda. Substantial remodelling of the mosque occurred in the late eleventh century, in the aftermath of a fire. The southern room was incorporated into the prayer hall (necessitating the addition of two more pillars), and a veranda was also constructed to the west. A large *mihrab* projecting beyond the *qibla* wall was added in the mid-twelfth century (following the practice of the Ibadi mosques of Oman, though direct parallels for the design can be sought in Zanzibar). In the early thirteenth century the mosque incorporated a walled area containing a well and a large water tank. The *mihrab* was reconstructed in the thirteenth or fourteenth century, and ornamented with inscriptions written in a degenerate cursive script which replaced the Kufic bands of the earlier structure. Changes in the orientation of the burials beyond the south, east, and north (*qibla*) walls of the mosque probably reflect the more accurate calculation of the direction of the *qibla* in the centuries after the initial construction of the mosque.

These layers of construction reflect the continuing importance of the mosque for the Muslim community. That the site had a long-term significance for the inhabitants of Shanga was indicated, however, by the excavations of *c.*1000 beneath the floor of the mosque. Here a sequence of seventeen phases was found, in which a series of small rectangular buildings, oriented further to the west than the standing mosque, were built one over another (Fig. 6.2). The last one of these, building H (dating from the early to mid-tenth century), was made of stone and comprised a prayer hall, a southern chamber, and a projection on the north wall (marking a *mihrab*). Prior to this, the physical evidence for structures comprised post holes, trenches, traces of plaster, and compacted mud (*kinyokae*) or pebble floors. The earliest timber structure, building A, was a simple rectangle, though later buildings comprised two rooms. The dating of the complete sequence is uncertain, though ceramic finds, carbon-14 readings, and comparison with modern ethnographic data suggested a regular replacement of buildings every ten or fifteen years (which gives a probable starting date between c.745 and 830).[7]

This sequence of early buildings raises some important questions concerning the identification of mosques – particularly small and architecturally undistinguished ones – in the archaeological record. Orientation is clearly an important aspect of this identification, though the example of Wasit shows how a substantially inaccurate calculation of the *qibla* might be corrected centuries later by a newly constructed mosque on the same site. The archaeological evidence from Shanga suggests that the area occupied by buildings A–H retained some significance as early as in the mid-eighth century; but can one be sure that all of them functioned as mosques? While some of the later structures, from the ninth century onwards, included what may be a *mihrab*, the earliest ones are devoid of the characteristic features of a mosque (though they are measured out according to the cubit commonly employed in the early Islamic world). This issue has proven controversial, not least because it would place the introduction of Islam to East Africa earlier than is indicated by the historical sources. If one accepts the contention of the excavator, Mark Horton, that the earliest structures are mosques, this leads a to further question: were they employed by Arab Muslim traders or by the native population? Horton points out that the former explanation is rendered less likely by the fact that the site is located at the centre of the settlement rather than on the periphery. Interestingly, ninth-century burials in the area contained locally minted silver coins bearing Muslim names. If Horton's interpretation is correct, it indicates that there was a dominant Muslim population in Shanga from the inception of the settlement or soon afterwards.

Located within the ruins of the abandoned Sasanian fort and surrounded on three sides by the market area, the congregational mosque in Siraf is the most impressive religious building of that area (Fig. 6.3a and b).[8] Built upon a 2 metre-high platform measuring approximately 55 metres on each side, the mosque is constructed of rubble and coarsely shaped sandstone masonry, bonded with gypsum mortar and, in the foundations, with a mixture of clay, lime, and ash (*saruj*). The rubble piers and arches were roofed with wooden beams, probably imported from East Africa.[9] The main entrance is located on the north-east side and creates a principal axis running to the *mihrab* on the south-west (*qibla*) wall. The rectangular stump of the minaret was found immediately south of the entrance. The mosque itself comprises a courtyard surrounded by a double arcade on three sides and a prayer hall with five aisles parallel to the *qibla* wall. The *mihrab* consists of a shallow rectangular niche on the interior, but is marked on the exterior by a pronounced salient. Indentations in the plaster floor and abutments to the piers suggest that the prayer hall of the twelfth-century mosque contained a wooden *maqsura*, a *minbar*, and perhaps a wooden platform (*dakka*). An extension to the mosque on the south-east side added a further three bays to the mosque (excluding the area of the east corner, which was occupied by a cistern and a latrine).

The recovery of a Saljuq *dinar* beneath the floor level fixed the final construction phase to after 1147–8/542.[10] Excavations revealed that a mosque had stood on the site for more than three centuries. The first construction phase was dated by coin evidence to soon after 803–4/188, and comprised a rectangular plan measuring 51 x 44 m. The interior possessed a single arcade around the courtyard and a prayer hall three bays deep. The initial *mihrab* was probably a shallow niche or plaque set into the wall, but soon after its completion this section of the wall was reconstructed to create a deeper niche, marked on the exterior by a salient. The decision to construct the mosque on a platform was probably necessitated by the presence of numerous abandoned buildings inside the Sasanian fort.

Like with the changes from Aqsa I to Aqsa II, an intriguing feature of the congregational mosque in Siraf is the rapid pace of the renovations made to the first building. In the second construction phase the superstructure of the mosque was torn down and the floors were removed. The second mosque extended the internal space through an additional bay on the *qibla* side which required the destruction of the original *mihrab*. The platform was extended on the south-east side to create three more bays to the prayer hall and an ablution area. The street level under the prayer hall extension comprises a series of chambers facing onto the market, which were utilised for a range of commercial functions. The courtyard was also transformed through the addition of a cistern and of a second arcade around all four sides. The principal excavator, David Whitehouse, concludes that the first two phases can be dated from c.803–804 to c.825 and c.825–850 respectively, though reconsideration of the numismatic and ceramic data suggests a more compressed chronology, with both phases occurring between c.803–4 and c.815.[11]

Although the second and third phases of the Siraf mosque certainly incorporated some decorative components, the chief importance of the building is not aesthetic; it was a provincial mosque built out of simple materials, on a plan that accords broadly with existing Abbasid models (chapter 3). Its primary interest lies in the initial mode of construction on top of the platform and in the subsequent adaptations. While the radical changes of the second phase may have been motivated in part by structural concerns, they also indicate that the builders were reacting to the changing needs of the inhabitants of Siraf. This fact may be indicated in the extension of the prayer hall and courtyard arcades, as well as in the introduction of commercial units at the street level. The use of imported timber in the roofing is a physical reminder of the vibrant mercantile economy of Siraf at the time of the first two phases of the mosque.

Similar dynamics are also apparent in the smaller mosques (*masjids*) of Siraf. Ten were identified and five were subjected to excavation. Like the congregational mosque, the neighbourhood mosques were all constructed (and often renovated) between the ninth and the twelfth century (the period of most intense commercial activity at the port – see chapter 8). Many of them were found to have traces of multiple building phases, and all were closely integrated into existing street plans.[12] The consistent use of a pronounced exterior salient to mark the presence of the *mihrab* – a feature also found in the congregational mosque – recalls the Ibadi mosques of Oman and of the coast of East Africa. Examination of the 'stone town' of Shanga also revealed small mosques incorporated into the urban plan beside domestic structures.[13] This appears to be a common pattern around the Islamic world, and can be seen in the standing architecture of many towns and cities. For instance in the excavated areas of Nishapur known as Tepe Madrasa and at Qanat Tepe (chapter 5), places of worship enjoy no greater prominence on the streetfront than the dwellings which abut them.[14]

Burial practices

Drawing on the authority of *Hadith*, Sunni Muslim law places great emphasis on speed and simplicity in the treatment of the dead. Thus the body should be placed in the ground before dusk, on the day of death or early on the following morning. The burial should be devoid of artefacts other than items of clothing and a shroud, and it should have no permanent grave marker or architectural structure above ground. While members of the immediate family were permitted to visit a grave after the funeral, Sunni Muslim jurists, particularly of the Hanbali school of law, inveighed against the practice of making pilgrimages (*ziyara*) to the burial places of holy men and women – an exception being made for the tomb of the Prophet at Medina.[15] Excavations have recovered many burials which conform to the strictures of Muslim law, but, predictably, many of the more austere regulations were routinely flouted as Islam came into contact with other, long-established funerary and commemorative practices in Asia and Africa.

The gravestone of 'Abd al-Rahman ibn Khayr dated 652/31 (chapter 2) is perhaps the earliest example of the widespread practice of marking the burial with an inscribed plaque. Apart from the evident piety manifested in the inscription, there is clearly also a desire that the name of the dead man should live on. The expression of kinship, tribal identity, social status, and human need for personal aggrandisement is at play in the proliferation of grave markers in later periods, though the precise format, medium, and ornamentation varies from region to region. The export of carved grave stelae from twelfth-century Spain to Gao in Mali or, later, from Gujarat to Indonesia illustrates not merely long-distance trade in luxury funerary items, but the importance of signalling Muslim identity in areas undergoing gradual conversion to Islam.[16] Social status is powerfully communicated through the practice, followed in Ottoman Turkey, of carving on top of the headstone the official headgear that had been worn in life. Less visible but equally significant are the clothes worn in death. The dry soils of Egypt and Sudan allow for the preservation of ancient textiles in Christian and Muslim cemeteries. That Coptic Christians from late antiquity into the Islamic period often favoured vividly coloured and patterned robes is demonstrated by the materials gathered from (often illicit) excavations at sites such as Armant, Manshiyya, and Akhmim. The last of these sites produced a textile made in Ifriqiya (Tunisia) bearing the name of the Umayyad Caliph Marwan (probably Marwan II, r. 744–50). This practice of adding *tiraz* with the titulature of the caliph is a common feature of later textiles. Often given as gifts on the recipient's being invested with an official post, these valuable items were taken by their wearers to their graves. Examples of Fatimid *tiraz* have also been found during controlled excavations at Fustat.[17]

The most conspicuous act of commemoration was the construction of a domed building (*qubba*) over a tomb. Picking up on architectural traditions as diverse as classical martyria, Sasanian fire temples, and Buddhist funerary architecture, Islamic mausolea become a major focus of architectural patronage, particularly from the eleventh century on. Early examples include the Qubbat al-Sulaybiyya in Samarra, an octagonal and domed building, probably housing the remains of three ninth-century Abbasid caliphs; and the so-called tomb of Isma'il the Samanid in Bukhara, dated to the tenth century. A fascinating group of relatively simple, domed structures at Aswan in southern Egypt has been interpreted as a commemoration of Fatimid martyrs (*shahid*) from military campaigns in Nubia. The evolution of monumental mausolea is the domain of architectural history, though an archaeological approach might consider aspects of spatial distribution (for instance along trade or pilgrimage routes), and partic-ularly the relationship between *qubba*s and cemeteries.[18]

A building at Emmaus (Amwas) in Israel has been associated, at least since the thirteenth century, with a companion of the Prophet. Excavations recovered large numbers of crudely made ceramic saucer lamps, mostly dating from the Mamluk and Ottoman periods. Accounts of *ziyara*s made to sites like this mention the lighting of candles or lamps as part of the veneration of the tomb.[19] Stamped clay tokens (*muhr*) are made at Shi'a pilgrimage sites such as Karbala' and Mashhad and taken back to their local mosques by pilgrims (Fig. 6.4). This practice is also noted by observers in the nineteenth century, and a pressed clay tablet of this type is reported from the excavation of a sixteenth or seventeenth-century grave at Qal'at Bahrain in the Persian Gulf.[20]

Although recent work in Spain provides evidence of intra-mural cemeteries (chapter 5), locations outside of the city or town walls are encountered in many other regions of the Islamic world. In the area known as Tal Aswad, in the north-east of modern Raqqa, the Christian cemetery was taken over by ceramic workshops in the period after c.771 (chapter 7). Excavations revealed, however, that burials continued during the time when the area was occupied by ceramic workshops. The association of burial and manufacturing can also be found at Damascus, where kilns coexisted with the cemetery beyond Bab Kisan to the south-east of the walled city. At Qal'at Bahrain the burial ground was located north-west of the town established in the late thirteenth century. As the cemetery grew, it expanded over the commercial warehouse of the port.[21] Although these extra-mural localities might combine industrial/commercial and funerary functions, this does not mean that cemeteries were not accorded considerable importance in Islamic society. The monumental architecture of the 'City of the Dead' in Cairo, or the Shah-i Zinda in Samarqand, demonstrate it well. For most Muslims, however, burial was a less elaborate affair, and the graveyards in which they were interred lack any inscribed headstones or other expensive forms of commemoration. Numerous Muslim cemeteries have been excavated in rural areas of the Middle East, and they provide valuable data concerning mortuary practices, health, and disease, as well as intriguing avenues of interpretation regarding socio-cultural values among the living. An extensively published cemetery of this type was excavated at Tal al-Hasi near Gaza, in southern Palestine.[22] The ancient mound was investigated by Frederick Bliss in the 1890s, and there is no indication that bodies were still being interred at that time. Nevertheless, it is clear that the burial area was relatively recent, occurring c.1400–1800. With the exception of the ruins of a small rectangular structure to the south – the shrine (*wali*) of a holy man – the graves lacked external markers.

Given the absence of inscribed headstones and the paucity of coins on the site, the investigation of the Tal al-Hasi graves concentrated upon questions of typology and distribution. The principal typological distinctions are reviewed below, but perhaps more important is a recognition of the considerable areas of consistency in burial. First, with very few exceptions, the bodies were aligned, according to orthodox Muslim practice, with the head to the west and the face directed toward the *qibla* (approximately south). The body lay roughly east–west and might be arranged on its back, or more commonly be turned on the right side, with the knees slightly bent (in a manner reminiscent of sleep).

The hands were often arranged to cover the genitals, particularly in burials of adult females. The occasional traces of textiles excavated in the burials were probably associated with shrouds and burial clothing. Second, the depth of the burial accorded to practices noted by nineteenth and early twentieth-century observers. According to tradition, the body had to be placed deep enough to be able to rise to a seated position beneath the earth. It was in this position that the deceased would be interrogated by angels.

Variations in the treatment of bodies included the pointing of the face to the north (perhaps towards Jerusalem) and the striking examples of a decapitated adult female and the possible case of the interment of a still living juvenile male. Most of the bodies were articulated, indicating primary burial, though evidence of secondary burial was recovered in the form of disarticulated bones. Grave goods were recovered, including ceramic jugs and – largely restricted to adult female or child burials – jewellery and other personal adornments. The grave itself might consist of a simple shaft, though in many cases the body was covered with large cap stones prior to the infilling with soil. Cap stones could be used to cover more than one body, and in more elaborate cases the sides of the grave were lined with stones, or a flat stone was placed under the head as a 'pillow'. Pressure of space in some areas of the cemetery was probably a factor contributing to the practice of placing a new burial into a previously used area, which often led to the disturbance of the bodies beneath (Fig. 6.5). Lastly, the treatment of infants showed considerable variability, ranging from burial with an adult – in most cases, presumably, the mother – to interment within a large unglazed ceramic jar.

The Tal al-Hasi cemetery was probably employed by bedouin rather than by settled villagers (*fellahin*). That the majority of the adults enjoyed relatively good health, and a balanced diet is indicated by the rarity of bone deformations and other signs of disease and malnutrition. The high occurrence of infant burial does indicate, however, that childbirth and early life were times of high mortality. Some burials were evidently more elaborate than others, but the interments did not show any clear spatial patterning beyond a tendency for the stone-lined graves to be closer to the grave of the 'holy man'. While tribal affiliation or social status could not be inferred from the distribution of burial types, some division by gender existed, adult females being accorded more elaborate burials than adult males. Changing social status was also suggested through the contrast between the rather haphazard approach to infants and the care taken over children aged three or more years (perhaps the age at which they were recognised as full members of the tribe).

Synthesis of information from other excavated burial grounds in Egypt, Greater Syria, Turkey, and Iraq reveals similar patterns to those of Tal al-Hasi, as well as a range of other, regionally specific practices.[23] Commonly cemeteries clustered around the tomb of a holy man or woman, and often on areas unsuited to cultivation. The outward expansion of cemeteries from a central point (such as a shrine) made it difficult to maintain family or tribal divisions over time, and this may be a reason for the vertical concentration of burial in some areas. In some regions infants and older children were placed in separate cemeteries. Graves vary in form and in the materials (stone, mud, bricks, pot sherds, and slag) used to line or cap the body. The placement of the body exhibited the consistent concern with orientation to Mecca, though the head might lie to the east or west, and variations existed in the pose of the arms and legs. While recorded grave goods included ceramics, glassware, coins, bells, and knives, the largest concentration of artefacts comprised personal adornments and cosmetic items such as mirrors and combs. Among the necklaces and pendants, the pref-erence for specific colours reflects popular beliefs (for instance, the idea that blue protects against the 'evil eye'). Thus many features of these burials contravene to 'orthodox' Muslim burial practices. Allowing for such phenomena as secondary burial or the employment of grave goods, it is however more important perhaps to emphasise the extent to which rural communities adhered to the fundamental principle of body orientation as a marker of Muslim identity.

Other religious communities before and after the Islamic conquest

Following the Muslim conquests of the seventh and eighth centuries, the adherents of other religions found themselves under the dominion of a new and, over time, assertive faith. From its inception, Islam recognised the legitimacy of religions that had received Divine Scripture, or of the 'Peoples of the Book' (*ahl al-kitab*). These groups (most importantly Christians, Jews, and Zoroastrians) were assigned the status of a 'protected group' (*dhimmi*) and were accorded freedom of worship and other rights in return for the payment of a head tax (*jizya*). While *dhimmi* did not enjoy all the privileges of their Muslim counterparts and there were outbreaks of religious intolerance against non-Muslim communities, peaceful coexistence appears to have been more the norm than the exception. A different picture emerges, however, in relation to Islam's interaction with religious practices that were, at times, considered idolatrous, such as Buddhism and Hinduism. The destruction of Buddhist monuments in Iran following the conversion of the Ikhanate to Islam in 1295 was so complete that only a few traces remain.[24] The capture and destruction of Hindu sculptures followed from military expeditions to India led by Mahmud of Ghazna (r. 998–1030) and by the Ghurid dynasty of Afghanistan (early eleventh century–1215). Figural sculpture defaced and looted from Hindu temples and from commemorative pillars (*stambhas* or *lats*) can also be found in thirteenth and fourteenth-century Indian mosques.[25]

The last part of this section considers the Christian communities of Palestine and Jordan. Before reviewing the evidence, some general comments should be made about the archaeology of late antique religious life in the other lands that were to form the Islamic Empire of the seventh and eighth centuries.[26] Archaeological work in the Persian Gulf has demonstrated the vitality of the Nestorian church in the two centuries before the rise of Islam. On the Arabian coast, Nestorian churches and monastic communities have been identified on the islands of Sir Bani Yas (Abu Dhabi) and Failaka (Kuwait), as well as at Jabal Berri in Saudi Arabia. At Sir Bani Yas the ceramic sequence indicated extensive activity during the sixth and seventh century, and abandonment not long after the Abbasid takeover in 750. Nestorian churches have been identified on Kharg Island (Iran) and on numerous Sasanian period sites – including Hira, Ctesiphon, and Veh Ardashir. A carved stucco panel carrying a Nestorian cross was recovered from excavations at Tulul al-Ukhaydir, a qasr west of Karbala' built in the late Sasanian period and reused in early Islamic times. Churches also appear in northern Iraq and south-eastern Turkey, most famously in the Tur 'Abdin.[27] Where the abandonment of sites such as Sir Bani Yas probably reflects a wider process of Islamisation of the Arabian peninsula that would also spell the end of Christianity in Yemen, the Nestorian communities in western Iran, Iraq, and south-east Turkey continued to thrive under Islam. The religious plurality of the Sasanian Empire can be seen both in the surviving architecture and in the conspicuous presence of Christians and Jews in the royal foundation of Gondeshapur in Khuzistan. The state-sponsored religion of Zoroastrianism has left its mark all over the former Sasanian lands in the form of fire temples and other ritual structures. The redating of the enigmatic complex at Sarvistan to the early Islamic period illustrates the continued architectural patronage of Zoroastrian communities beyond the fall of the Sasanian dynasty.[28]

Syria provides abundant evidence for the construction of churches and monastic buildings during the late antique period. This might involve imperial patronage – as is seen in pilgrimage centres such as Qal'at Siman and Rusafa – but more frequently the impetus came from the diverse Christian communities of the region and from local elites. Less evidence survives of the great urban cathedrals, though architectural elements are preserved in Muslim religious structures such as the Madrasa al-Halawiyya in Aleppo and the Ulu Cami in Diyarbakr.[29] Similarly energetic patronage of churches can be found in Egypt, and there exists an impressive catalogue of Coptic churches and monasteries from the centuries prior to the Islamic conquest. The great pilgrimage church associated with the tomb of St Menas was constructed under the auspices of Byzantine emperors between the fourth and the early sixth century.[30] Churches in Algeria, Tunisia, and Libya vary from the converted Severan basilica in Lepcis Magna to newly constructed foundations in cities, ports, and smaller settlements. Sometimes built on a very large scale (as were the basilicas of Tebessa and Damous al-Karita at Carthage), the churches of these regions are architecturally conservative, lacking the structural experimentation found further east in Syria, Anatolia, or Constantinople.[31] The evidence for religious architecture in Visigothic Spain consists largely of small-scale provincial churches, though excavations undertaken in the 1930s beneath the floor of the Great Mosque of Cordoba revealed part of the Cathedral of San Vicente.[32]

Jewish religious life in Palestine appears to have flourished under Byzantine rule; from the fourth to the seventh century many synagogues were built, often being ornamented with mosaic pavements. Intriguingly, the design and ornamentation of these places of worship exhibit distinct similarities to contemporary churches, indicating a period of fruitful interaction between different religious communities. Late antique *diaspora* synagogues present a less complete picture, though the scale of the famous structure at Sardis (adapted for ritual use in the second half of the third century and renovated in the fourth) demonstrates that some Jewish communities enjoyed considerable status. Synagogues have also been excavated at Dura Europos, Apamea, and Jarash (Gerasa). The lavishly painted building at Dura operated until the Sasanian sack of the town in 256, while the two fourth-century synagogues of Apamea and Jarash were subsequently replaced by churches. Excavations at Hamman Lif, south of Tunis, revealed a substantial villa of the fourth or sixth century, with an attached synagogue. Another probable late antique example was found at Elche in southeastern Spain, though it is to the periods of Islamic rule and of the *Reconquista* that one must look to find the most impressive Jewish art and architecture.[33] Jewish communities prospered in many regions of the Islamic world; the activities of the Jews of medieval Cairo are particularly well known through the documents of the Cairo *Geniza*. Recently, the city's oldest synagogue (Ben Ezra) has been the subject of a major renovation project.[34]

Archaeological research has demonstrated the immense resources that must have been put into church construction in Jordan and Palestine from the fourth to the early seventh century: for instance Jerash (Gerasa) boasts a cathedral and at least fourteen smaller churches, while the smaller settlement at Umm al-Jimal contained thirteen.[35] Whether this indicates doctrinal differences among Christians or simply the extent of personal and communal piety is unclear. Analysis of the churches of Jordan and Palestine has revealed that substantial numbers of churches of the sixth and early seventh centuries survived the initial years of the Muslim conquest and continued to function into the eighth century. Many of them were abandoned by the end of the Umayyad caliphate in 750, though this may be something to do with economic and social factors affecting Greater Syria (including the devastating earthquake of 749) as much as with any repressive policies instigated by the new Abbasid regime. Even more significant is the evidence for the foundation or renovation of new churches and monasteries after the conquest. While most of the building work appears to be concentrated in the seventh century, significant projects such as the acropolis church at Ma'in (719–20) and the new mosaic pavement in the Church of St Stephen in Umm al-Rasas (718 and 756; Fig. 6.6) provide evidence for continued vitality in the eighth-century Christian community of Jordan. An even later refurbishment of a church is recorded at Khirbat al-Shubayka in western Galilee; mosaic inscriptions give the names of the Metropolitan Anastasius and of the Abbot Procopius, as well as a date of 785–6.[36]

Although there is ample evidence for the employment of Roman–Byzantine spolia in mosques, the conversion of churches appears to have been rare. Examples have been identified at Hama in Syria and at Umm al-Jimal in the north of Jordan, while the monastic church of the Kathisma, located on the road between Jerusalem and Bethlehem, appears to have been partially converted for Muslim use.[37] Constructed in three phases between the fifth and the early eighth century, the church is remarkable for its octagonal plan around an exposed rock (bringing to mind the Dome of the Rock) – which, according to tradition, was the one on which the Virgin rested on her way to Bethlehem. The eighth-century refurbishment included the introduction of new mosaic panels – one with a palm tree design, perhaps deriving from prototypes in the Dome of the Rock – and a *mihrab* built into the threshold of the blocked-up south entrance. That the building was not wholly given over to Muslim use is indicated by the dedicatory inscription naming two Christians, Basilius and John.

The study of iconoclasm – the destruction of two and three-dimensional religious art – in this period has focused largely upon the attitudes towards the representation of animate life, and particularly of the human form; but these were not the only images to evoke strong responses. Historical sources indicate that, at different times in the seventh and eighth centuries, Jews and the Muslim authorities displayed hostility to the public exhibition of the cross.[38] There were episodes of destroying crosses atop churches and of forbidding the use of ceremonial crosses during public processions on feast days. The archaeological evidence does not indicate a consistent policy of destruction, however; crosses were carved onto tombstones after the conquest, while a cross is also to be found in an inscription of 662/42 from Hammat Gader naming both the Caliph Mu'awiya and a Christian called John. Crosses also appear on the mosaic floors of churches (even though this practice was prohibited by the authorities in Constantinople), and on the lintels of many churches. In neither case is there evidence that such motifs were destroyed, and at the church of Masuh the damaged figural designs of a mosaic were replaced by a cross. Strikingly, a lintel carrying a cross was left in place during the renovation of Qasr al-Burqu' in 710. Crosses have also been found on ceramic lamps from the Umayyad *qasr* further north, at Jabal Says, and from the late eighth-century pottery workshops of Raqqa (chapter 7).[39]

Antipathy towards the representation of humans and animals has been expressed periodically by religious groups, from ancient times on. Excavations of synagogues indicate that Jews abandoned figural imagery in religious contexts during the sixth century, while there is evidence for some Christian sects in Syria adopting purely aniconic forms in church decoration in the same period.[40] The Byzantine Empire adopted iconoclasm as an official state policy in two phases (726 or 730–87 and 815–43), but it is clear from the historical record that there was little consensus on the issue throughout the empire. Iconoclasm also divided Christian communities in the areas conquered by Islam; prominent churchmen like John of Damascus (d. c.753–54) wrote strongly in support of icons during the first phase of Byzantine iconoclasm. The aniconic nature of Islamic religious art and architectural decoration is, of course, well known, though it is worth noting that no explicit prohibition exists in the *Qur'an*. Further, the pronouncements against figural images found in collections of *Hadith* cannot be traced with certainty earlier than the beginning of the eighth century. Of greatest relevance to the present context is the possibility that Muslims concerned themselves with the figural art employed by Christians within their churches. The key piece of evidence in this regard is a Byzantine report – the historical veracity of which remains unresolved – that in 721 Caliph Yazid II (r. 720–24) issued an edict ordering the destruction of figural representations.[41]

It is possible to get some picture of the effect of iconoclasm in the late seventh and eighth centuries by reviewing the mosaic pavements of the churches. Some words of caution are in order before assessing this evidence, however. First, it is the decorated pavements, and not the superstructure, that survive in most churches. Strikingly, many of the pavements contain little that is explicitly religious in nature – apart from crosses and inscriptions – and archaeology allows us no way to establish what happened to the portable icons and wall paintings which would have existed above floor level. Not only were these paintings more visible, but they would have comprised representations of Christ, of the Virgin, of saints, and narrative scenes drawn from the Old and New Testament. Second, establishing the date at which a mosaic was damaged is not always possible. Third, damage to a mosaic might occur through deliberate iconoclastic actions or simply through the later use of an abandoned church.

To assess the churches that remained in use through the Umayyad period: about ten in Jordan and Palestine suffered no alteration to their mosaic pavements. This may be contrasted with the larger number of fifty-five churches that exhibit clear signs of damage.[42] What is perhaps more significant, however, is that the nature of the damage (and of the subsequent repairs) varies considerably within this second group. There are pavements where the iconoclasts systematically obliterated every human and animal found within the mosaic. More often the approach was less thorough: most figural representations were destroyed, but a few were left undamaged (perhaps because they were obscured by liturgical furniture within the church). Another aspect of this phenomenon was that the heads and upper bodies of humans or animals were removed, but some elements remained visible (Fig. 6.7). In other examples the heads remained, but the bodies were removed. Turning to the subsequent repairs, one finds possible evidence concerning the motivation for adjusting these mosaic designs. The crudest repairs – filling the gaps in the pavements with plaster or architectural spolia – suggest that the aesthetic and symbolic qualities of the mosaic were no longer valued by the occupants. This might occur when a church has been converted to domestic use. More interesting, however, are the examples where the iconoclastic damage was carefully repaired. This might take the form of scrambling the tesserae that had been removed or of inserting new ones into the gaps. For instance at the east end of the nave in the Church of St Stephen in Umm al-Rasas the mosaicists replaced the figures with vertically arranged designs made up of simple geometric figures (Fig. 6.6).

The presence of undamaged figural mosaics in churches operating in the seventh and early eighth centuries is a sign that the Umayyad authorities did not instigate a systematic purge of church decoration. Likewise, the abundant evidence for the careful repair of the damaged pavements makes it improbable that either the damage (which itself was highly selective in character) or the subsequent repairs were done by Muslim troops or officials. It would seem, therefore, that both damage and repair were conducted by Christians. What remains unclear, however, is whether they were carried because of iconoclastic disputes among the Christians or by the order of the Islamic state. It is intriguing that the mosaic pavements laid just before the supposed iconoclastic edict of Yazid II in 721 and the first phase of Byzantine iconoclasm – for instance those in St Stephen at Umm al-Rasas (718) and in the acropolis church at Ma'in (719–20) – contained extensive figural elements. Presumably the subsequent eradication of the human and animal content in each case can be dated to within a decade or two of the initial creation of the pavement. Finally, iconoclasm was not limited to churches; synagogues operating in this period also seem to have suffered damage done to the figural reliefs and mosaic pavements. In the case of the mosaics of the synagogue at Na'ara, signs of the zodiac – perhaps the chief cause of offence – were removed, but Hebrew inscriptions and animals elsewhere on the pavement remained intact.[43]

Notes

1 Avni (2004); Johns (1999), 81, fig. 17.
2 On Coptic portable arts of the late antique and Islamic periods, see Badawy (1978), 282–363; Anon. (2000), 146–227. For cultural assimilation in the arts of Spain, see Mann, Glick and Dodds, eds (1992); chapters by Marilyn Jenkins and O. Werckmeister in Anon. (1993): 76–163.
3 On Isfahan, see Galdieri, ed. (1972–4); Grabar (1990). On San'a', see Finster (1978b) and Finster and Schmidt (1979). On Cordoba, see Dodds, ed. (1992), 11–25. On Qayrawan, see Lézine (1966), 11–52; Lézine (1967), 73–7; Ewert and Wisshak (1981), 31–54. See also Creswell and Allan (1989), 83–8, 291–302, 315–30, 345–6. Good examples of other studies of individual mosques are those of Kilwa (Tanzania), Susa (Iran), Rusafa and Rafiqa (Syria). See Chittick (1974), 1: 61–99; Kervran and Rouguelle (1984), 13–31; Sack (1996); Hagen, al-Hassoun and Meinecke (2004).
4 Bloom (1989), 131–6.
5 Hamilton (1949) and (1992). See also Stern (1963); Creswell and Allan (1989), 73–82; Grabar (1996), 117–22. Grafman and Rosen-Ayalon (1999) reject Hamilton's interpretations and offer a radically different chronology of the earliest phases of the Aqsa.
6 Discussed in Johns (1999), 62–4, fig. 9.
7 Horton (1996), 170–223; Horton (2004). Horton (2004) discusses the controversy concerning the dating and identification of the early mosques on p. 76 (with citations to the opinions of other scholars on these issues). See also Whitehouse (2001), 417.
8 Whitehouse (1980).
9 Whitehouse (2001), 416–17.
10 Whitehouse (1980), 24, fig. 12; Lowick (1985), 43–4, 88–9.
11 Whitehouse (1980), 9–19; Tampoe (1989), 77–8. See also Allen (1982).
12 Whitehouse (1980), 30–57.
13 Tampoe (1989), 111; Horton (1996), 26–62. On the Ibadi mosques of Oman, see Costa (2001).
14 Wilkinson (1986), 59–70, 76–82, 223–7, 264–7; Finster (1994), 226–9.
15 For instance, see Malik ibn Anas (1989), 85–92. On the veneration of the dead (and jurisprudence on the subject) in medieval Syria, see Meri (2002).
16 Insoll (1999), 189; Lambourn (2008).
17 Contadini (1998), 40. On Coptic textiles from funerary contexts, see Badawy (1978), 282–304; Anon. (2000), 136–40.
18. Grabar (1966); Insoll (1999), 183–7.
19 Gichon and Linden (1984). For vivid accounts of such practices in the twelfth and thirteenth century, see Meri (2002), 129, 134–5. Similar devotions were observed around shrines by Tawfiq Canaan in early twentieth-century Palestine. See Canaan (1927).
20 Kervran, Hiebert and Rouguelle (2005), 342–3, pl. 100. Amulets of dried earth mixed with the blood of sacrificial animals were made in Mecca to be taken home after pilgrimage. See Canaan (1927), 99, 106, 110.
21 Henderson et al. (2005), 139; Wolska in Miglus, ed. (1999), 11–15; Kervran, Hiebert and Rouguelle (2005), 334–42.

22 Toombs (1985), 16–250; Eakins (1993). On the identification of injuries, disease, and medical interventions from human skeletal remains, see Hodges in Redford (1998), 281–98; Mitchell (2004).

23 Simpson (1995a). For the patterning of graves within Muslim cemeteries in other regions, see Chittick (1974), 1: 224–7; Horton (1996), 63–76; Insoll (1999), 169–76.

24. Ball (1976).

25 Flood (2003).

26 For an introduction to the religious environment of late antiquity, see Fowden (2001).

27 King (1997); Elders (2001), Finster and Schmidt (2005), 340, fig. 7; Krautheimer (1986), 160–6, 301–4.

28 Bier (1986).

29 Peña (1996); Krautheimer (1986), 137–56. On the employment of classical spolia in Islamic architecture, see Ewert and Wisshak (1981), 135–84; Allen (1986).

30 Badawy (1978), 62–92; Krautheimer (1986), 110–17, 304–8.

31 Krautheimer (1986), 187–95. On the Christian architecture of Carthage in the late antique and Islamic periods, see also Humphreys (1980), 7–123; Stevens, Kalinkowski and van der Leest, eds (2005).

32 Ruggles (forthcoming). For a review of the historical evidence, see Ocaña (1942).

33 Levine (2005a), 252–83; Milson (2007). On the synagogues of medieval Spain, see Mann, Glick and Dodds, eds (1992), 113–31.

34 Goitein (1967–88). On the structural history of the Ben Ezra synagogue, see contributions by Sheehan and Le Quesne in Lambert, ed. (2001), 65–97.

35 Michel (2001), 166–84, 224–74. For a brief survey of church architecture in these regions, see Krautheimer (1986), 156–60.

36 Syon (2003); Tzaferis (2003), 84–5.

37 Creswell (1969), 1.1: 17–22; Schick (1995), 130; Avner (2003).

38 King (1985).

39 Schick (1995), 164–5; Gaube (1974), 97; Brisch (1965), fig. 33.

40 Levine (2005b); Mundell Mango (1977).

41 Van Reenan (1990); Vasiliev (1956); Schick (1995), 215–17.

42 Schick (1995), 187–91, tables 8–10. For illustrations of the mosaic pavements, see Piccirillo (1993).

43 Chiat (1982), 256–60; Schick (1995), 202–4.

7

Crafts and industry

Islamic culture is justly famous for its achievements in crafts which include the making of textiles and carpets, the carving of wood, ivory, stone and stucco, and the manufacture of vessels in ceramics, glass, and metal. Given the high reputation of Islamic craftsmanship among modern audiences, it is perhaps surprising to find that the makers of the diverse artefacts exhibited in major public and private collections were seldom accorded much status in their own societies. While Islamic law has quite a lot to say about the regulation of craft practices in urban markets (a body of literature known as *hisba*), jurists and other scholars generally held craftspeople in low esteem. This happened despite the admission, made by the North African polymath Ibn Khaldun (d. 1406) and echoed in other sources, that the crafts (*sina'a* in the singular) were essential to the maintenance of urban life. It is striking that so few artefacts – apart from manuscripts – bear the names of the artisans responsible for their manufacture, and these men and women are almost completely absent from the voluminous biographical dictionaries produced in the medieval Islamic world. Only scribes and, from the sixteenth century on, the best manuscript painters appear to have enjoyed a more privileged social status.[1] While valuable information concerning craft practices, the economics of manufacturing, and the lives of artisans can be gleaned from contemporary written sources (including a few manuals written by craftsmen) and from inscriptions on artefacts, it is the objects themselves and the archaeology of manufacturing practices that remain the foundations for research.

Some comments are needed concerning the wider context of manufacturing in the Islamic world and the areas where archaeology has had a more limited impact on our understanding of craft practices. The three sections that make up the bulk of this chapter are concerned with the manufacture of artefacts in inorganic media, ceramics, glass and metal. The restriction is not meant to imply that artefacts in these media were necessarily the most important products from the urban workshops of the Islamic world; for instance pre-modern Arabic, Persian or Turkish written sources illustrate that fine textiles were valued much more highly than glazed pottery.[2] What dictates the choice of inorganic

An introduction to Islamic archaeology

materials is the extent of the contribution made by conventional archaeological practices. Two factors are relevant in this context: first, inorganic artefacts, and particularly ceramics and glass, survive in much greater numbers in excavated contexts; and, second, the requirement for architectural infrastructure (such as kilns and furnaces) and the application of intense heat means that ore smelting installations and the workshops of potters, metalworkers and glassworkers are more readily identifiable in the archaeological record.

That said, the study of epigraphic evidence and of physical evidence from other media does provide some important avenues of interpretation, as well as highlighting the complex nature of patronage and craft organisation in Islamic societies. For instance *tiraz* bands bearing the names of caliphs or sultans appear on numerous textile fragments (Fig. 7.1), and there is abundant textual evidence for the existence of workshops operating under some degree of state control.[3] Many Islamic dynasties also operated court workshops specialising in the production of luxury artefacts. While the names of the artisans very seldom survive, luxury artefacts such as the ivory pyxides and precious metal caskets of Umayyad Spain often carry inscriptions noting the patron, the recipient, and even the overseer of the project.[4]

There exists another, larger stratum of craft activity within the cities and towns of the Islamic world. Workshops might undertake specific commissions from the court (as is well documented in the case of the potters of Iznik in Ottoman Turkey) or from wealthy individuals, but they also produced more generic objects for sale in the market place. Considerable specialisation existed within individual crafts, and the manufacture of a decorated glazed bowl, inlaid metal vessel, or silk carpet was frequently undertaken by several artisans. The *Geniza* archive illustrates gender divisions in craft activities, women being largely engaged in manufacturing processes that could be done within the home, and men working in the more public sphere of the urban workshop.[5] While inscriptions on famous objects such as the twelfth-century 'Bobrinsky bucket' are fascinating for the insights they provide into the identities, roles, and social status of skilled craftsmen, it should be emphasised that most of the artefacts in museum collections do not carry the names of their makers. This is even more evident in material recovered from excavations; inscriptions, when they occur at all, usually record only formulaic messages of good will, or moralising aphorisms. It is not uncommon for the words to be garbled and incomprehensible, as they have been copied from another source by semi-literate craftsmen. As a result, it is often through stylistic or technical similarities that a group of vessels is assigned a common workshop or region of production. The diffusion of a given style or technique might be due to the movement of artefacts or artisans. In the case of architectural decoration, it was common practice to move craftsmen to the building site; examples include the manufacture of tiles to clad the Dome of the Rock in the sixteenth century and the elaborate stucco *mihrabs* of Iran and Oman. The movement of stucco workers may also explain the wide geographical spread of the so-called 'bevelled style' from its probable source in ninth-century Samarra.[6]

Tracing industrial activity in the archaeological record

Recent archaeological research has demonstrated the promotion of trade by the Umayyad elite during the early eighth century in the centres of established towns in Greater Syria (chapter 3). Caliph Hisham was particularly active in this regard, establishing many new market places. One of Hisham's markets has been excavated in Bet Shean. While commerce was evidently the chief concern in the construction of the market area in the town, one can assume that some of the spaces were reserved for crafts such as weaving, goldsmithing, carpentry, or leatherworking. Although such activities tend to leave little trace in the archaeological record, this is not the case with industries that require the use of bulk raw materials, toxic substances, large spaces, copious supplies of water, and the application of intense heat. Most important in this regard are the manufacture of ceramics and glass, and the smelting and working of iron, steel and copper. Archaeology also has at least the potential to recover signs of tanning, paper-making, and the burning of lime or gypsum.

Returning to Bet Shean, one industrial activity – a substantial pottery workshop – was discovered in the excavation of the early Islamic phase on the site. In contrast to the grand market place with its mosaic inscription panels, the kilns and other parts of the workshop were located on the periphery of the settled area of the town (evidently, the eighth-century population was smaller than it had been in earlier centuries), and made opportunistic reuse of existing architecture. Jarash presents a remarkably similar picture: there was Umayyad refurbishment of the town centre, while the potters located themselves in a disused building – the north theatre. In order to build the kilns into the ashlar masonry structure, the potters erected crude rubble and mortar walls and cut flues through the walls of the theatre.[7] It would be easy to view this process as evidence of decline, since a theatre – an emblem of Graeco-Roman cultural sophistication – was reassigned a humble industrial use. It is worth considering, however, that theatres had ceased to have a meaningful function in the Middle East and North Africa centuries before. Like other developments in the late antique/early Islamic city, such workshops can be interpreted as signs of economic vitality. The intrusion of olive oil presses and of other installations into the public spaces of towns in North Africa, and the coexistence of domestic and craft activities in the Sasanian city of Veh Ardashir, are further signs of the increasing presence of manufacturing within the urban spaces of late antiquity and early Islam.[8]

While the excavations at Tabariyya (Tiberias) illustrate the continued practice of reusing abandoned buildings (such as churches, bathhouses, or synagogues) for commercial or industrial purposes after the Umayyad period,[9] it is evident that the rise of the Abbasids, and particularly their patronage of huge cities in Mesopotamia, brought a new dynamics to Islamic industry. Two points should be highlighted about this phase of activity. First, the creation of immense urban foundations like Baghdad, Samarra, and Rafiqa necessitated the formal allocation of zones devoted to the industrial activities required during in the initial period of construction. Industries then needed to adapt to the demands of the influx of new city dwellers. Second, the unprecedented size of the Abbasid urban foundations required the transfer of skilled craftsmen from different regions to work on these new projects. In the case of Baghdad, the eleventh-century chronicler Khatib al-Baghdadi records in his *Tarikh Baghdad* that Caliph Mansur 'wrote to every town asking them to send inhabitants with some knowledge of the building trade. But he did not begin construction until the number of craftsmen and skilled labourers in his presence reached many thousands.' The need to house the craftsmen and engineers also stimulated the renewal of the nearby town of Karkh and the construction of the district of Rusafa.[10] It seems likely that the interaction of artisans is one of the factors which contributed to the technological and artistic innovation so evident in the portable arts and architectural decoration of Iraq between the late eighth and the tenth century.

Archaeological reconnaissance in Samarra has led to the identification of glass-working and brick-making sites,[11] but it is the Syrian city of Raqqa on the Euphrates that preserves the most extensive evidence of the evolution of an industrial district (Fig. 5.5). By correlating these physical data (excavated structures and finds, coins, and aerial and satellite photography) with written sources, it is possible to trace the phases of activity over the course of nearly five hundred years, until the final demise of manufacturing in the city prior to the Mongol invasion of Syria in 1258–60.[12] Two issues are addressed in this chronological survey: first, how did the planners of the late eighth century incorporate the industrial zone into the larger urban plan; and, second, what did the artisans of this area produce during the different phases of its history?

Large-scale industrial activity began around the time of the commencement of the construction at Rafiqa in 771 (chapter 5). A glass workshop further east, at Tal Zujaj, dates from this phase (this site is discussed in greater detail in the next case study). The lowest levels of the most westerly excavated site, known as Tal Fukhkhar, produced what could be evidence for brick-making in the late eighth century. X-ray magnetometer surveys and excavations have revealed an extensive series of pottery workshops north of the sixth-century walls of Raqqa (formerly Kallinikos), at a site known as Tal Aswad. Such extra-mural locations are common for ceramic and glass workshops; examples of this practice can be seen for instance in the *misr* of Ayla on the Red Sea and, later, outside the south-eastern and eastern gates (Bab Kisan and Bab Sharqi) of Damascus.[13] At Tal Aswad there is no evidence of industrial activity prior to 771 (the area had been a cemetery), but in a short time numerous pottery kilns and related structures were erected (Fig. 7.2). Some kilns were reconstructed once or several times in the course of a few decades. Analysis of the ceramics and coins suggests that Tal Aswad enjoyed a relatively short life-span, ceasing to operate shortly after 825.

Simple unglazed wheelthrown vessels – including jars, bowls, large storage vessels, chamber pots, and drainpipes – were common in the refuse around the kilns of Tal Aswad. The potters also produced smaller numbers of relief-moulded slipper lamps and pitchers, as well as a range of glazed earthenware with splashed or simply painted decoration. In other words, the primary focus of the workshops of Raqqa was to satisfy the everyday needs of the new inhabitants of the garrison city of Rafiqa and of the northern palaces. It is clear that luxury ceramics – such as the blue and white and lustre-painted vessels – continued to be imported from Iraq. One unglazed vessel carries a moulded inscription naming the potter as one Ibrahim, a Christian from the Iraqi city of Hira. A Christian connection among the potters of Raqqa is also suggested by the crosses marked on the undersides of some slipper lamps.[14] Analysis of the glaze technologies employed at Tal Aswad indicates that potters were probably also brought from Basra to work in Raqqa.[15] The presence of walls demarcating groups of kilns and associated structures is perhaps an indication that the teams of craftsmen imported to Abbasid Raqqa maintained their independence within the area of Tal Aswad. Similar divisions of space, using walls and alleys, were also found in excavations of the ceramic workshops of Balis, further west on the Euphrates river.[16]

Tal Aswad was integrated into the larger urban plan of Raqqa–Rafiqa (Fig. 5.5). Of crucial significance in this respect is a gateway in the eastern section of wall (known in historical sources as Bab Sibal) providing direct access to Tal Aswad through a road visible in aerial and satellite photographs. In addition, a canal skirted the western edge of Tal Aswad and provided the large quantities of water needed for pottery manufacture. The placement of Tal Aswad on the north-eastern extremity of Raqqa–Rafiqa took account of the prevailing winds of the area (the smoke from the kilns would be carried away from the city); but it was also beyond the walls and vulnerable to attack. With the breakdown of security in northern Mesopotamia in the ninth century, Tal Aswad was abandoned. The next phase of activity was located in the region between Raqqa and Rafiqa. This intermediate area was enclosed by a wall in 815, and in later sources it is described as an independent city (*madina*) called 'the burning Raqqa' (*al-Raqqa al-Muhtariqa*).[17]

The most important phase at Tal Fukhkhar can be dated to the eleventh and twelfth centuries. Although the population and political importance of Raqqa–Rafiqa were much reduced by this time, the pottery workshops were evidently highly active, producing both unglazed and glazed earthenware (Fig. 7.3). The latter was made to a high standard involving two firings – a biscuit firing and a glaze firing (within saggers) – and a range of decoration, most commonly sgraffito.[18] While in the early phase the potters appear to have been manufacturing their wares for consumption within the new Abbasid city, the sgraffito wares from eleventh/twelfth-century Raqqa were traded widely in Syria and Iraq. Clearly the riparian location of the city facilitated the trade to Iraq, as well as providing a means to transport vital supplies of fuel (the vicinity of Raqqa has little timber) down the Euphrates, from southern Anatolia.

The last and most famous phase of industrial activity can be dated from the second half of the twelfth to the mid-thirteenth century. At this time potters in Raqqa started to produce a range of decorated glazed stonepaste wares – the best known are lustre-painted – that were exported all over the Middle East, and as far afield as southern Europe (chapter 8; Fig. 8.4 a). The presence of many pottery and glass workshops in an area encompassing the northern and eastern sectors of the walled city of Rafiqa suggests that the area given over to the domestic and administrative components of the town had dwindled to the regions south and west of the congregational mosque.[19] In other words, the scale of industrial activity is not contingent upon the size of the neighbouring town or city. Rather it needs to be seen in the wider context of the transport infrastructure and of the trading relationships established by skilled artisans and merchants.

Other Islamic sites offer interesting evidence of industrial activity, either during a relatively short phase or, like Raqqa, over the course of centuries. Large areas of the old city of Fustat were devoted to industry, particularly the production of glazed and unglazed ceramics. Numerous kilns have been excavated on the site since the early twentieth century, though the quality of much of the published data is variable. The same can be said of the poorly published French excavations, in the 1920s, of the ceramic and glass workshops in Damascus.[20] Other major industrial areas have been discovered at Samarqand and Nishapur, while evidence of ceramic production is known in numerous sites in Central Asia, the Middle East, North Africa, and Spain. Apart from large extra-mural industrial zones attached to cities, there were towns, and even villages, that specialised in the production of specific media. Some are known only from written sources, though a few have been examined archaeologically, the famous pottery production centre of Iznik among them.[21]

The mining, smelting, and working of metal have been the subject of archaeological and scientific investigation on Islamic period sites, from Spain to

Central Asia. Evidence for mining and smelting copper has been recovered from such sites as Huelva in Spain and Timna and Wadi Faynan on the Israeli and Jordanian sides of the Wadi 'Araba. These last two are interesting in that they represent the continuation or revival of an industry stretching back millennia. Some of the activity during the Islamic centuries was directed at the resmelting of slag rather than at the processing of newly mined ore.[22] Ingots of smelted metal would often be transported in order to be processed elsewhere. This is demonstrated by the late ninth or early tenth-century steel-making workshop recovered from Merv in Turkmenistan, a city lacking nearby iron deposits. Found among the crucibles and other industrial waste on the site was a corroded ingot of steel, probably meant to be forged into a sword or piece of armour. Examination of thin sections of the ingot indicated that the manufacturing corresponded to a description of the process given by the polymath al-Biruni (d. 1048). The steel from Merv probably made use both of plain iron (bloomery or wrought) and of cast iron to achieve the desired alloy.[23] The use of a variety of metals – from ingots to reused scrap metal – is a feature of coppersmithing throughout the Islamic period. The discovery in Tabariyya of a cache of over one thousand metal artefacts (mostly fragmentary), bronze coins, and tools packed into three ceramic jars probably represents the hoarded resources of a metal-worker. Dating to the Fatimid occupation of Palestine (969–1099), the more complete objects exhibit stylistic and technical affinities with a cache of copper alloy vessels discovered in a well in Caesarea, further south.[24]

Technological innovation and the movement of craftsmen and artefacts

The creative interaction of craftsmen in urban centres such as Basra, Raqqa-Rafiqa, Cairo-Fustat, Mosul, and Kashan contributed to the inventiveness of the portable arts of the Islamic Middle East. Technologies and new artistic styles were generated in such centres, but their further diffusion relied upon the migration of craftsmen and of the objects they produced. Techniques like lustre-painting on glass and glazed ceramic, or precious metal inlay, are thought to have been transferred between urban centres by skilled artisans. Excavations in Turkmenistan indicated that the decorative moulds used in the production of glazed and unglazed pottery travelled from one town to another.[25] Occasionally personal names appear on vessels, and the inclusion of a *nisba* may allow one to reconstruct the movement of a master craftsman. That fourteenth-century Cairo represented both a huge market for imported pottery and an opportunity for immigrant craftsmen is indicated by the wealth of *nisbas* written onto the bases of glazed bowls and jars excavated in Fustat. The career of one skilled potter, Ghaybi al-Tawrizi, can be traced as he moved from north-western Iran to

Damascus and finally to Cairo (Fig. 5.10). The control of his Egyptian workshop was later passed on to his son, who signed his works as Ibn Ghaybi ('son of Ghaybi').[26] The presence of numerous thirteenth-century inlaid vessels bearing the *nisba* 'al-Mawsili' ('of Mosul') illustrates both this city's fine metalworking tradition in the early decades of the thirteenth century and the subsequent migration of its talented artisans to other localities in Syria and Egypt. Mosul itself probably benefited from an influx of metalworkers from great eastern centres such as Herat who were fleeing the Mongol invasions after 1219.[27]

The movement of craftsmen and technologies can also be inferred from the spatial and temporal distribution of artefacts. An early example of this is the switch that occurs in eighth-century Greater Syria, from the native red-coloured to cream-coloured earthenware. The adoption of this Iraqi technology is allied to a new repertoire of vessel shapes and decorative modes.[28] By the end of the eighth century, potters in Raqqa and elsewhere in Syria started to employ the new glazes developed in the ceramic manufacturing centres of southern Mesopotamia. The rapid spread of the sgraffito technique around the Islamic world, and ultimately to the Byzantine Empire and Europe, maybe due in part to the migration of craftsmen.[29] In the case of lustre-painting, it seems most likely that its dispersal can be attributed to the movement of potters and master painters. First appearing as a decoration on glass, lustre-painting was transferred to tin-glazed earthenware in southern Iraq during the early ninth century. The demise of Iraqi lustre pottery production broadly coincides with its emergence in Fatimid Cairo in the late tenth century (Fig. 7.4). By the last quarter of the eleventh century a short-lived production centre was established in central Syria (probably at Tal Minis near Ma'arrat al-Nu'man), and between the twelfth and the fourteenth century evidence of lustre manufacture can be seen on sites along the upper Euphrates in Syria and Turkey, as well as in Iran (where it was centred in the city of Kashan). To the west, both the skilled Iraqi potters and their lustre-painted vessels and tiles made their way to Qayrawan (adorning the *mihrab* of the mosque) and to the Umayyad court in Spain.[30]

This complex transmission is explained by the technically demanding (and financially risky) nature of lustre-painting. Apart from the costly materials, the vessels required at least two firings, the kiln atmosphere and temperature of the last firing being tightly regulated to ensure success.[31] The skills needed to produce these wares were probably known to a few workshops, though the proliferation of production centres along the Euphrates perhaps suggests that the previous exclusivity of the craft had eroded in the twelfth century. Technical examination of lustre-painted vessels also indicates that craftsmen had to adapt, making use of new materials as they migrated from one region to another. Also important is the move from tin-glazed earthenware to lead-alkali or alkaline-glazed stonepaste as the carrier of lustre-painting. In other words, adaptation to new circumstances is an important characteristic of technological change. These issues are addressed in greater detail in the following summaries of scientific research into glass and glazed ceramic technology.

The manufacture of glass is a labour-intensive process requiring considerable specialised knowledge, abundant fuel, and access to a range of mineral and organic resources. Silica, the basic raw material of glass, is readily available in the form of sand and quartz, though relatively few sources are uncontaminated by metallic impurities. Lead may be employed as a flux, but the glass of the early Islamic period – known as soda-lime glass – tends to make use of alkalis for the same purpose. Scientific analysis has identified two main sources: ashes made from the burning of desert plants such as those from the genera *Salicornia* and *Salsola*; and ashes from minerals such as natron and trona. While organic alkali sources of the first group are widely available in arid regions as well as in marine environments, the alkali-rich mineral are more scarce. Egypt is the most abundant source in the Middle East, particularly in Wadi al-Natrun and in the southern province of Buhayra. Both organic and mineral alkalis have high percentages of sodium compounds, but plant ashes contain a significantly higher percentage of magnesium oxide (magnesia). Calcium oxide is an essential component of glass made by using these alkali compounds. Crushed seashells were often employed (beach sand would usually contain sufficient quantities), though other mineral and organic sources were employed when glass was produced away from coastal areas. A range of minerals were utilised as colourants and opacifying agents.[32]

Variations in the percentages of magnesia and aluminium oxide (aluminia) in Islamic soda-lime glass have helped to establish the chronology of the crucial shift from the use of mineral alkalis (natron and trona) to that of alkalis derived from plant ashes. One useful source of information on this development is the glass weights produced in early Islamic Egypt. These weights are often stamped with the year of their manufacture, and the testing of the composition of the glass indicated the transition from low to high magnesia content, which occurred in Egypt c.845.[33] Egypt was the principal source for mineral alkalis, and one might suspect that glass-makers in that country retained the familiar technology – one which can be traced back to Hellenistic and Roman glass manufacture – longer than in other parts of the Islamic world. The possibility of testing this general hypothesis came with the discovery of the remarkably well preserved glass workshop of the early Abbasid period in Raqqa.

Constructed on top of the hypocaust of an abandoned eighth-century bath-house, the industrial installation at the site known as Tal Zujaj comprises a series of furnaces built into, or abutting, the walls (Fig. 7.5). Some of the furnaces were found to connect to underground flues. The best preserved furnace in the south-east corner of the workshop comprised a lower firing chamber, a middle chamber for melting the glass, and an upper annealing chamber topped with a clay dome. Equally important for the study of ancient technology were the furnace bricks, lumps of raw glass, sherds from broken vessels, drips, and moils associated with glass-blowing, sections of the trays in which glass was melted, and pieces of glass frit (the preliminary stage before the silica is vitrified). The operation of the workshop was relatively short, probably extending from the last quarter of the eighth century until some time soon after the departure of the court of Harun al-Rashid in 808.

Fragments recovered from this site were analysed in conjunction with glass from elsewhere in Raqqa–Rafiqa. By focusing upon the content of aluminia and magnesia, Julian Henderson was able to demonstrate the presence of clusters of samples with equivalent chemical compositions. Only one group – associated with window glass from one of the Abbasid palaces – was made using low magnesia soda-lime glass (that is, employing a mineral alkali source), while later, eleventh or twelfth-century samples were made from a lead-rich glass with little alkali content. The glass and glass frit from the workshop of Tal Zujaj comprised soda-lime glass with a high magnesia content, indicating that, by the late eighth century/early ninth century, artisans in north-eastern Syria had already taken advantage of the ubiquitous alkali-rich plants. This loosening of reliance upon expensive imported natron would certainly have had considerable financial benefits for the glass-makers, though it is not known what caused them to experiment in this way. Perhaps the influx into Raqqa of skilled craftsmen from many regions encouraged an atmosphere of technological innovation; or maybe the supply of minerals from Egypt became unreliable and necessitated a search for alternatives. Analysis of the glass frit also revealed another local adaptation in the manufacturing process: electron micrographs of the frit indicated that bones were substituted for sea shells as the principal source of calcium oxide.[34]

Petrography, lead-isotope analysis, neutron activation, and scanning electron microscopy have been combined with conventional archaeological techniques to examine technological innovations in Islamic glazed pottery.[35] Of particular interest are the invention of the tin-opacified glaze, the evolution of stonepaste, and the use of lead-alkali and alkaline glazes. Tin-opacified glaze (or simply 'tin-glaze') was used over fine earthenware ceramics and provided a white ground that allowed for painting with cobalt (blue) and copper (green) as in-glaze pigments, as well as for the famous over-glaze technique of lustre-painting. The stonepaste body had the great advantage of being white in colour, thus obviating the requirement to use a layer of pale clay slip prior to the application of the glaze. The specific chemistry of the stonepaste body also necessitated the development of new glazes, first fluxed with lead-alkali and then solely with alkali. The transparent and glassy qualities of these new glazes – which were colourless in their natural state, although cobalt, copper, and manganese could be employed to create blue, turquoise, and purple respectively – facilitated a wide range of decorative techniques, from overglaze lustre and enamel painting ('*mina'i* ware') to the application of raw pigments, or pigments held within a clay slip, onto the stonepaste body prior to the addition of the glaze (a technique known as under-glaze painting).

It has proved difficult to establish when and where each breakthrough occurred and how these new techniques were later dispersed to different regions of the Islamic world. Several factors have compounded this problem. First, the record of controlled excavations in many of the key areas (particularly Iraq and Iran) is patchy, relatively few production sites being subjected to archaeological investigation. Scholars have also relied too much on some sites – most notably Samarra and the so-called 'Samarra horizon' (chapter 1) – for the provision of chronological parameters for key ceramic wares.[36] Second, many of the finest examples of Islamic glazed wares in museums and private collections were recovered through illicit excavations. As a result, we lack both the geographical location and the precise context in which the object was discovered. Third, Arabic and Persian written sources from the eighth to the sixteenth century provide little evidence concerning either the manufacturing processes of skilled potters or the locations of the major workshops. The treatise on ceramics written c.1301 by the Persian potter and metalworker Abu al-Qasim is an important exception, and further data have been gathered from documentary sources relating to the famous Ottoman pottery workshops in Iznik.[37] Ethnographic observations of modern potters in Turkey, Iran, and Pakistan may also be used, with some caution, to infer aspects of earlier practice.[38]

Given the limitations outlined above, scientific analysis of pottery samples from both museum collections and controlled excavations has much to offer. Petrographic examination concentrates upon the mineralogical composition of the earthenware or stonepaste body, and can provide evidence concerning provenance (particularly when correlated with wasters or kiln furniture recovered from a production site) or concerning technical issues such as the addition of tempers. Scanning electron microscopes are employed to reveal the chemistry of ceramic fabrics and glazes. Recent research into the use of tin oxide as an opacifying agent indicates that its technical origins lie in the turquoise glazes of Sasanian pottery. The earliest Islamic opaque glazes made use of tin oxide, a range of other minerals, and gas bubbles locked in the glaze during the firing in order to reduce transparency. According to the chronology offered by Robert Mason, between c.750 and 800 potters gradually took to adding more tin oxide (Fig. 8.3). This compound becomes the principal opacifying agent in the early ninth century (a development broadly coeval with the appearance of lustre-painted decoration). Petrographic analysis suggests that the greatest production centre of the Abbasid period was probably the southern Iraqi port–city of Basra.[39]

In the absence of the kaolin-rich clays available in China, Islamic potters developed an artificial ceramic composed of a small proportion (c.10 per cent) of white, sticky clay mixed with c.10 per cent ground glass and c.80 per cent finely ground quartz. Despite the common employment of the term 'fritware', this artificial paste was seldom made using frit (fully vitrified glass was preferred). While this paste certainly lacks the stone-like quality of true porcelain, it does succeed in imitating the white colour. The basic composition of stonepaste is confirmed in the account written c.1301 by the Persian craftsman Abu al-Qasim. Scientific analysis now suggests that the true stonepaste body came about, not as a sudden reaction to an external stimulus (the desire to imitate the porcelaneous bodies of Ting wares from China), but through the gradual addition of quartz and glass to conventional clays, perhaps as a means to enhance the adherence of the body and the glaze. So-called 'proto-stonepastes' dating from the ninth and tenth centuries have been identified in Iraq, northern Syria, and Egypt.[40] The true stonepaste body probably originated in Egypt, roughly after 1025. Around 1075, stonepaste was being used in Syria for the production of lustre-painted vessels known as 'Tal Minis' wares. Within two or three decades, the same technologies were employed in the potteries of Raqqa and Damascus and in Iran.

In the case of 'Tal Minis' we seem to have evidence of the migration of a group of skilled potters from Egypt, who were in search of new patrons for their costly lustre-painted ceramics. This link is suggested by similarities between the vessel shapes and painting styles of Egyptian lustre wares and those of Tal Minis. Other connections are indicated by the analysis of the composition of the stonepaste and by the glaze chemistry. Often migrating potters adapted their new techniques, initially as a response to different local resources, and later out of a desire to create new visual and decorative effects. For instance potters in Syria soon abandoned the lead-alkali glazes of Egypt in favour of fully alkaline glazes. This shift, occurring around 1100, could reflect continuity with native Syrian glaze traditions, though it may be that the absence of lead in the glaze facilitated the application of the copper-rich lustre pigments favoured in Syria. Lead-alkali variants are absent in Iran, which points to Syria (and not Egypt) as the source of these new techniques. Iran, in turn, appears to have exerted a considerable technological influence on the practices of potters working in the Ottoman ceramic centre of Iznik.[41]

The revival of handmade pottery

Ethnographic research has recorded practices associated with village crafts, including the making of flat-weave textiles and rugs, embroidery, knotted pile carpets, felts, baskets, reed mats, and leather artefacts. It is often difficult, however, to relate this wealth of contemporary data to the archaeological record, due to the poor survival of organic media in excavated contexts. In order to develop some understanding of rural craft practices in earlier periods it is necessary to turn to the most common form of occupational debris, ceramics. Of particular interest are pottery vessels manufactured by hand (that is, without the use of a kick-wheel) in the villages of the Islamic world.

There exist numerous nineteenth- and twentieth-century written accounts of handmade pottery manufacture in rural towns and villages from the Maghrib, Palestine, Jordan, and Iraq.[42] While the vessel shapes and decoration vary by region, there are some significant commonalities in the manufacturing processes and in the identities of the practitioners. It is generally the women of the village who are responsible for making these objects. Clays are subjected to minimal preparation with sand, grog (ground-up pot sherds), dung, or straw added as temper. The vessels (usually jugs, bowls, braziers, and lamps) are formed by hand, often using a basket or a bag of sand around which the coils of clay are shaped. The surface of the vessel may be burnished, but the most common form of decoration consists of painting with coloured slip clays. The firing is usually done in an open fire or a clamp (a fire covered with turf). Among the marsh Arabs of southern Iraq, only the *kuz* (water jar) was baked, other vessels, utensils and containers being merely sun-dried before use. With some exceptions, these handmade wares are made for personal use rather than commercial distribution. While handmade wares can often be visually appealing, the poorly prepared clays and low firing temperatures make these objects relatively fragile.

Some archaeologists who encountered handmade pottery production in Palestine in the early twentieth century assumed that they were witnessing continuity of village craft practices tracing back to the iron age.[43] Certainly, some iron age pottery of the region shares visual characteristics of vessel shape and painted ornament, but an examination of the archaeological record in Greater Syria suggests a different picture of the evolution of Islamic handmade pottery. In rural ceramic assemblages dating from the seventh to the eleventh century, vessels were for the most part formed on kick-wheels and baked in kilns. Large storage jars were made by hand but, like their wheelthrown counterparts, they were kiln-fired. The only ceramic artefacts of this period to share the poorly mixed ceramic fabrics tempered with organic matter and low firing seen in later handmade wares are clay ovens (*tabuns*, Fig. 7.6) and grain bins. In the south of Jordan a new mode of production can be detected in the eleventh century. Potters in sites like Ayla, Gharandal, and Wu'ayra abandoned the kick-wheel and started to produce small handmade bowls and jugs, often simply painted with lines and dashes of red slip.[44] Through the course of the twelfth century the simpler style of slip-painting was replaced by an intricate geometric style, perhaps influenced by basket-weaving or textiles (Fig. 7.7).

Field surveys and excavations reveal that, during the thirteenth and fourteenth century, handmade pottery with geometric slip painting spread to every part of Greater Syria and into southern Anatolia. That this ware spread over such a wide area in the course of a half-century is remarkable, and can be explained through the trade of the pots and/or the movement of itinerant potters. In other words, despite the evident fragility and rustic appearance of this ware, there may have been an initial phase of commercial distribution and some degree of trade in the thirteenth and fourteenth centuries (also suggested by the occurrence of handmade vessels in cities like Jerusalem and Hama).[45] It seems likely, however, that the simple manufacturing techniques were soon assimilated into the domestic environment and that the bulk of later production was non-commercial in character. Styles of painting became very localised, individual motifs and larger compositional modes possibly being passed down through generations. Quite how handmade pottery evolved in Greater Syria from the fifteenth century on is difficult to trace in the archaeological record, though there appears to be a tendency toward simplification in the painting styles.

Perhaps what is most important about this widespread phenomenon is that, at different times, the inhabitants of rural areas have chosen to abandon the existing manufacturing methods in favour of more 'primitive' technologies. Technological regression is commonly associated with periods of economic and cultural decline, and one might ask whether this interpretation is supported in the archaeological record. In the case of Greater Syria, the period between the twelfth and the fourteenth century was – as far as it can be judged from field surveys, excavations, and historical sources – a time of relative prosperity, with high levels of rural settlement. Looking elsewhere, it is also apparent that the rise of handmade pottery is not necessarily tied to economic decline; for instance the increasing dominance of handmade wares at Qasr Ibrim in Nubia (southern Egypt) occurs in the fifteenth century, the last period of Christian rule. This phase contains the highest percentage of imported glazed wares from Lower Egypt (probably Fustat), indicating continued economic vitality on the Nubian site. Thus we have to look to the potential advantages that this new mode of production may have possessed. While the wheelthrown and glazed ceramics of the urban workshops were more durable and there continued to be a market for them in rural areas, locally manufactured handmade pottery was cheap and allowed for greater flexibility, as one could make as many vessels as were needed each year. This reduced reliance upon commercial manufacturers had the effect of increasing the financial autonomy of the inhabitants of rural areas. Thus the apparent 'technological regression' represented by the adoption of handmade pottery should perhaps be seen rather in the context of economic choices made by producers and consumers.

Notes

1 Ibn Khaldun (1958), 2: 347–52. On the status of craftsmen in traditional Islamic society, see Abdul Jabbar Beg (1972) and Rezq (1988). For a wide-ranging discussion of the crafts in the Cairo *Geniza*, see Goitein (1967–88), 1: 75–147.

2 On the status enjoyed by textiles in Islamic society, see Golombek (1988); also Goitein (1967–88), 4: 107–29, 150–200.

3 On the significance and interpretation of *tiraz*, see Blair (1997); Contadini (1998), 39–58.

4 Dodds, ed. (1992), cat. nos. 4, 5, 9; Anon. (1993), cat. nos. 38a, 39, 45.

5 Goitein (1967–88), 1: 127–30.

6 A translation of the inscription on the 'Bobrinsky bucket' is given in Ward (1993), 74. For the stucco *mihrabs* and the dispersal of the 'bevelled style', see Ettinghausen (1952); Shani (1989); Costa (2001), 212–23.

7 Tsafrir and Foerster (1997), pp.136–8, figs 51–2; Schaefer (1986). See also Foote (2000).

8 Gelichi and Milanese (1998) and (2002); Leone (2003); Simpson (2000), 61.

9 Walmsley (2007), 78–9.

10 The passage from Khatib al-Baghdadi is translated in Lassner (1970), 45 (for Rusafa, see p. 64). On the question of skilled and unskilled man-power employed in the building of the Abbasid cities, see Milwright (2001b), 89–101.

11 Northedge and Falkner (1987), pp.149–51, figs 2, 3, 7.

12 For recent research on the industrial districts of Raqqa, see Miglus, ed. (1999); Challis et al. (2004); Henderson et al. (2005); Heidemann (2006).

13 For archaeological and textual references, see Carswell (1979), 19; Milwright (1999), 506.

14 For a reading of the inscription with the name of Ibrahim, see Gonnella in Miglus, ed. (1999), 57–8. The inscription seems to indicate that the vessel (or at least the decorative mould) was manufactured in Hira, though it was found in excavations at Raqqa. On the pottery of Hira, see Rousset (1994). The region of Raqqa already contained a vibrant Christian population. See Robinson (2003a).

15. Links between the glazed wares of Raqqa and Basra are explored in Mason and Keall in Miglus, ed. (1999), 141. Cf. Mason and Keall (1991).

16 Henderson et al. (2005), 139.

17 Muqaddasi (d. 990), translated in Heidemann (2006), 45–8. Also Heidemann (2003), 43–4; Challis et al. (2004), 147–8, fig. 6.

18 On the pottery of this phase, see Tonghini and Henderson (1998); Milwright (2001a), 15.

19 Heideman (2003), 50–1; Heidemann (2006), 48; Porter (2004).

20 See sources collected in Tonghini and Grube (1989), 67–73.

21 For the pottery and kilns of Nishapur and Samarqand, see Wilkinson (1973); Anon. (1992). See also Lane (1957), 17–18 and plates; and Watson (2004), 205–51. On the excavation of the tile kilns at Iznik, see Aslanapa, Yetkin and Altun (1989). Also Atasoy and Raby (1994), 57–64 and notes.

22 On the mining operations in Spain and Oman, see Trauth (1996); Weisgerber (1980). For Islamic mining and smelting in the Wadi 'Araba, see Rothenberg (1999), 163–9; Hauptmann and Weisberger (1987), 423–4; Hauptman (2000), 86–7, fig. 62. See also Walmsley (2007), 119–20 and Milwright (2008a), 123–4.

23 Allan and Gilmour (2000), 50–5. See also Allan (1982), 56–9, 203–4.

24 Rosen-Ayalon (2006), 73–81. Also Walmsley (2007), 78–9, 118–19.

25 Wilkinson (1973), 261.

26 Jenkins (1984), 104–12. For other 'signatures' on glazed pottery, see 'Abd al-Raziq (1967); Contadini (1998), 81–2; Watson (2004), 417–25.

27 For a list of craftsmen with this *nisba*, see Rice (1957), 325–6.

28 Walmsley (2001); also Northedge and Kennet (1994), 23.

29 Allan (1974); Morgan (1994); Milwright (2003), 87.

30 For the most comprehensive discussion of the evolution of lustre-painted pottery in the Middle East, see Mason (2004). For specific regions, see Contadini (1998), 74–82; Porter and Watson (1987); Watson (1985); Redford and Blackman (1997); Marçais (1928); Anon. (1993), cat. no. 53.

31 Caiger-Smith (1985), 197–236.

32 Henderson (2000), 25–38.

33 Sayre (1965), 152–3, fig. 8. See also Matson (1948); Gratuze and Barrandon (1990).

34 Henderson (1999); Henderson (2000), 84–7.

35 On these techniques and their application, see Mason (2004), 5–22 and Bernsted (2003).

36 Northedge and Kennet (1994); Northedge (1996).

37 For Abu al-Qasim's text, see Allan (1973). See also Allan, Llewellyn and Schweizer (1973); Bernsted (2003), 23–8. On the manufacturing practices at Iznik, see Raby in Atasoy and Raby (1994), 50–64 (also the contribution by Henderson, 65–69).

38 Wulff (1966): 160–7; Rye and Evans (1976); Crane (1988). Additional studies are cited in Atasoy and Raby (1994), 50–64.

39 Mason and Keall (1991); Mason and Tite (1997); Mason (2004), 39–44. See also Tamari (1995), 137–40. On the use of lead as a flux in Islamic glazes, see Tite et al. (1998).

40 Mason and Tite (1994).

41 Mason (2004), 91–155; Tite (1989); Henderson (2000), 189–200.

42 For instance, Balfet (1965); Fayolle (1992); Einsler (1914); Mershen (1985); Ochsenschlager (2004).

43 See examples discussed in Johns (1998), 77.

44. Whitcomb (1988), 212, fig. 5a and b. For further bibliography on this phenomenon, see Johns (1998), 72; Milwright (2008a), 146–54 and notes.

45 Johns (1998), 72–3. The presence of handmade pottery on a site may also indicate some change in function. For instance, handmade wares appear at the castle of 'Athlit only after the departure of the Frankish occupants in 1291. See Johns (1935), 54.

8

Travel and trade

The distribution of Indian and Chinese ceramics in the Persian Gulf and the occurrence of substantial hoards of *dirhams* in 'European Russia' and Scandinavia are significant indicators of increasing economic activity in the early Islamic centuries (chapter 3). The latter phenomenon should give grounds for caution, however, concerning the modes of exchange that led to this widespread dispersal of coins from mints in the eastern Islamic world. Certainly the demand for luxury goods among the wealthy occupants of Baghdad, Balkh, or Samarqand would have provided a powerful stimulus for Islamic merchants to travel to entrepôts on the Volga river and elsewhere to exchange silver coins for slaves, furs, wax, and honey, but the flow of currency northwards need not have occurred only by means of trade. Allowing for the existence of northern entrepôts such as Ladoga, it seems likely that the largely non-monetarised economies of dark age Russia, Scandinavia, and north-eastern Europe exchanged goods through other means: barter, theft, 'protection money' (such as the Danegeld paid to the Vikings by the English kings), gift-giving, and the redistribution of wealth by ruling elites.[1] Nor should it be assumed that trade was the only mode of exchange in the more sophisticated economies of the pre-modern Islamic world; written sources record examples of expensive wedding dowries, of elaborate diplomatic gifts, and of the spreading of largesse by Muslim rulers during religious festivals, celebrations of the circumcision of their sons, and the investiture of state functionaries. In rural areas exchange could take the form of barter, with annual taxes paid in agricultural produce or in the seasonal provision of *corvée* labour.

The key point is that the analysis of the spatial distribution – a method commonly employed by archaeologists in both pre-historic and historic periods – is limited by the fact that, other than in exceptional circumstances, we cannot know precisely what modes of exchange resulted in the movement of an artefact from its place of manufacture (if known) to its place of deposition. Furthermore, the objects recovered through excavation and field survey tend to be those that survive in the soil (such as ceramics and glass), and these represent only a fraction of the totality of exchange. Foodstuffs and other organic commodities such as medicaments and textiles remain largely invisible in the archaeological record.

Nevertheless we are justified in viewing trade as a major dynamic factor in the movement of artefacts during the Islamic centuries, and study of the distribution patterns of ceramics, glass, and textiles can tell us much about this activity. The centrality of the market within the traditional 'Islamic city' displays the significance of trade. The positive stance to trade taken in early Islam is exemplified in a well known saying attributed to the second caliph, 'Umar: 'I prefer to die between the two upright pieces of my wooden saddle as I travel through the land seeking God's bounty, rather than be killed as a fighter in the *jihad* for the sake of God'. That the honest pursuit of profit (though not the hoarding of wealth) by the merchant was a meritorious act of benefit to the Muslim community as a whole is also a theme in Islamic legal writings, particularly of the Hanafi school of jurisprudence (*madhhab*).[2]

Another area of considerable interest for archaeology is the means by which goods and people travelled from one region to another. Maritime travel can be studied through the excavation of shipwrecks and ports. A good example of the way in which a shipwreck can illuminate the process of trading is provided by the underwater excavation in the harbour of Serçe Liman, on the southern Anatolian coast. A Byzantine ship plying the coastal routes as far south as the Palestine coast, it contained a diverse range of commodities, including amphorae for storing wine and olive oil, decorative water jars, glazed ceramics, and about two tons of glass cullet (broken vessels and glass-making waste) stored in wicker baskets. Probably bought from glass workshops in Fatimid-controlled Palestine to be reused further north, this cullet represented a marketable ballast. The dating for the wreck was confirmed by the coins and glass weights, the latest of which was inscribed with the year 1024–5. Probably taking advantage of the improved relations between the Constantinople and the Fatimid caliphate following a treaty signed in 1027, the presence of both Byzantine and Fatimid weights on the ship illustrates the ability of the crew to negotiate transactions across cultural and political borders.[3]

Travel by land was often done along routes established centuries before the birth of Islam (chapter 2), though the political and religious reorientation of the regions encompassed by the Islamic conquests of the seventh and eighth centuries naturally led to changes in the volume of traffic employing different routes. The increased emphasis placed on some arteries of communication can be traced through the distribution of state-funded architectural and engineering projects, while the richness and diversity of the artefacts located along such routes is an indication of economic activity. Many routes performed multiple functions, including the movement of armies, merchant caravans, and pilgrims, as well as the carrying of official mail.

The first section of this chapter is devoted to a discussion of pilgrimage and trade routes. This is followed by some general comments concerning the role of archaeology in tracing fluctuating patterns of Mediterranean trade between the eleventh and the fourteenth century. In the final section of the chapter the archaeology of two Middle Eastern ports, Siraf and Quseir, is examined in the context of trade in the Indian Ocean.

Pilgrimage and trade routes

The performance of the pilgrimage (hajj) is one of the five 'pillars' (rukn in the singular) of Islam. Before the advent of air travel, the Muslim pilgrimage was often an arduous undertaking, involving weeks or months of travel. Pilgrims had to contend with challenging terrain and climate, as well as with the ever-present danger of banditry. From the earliest phases in Islamic history, the ruling elites have striven to protect the annual passage of pilgrims coming to Mecca and Medina. The protection of the hajj caravans that set out from different cities of the Islamic world and the construction of the physical infrastructure – bridges, fire beacons, road markers, water storage facilities, forts or fortified enclosures (khans), and even sections of paved road – were seen as the responsibility of Muslim states.

The Islamic conquests in the Middle East, Central Asia, North Africa, and Spain had the effect of establishing populations of Muslim populations at a considerable distance from Mecca and Medina. This geographical expansion of the Muslim community meant that the caliphate had to find means to facilitate the passage of the annual pilgrimage from these newly conquered regions. Some of these routes were well established in the pre-Islamic period. For instance, both the routes south, to Yemen, and north, to Syria and Palestine, had long served for the movement of trade caravans, particularly those bringing commodities such as incense and spices from southern Arabia and the Horn of Africa to the Mediterranean.[4] The economic importance of this traffic through the Hijaz is illustrated by Qaryat al-Faw, a pre-Islamic settlement in the south of Saudi Arabia. Operating from the fourth century BCE through to the fourth or fifth centuryCE, this entrepôt grew wealthy through its control of part of this north–south route. The rich finds from the site included glass, ceramics, and metalwork (the last category included classicising statuary).[5]

In later times it is also possible to detect evidence of state patronage in the protection of the Syrian hajj. In the Mamluk and Ottoman period this expenditure covered some of the provisions, the allocation of troops to protect the pilgrims, and purses of money – essentially bribes – to the bedouin tribes to ensure that they did not molest the pilgrimage caravan. Most striking, however, is the creation, from the sixteenth to the eighteenth century, of a series of forts in Jordan and northern Arabia. This policy was instigated by Süleyman II (r. 1520–66) and continued by later Ottoman sultans. The route of the Syrian hajj was moved from the ancient Darb al-Hajj (which followed the course of the Roman Via Nova Traiana through the plains of Jordan before diverting southeast to Ma'an and then to Tayma') to a more easterly route on the margins of the desert. This extensive record of patronage has left a series of well preserved forts, bridges, and sections of paved road. The forts would each guard a cistern, and there was usually a cemetery in the vicinity.[6]

Another route that has left considerable evidence of state patronage is the Tariq Sadr wa Ayla, running through the southern Sinai and connecting Cairo to the Red Sea port of Ayla.[7] While this route offered a means for Egyptian pilgrims to follow the land by skirting the north bank of the Red Sea before heading south to Mecca and Medina, the majority – as the Spanish Muslim pilgrim Ibn Jubayr (d. 1217) is known to have done – made the sea crossing from the southern ports of Quseir and 'Aydhab to Yanbu' or to Jidda, on the coast of the Hijaz. The primary motivation for the late twelfth-century architectural patronage of Tariq Sadr wa Ayla was strategic; it facilitated the movement of Salah al-Din's (Saladin, r. 1171–93) troops and military supplies from Egypt to fight in his campaigns against the crusader kingdom of Jerusalem and the Zengid princes of northern Mesopotamia. The Mamluk sultans also appreciated the strategic importance of the roads running through Egypt and Greater Syria. A significant area of patronage was the postal system (barid); official communications were relayed by horse and camel riders and by homing pigeons (these methods were also employed in the Mongol khanates of Asia). Relay stations and dovecots dating from the later thirteenth and fourteenth centuries have been identified along the major north–south and east–west routes through Greater Syria.[8] To the east, the Saljuq sultans constructed networks of fortified caravanserais along the major trade routes of the Islamic east and Anatolia that could be used by merchants, pilgrims, and the peripatetic royal elite. Excavations at Ribat-i Sharaf (Fig. 8.1), located in north-eastern Iran, on the road to the city of Merv, led to the recovery of a rich assemblage of metal vessels and other items dating from the twelfth century to the Safavid period (1501–1722).[9]

That the pilgrimage routes might also have military or economic significance has considerable relevance for the interpretation of the roads leading from the Hijaz into southern Iraq. The two major routes from Mecca lead to the amsar of Basra and Kufa. These routes were employed in pre-Islamic times – the northern one leading to the Lakhmid capital of Hira and the southern one providing access to the delta of the Euphrates and Tigris rivers. Arab armies used these routes during the campaigns against the Sasanians, and later military expeditions by 'Ali b. Abi Talib (r. 656–61) and his son Husayn (d. 680) used the road to Kufa in 656 and 679 respectively.[10] The increasing population of Muslims living in Iraq and further east necessitated improvements to the facilities, particularly on the road from Kufa to Mecca (known as the Darb Zubayda). Some work on this road was evidently ordered by Rashidun and Umayyad caliphs, but the greatest period of patronage occurred under the Abbasid caliphs Saffah (r. 749–54), Mahdi (r. 775–85), and, most importantly, Harun al-Rashid and his consort Zubayda (d. 831), after whom the route was later named.

The Darb Zubayda (also known as Tariq Zubayda and Darb al-Sitt Zubayda) stretches across approximately 1,400 km of arid land between Kufa and Mecca (Fig. 8.2). The diverse geological conditions of the road present numerous challenges; the road had to be cut through mountainous regions; rocks and boulders were cleared from other zones; and paving was employed where the road passed over sand or soft loess soil. Arabic geographical sources indicate that the road was furnished with fifty-four major stations (that is, about every 25–6 km, or within one day's march) with other smaller resting places in between. Other features identified along the road are milestones and fire beacons. Most important of all, however, were the installations designed to provide water for the pilgrims and travellers who undertook the arduous journey through this harsh terrain. The larger, semi-fortified structures along the route exhibit points of continuity with the Umayyad *qusur* of Greater Syria (chapter 2). For instance the small *qasr* at 'Atshan in Iraq is one of the earliest structures on the road and may date to the late Umayyad period. Unlike the stone construction of the Syrian *qusur*, 'Atshan is constructed of brick – the common building material of southern Iraq – and incorporates adaptations to the standard Umayyad plan, including a projecting entrance. The *qasr* at Kura' creates a tripartite division of the internal space similar to those of the *dar al-imara* in Kufa and of the Umayyad palace of Mshatta. Other variations on this basic plan may be found in the later Abbasid structures located along the Iraqi and Saudi stretches of the road.[11]

The extensive water-storage and collection facilities are among the most impressive engineering projects on the Darb Zubayda. These consist of reservoirs (*birkas*), cisterns, wells, *qanats*, and dams built across wadis. The *birkas* are usually located in depressions in flat plains or near wadis, and they are designed to collect water from the winter rain. Additional walls create a wider catchment area and funnel the water towards the *birka*. While the annual rains would usually provide sufficient water to fill them, the build-up of sediment – particularly in water collected from the flash-flooding of wadis – presented problems. The accummulation of sediment was minimised by the angling of the channels leading into the main water tank and, in the case of Birkat al-Kharaba near Ta'if, by the use of a preliminary filtering tank. The reservoirs have different plans, ranging from square or rectangular to roughly circular ones. The circular *birkas* are often given buttresses around the perimeter wall. While the square and rectangular forms may be compared with the Roman constructions of Syria and Jordan, the circular buttressed type are similar to the ninth-century reservoirs constructed by the Aghlabid governors of Tunisia. Like in the case of other the great Abbasid construction projects of this period (chapter 5), it seems likely that craftsmen were brought from diverse regions to work on the Darb Zubayda.[12]

Pottery sherds collected from sites in the southern half of the route include significant numbers of glazed and unglazed ware from Iraq. The glazed ware falls into two main categories. The first are the turquoise, blue or green-glazed storage vessels employed for the transport of products such as date syrup (*dibs*) – a major export from southern Iraq. The second are the high-quality tin-glazed earthenwares decorated with blue or green pigments or lustre-painting, probably produced mainly in Basra (Fig. 8.3). The southern Iraqi ceramic bowls and containers found along the Darb Zubayda are also encountered at Persian Gulf ports like Siraf (from which they were distributed via maritime routes around the Indian Ocean). Further insights into the commercial activity of the Darb Zubayda came from the excavation of Rabadha. Important from pre-Islamic times on account of its fine pasturage, the town also benefited from the presence of gold mines and deposits of steatite (a soft stone that was carved into vessels) in the nearby hills. Excavation of the palatial and residential areas revealed the types of glazed ceramic described above as well as Umayyad and Abbasid *dinars* and *dirhams*, metalwork, carved stone, woodwork, textiles, and glass. The evidence for local glass and ceramic manufacture shows that Rabadha maintained a healthy craft sector of its own.[13]

Mediterranean trade from the eleventh to the fifteenth century

In chapter 2 it was noted that the volume of commercial traffic across the Mediterranean declined (though it did not disappear entirely) in the fifth and sixth centuries. The available evidence for the period from the Islamic conquests to the tenth century suggests that maritime trading contacts between southern Europe and the regions of North Africa and the Levant remained at a relatively low level.[14] Changes can be detected in the tenth century, however, with the rise of the Italian ports of Bari and Venice on the Adriatic coast and Amalfi, Naples, and Gaeta on the Tyrrhenian coast. Of these, Venice became the dominant player in international trade with the Byzantine Empire, Egypt, and Syria. Two other ports, Genoa and Pisa, rose to prominence in the eleventh century following raids on Muslim territories in Sardinia, Sicily, and the North African ports of Annaba and Mahdiyya. The poor survival of archival data from the Islamic world hampers our understanding of parallel developments in ports on the southern and eastern shores of the Mediterranean, though the activities of Jewish merchants, particularly from the eleventh to the thirteenth century, have been reconstructed from the papers of the Cairo *Geniza*. Among these documents there are references to Jewish traders taking merchandise to Amalfi,

Marseilles, Palermo, and Mahdiyya. Merchants in Cairo evidently also enjoyed active contacts with Jewish traders operating in the Red Sea.[15]

Archaeologically, this revival of international trade is manifested in finds of Islamic pottery and, less frequently, in glass on sites all over Europe. The fascination with Islamic glazed pottery is also demonstrated by the practice of embedding glazed bowls (known as *bacini*) into the façades of churches, and even into their pulpits (Fig. 8.4 a and b). This type of architectural ornament was popular in central and northern Italy and in southern Greece. Chinese bowls (particularly celadon and blue and white porcelain) or Persian stonepaste wares were sometimes embedded into the walls of private houses, into the façades, vaults, and *mihrabs* of mosques (Fig. 8.5), and even into the sides of grave markers in different parts of the Islamic world.[16] The largest group of *bacini* (more than 600 items) is located in Pisa. One of the earliest among the decorated churches is San Piero a Grado, of the late tenth or early eleventh century (Fig. 8.4 b). This assemblage allows for the formation of some tentative conclusions regarding the evolution of Pisan trading contacts from the eleventh to the thirteenth century.

The earliest Pisan *bacini* comprise a few exotic imports from Fatimid Egypt, and this engagement with the eastern Mediterranean is also seen later, in a small group of early thirteenth-century glazed stonepaste wares from Syria. More significant, however, is the presence of less sophisticated glazed bowls from Tunisia and elsewhere along the western part of North Africa. These North African imports make up nearly 90 per cent of the eleventh-century *bacini* and around 70 per cent of those of the twelfth and early thirteenth century. The influx of Tunisian glazed ware is also apparent in excavations in Pisa, Genoa, Rome, and Naples. Trading records from Pisa suggest intense mercantile contacts with coastal regions of North Africa as well as with Sicily and the Mediterranean coast of Spain. Skilled potters from Islamic Spain, North Africa, and Sicily appear to have been transported (presumably, often against their will) to set up workshops in Marseilles, Pisa, Pavia, and Lucera. They brought with them new vessel types such as the *alberello* storage jar and techniques, most importantly, the practice of tin glazing. In the case of Pisa, the increasing volume of tin-glazed pottery production (known as 'proto-Maiolica') removed the former reliance upon imports from Tunisia, and by the fourteenth century the *bacini* were composed of native glazed wares, with a few imported lustre-painted bowls from Spain.[17]

The formation of the crusader states after 1098 is a phenomenon of huge importance for the political history of the Islamic Middle East. The arrival of a new European (Frankish) colonial presence along the Syrian littoral, and more briefly in Jordan and southern Anatolia, also had a significant impact upon economic life around the eastern Mediterranean (Fig. 8.6). This issue can be addressed archaeologically through the analysis of the distribution of glazed ware on sites in Greater Syria, particularly in the south, which has the greatest concentration of published excavations and field surveys. Two points should be noted about this considerable corpus of sites: first, they comprise a wide range of settlement types (villages, small towns, cities, fortifications, and ports); and, second, while all the territories of the southern crusader states of the kingdom of Jerusalem and county of Tripoli finally reverted to Muslim control between the battle of Hattin in 1187 and the fall of Acre to the Mamluks in 1291, many sites were contested, shifting between Frankish to Muslim control – Ayyubid, Mamluk, and, in the Jabal Ansariyya, Isma'ili – during the twelfth and thirteenth centuries. This latter point brings up again the knotty question of the extent to which different ethnic or confessional groups can be identified in the material record (chapter 1).

What, then, can be defined as 'Frankish' material culture in the archaeological record? In architecture, there are relatively clear-cut examples of castles and religious buildings constructed or renovated by the kings of Jerusalem, the nobility, and the religious orders. The Franks also built for themselves rural dwellings akin to European manor houses in regions such as the Galilee and Samaria.[18] Portable artefacts – most importantly, glazed pottery – provide, however, a rather different picture. Some distinctive styles of glazed pottery were produced in the crusader states, the best known of which are the decorated wares of Port St Simeon (Mina) near Antioch. Less elaborate objects such as shallow frying pans (like the Italian *tegame*) and slip-painted or sgraffito bowls were also circulated in Frankish territories. In addition, proto-Maiolica bowls were imported from Italy, and sgraffito wares from Cyprus, the Aegean region, Sicily, and North Africa. The most expensive ceramics produced in Muslim-controlled territories were stonepaste wares, usually decorated with pigments painted beneath a colourless alkaline glaze. Most of the glazed stonepaste wares circulating in the south of Greater Syria were manufactured in Damascus, though small quantities may have come from manufacturing centres in northern Syria and Egypt (Fig. 5.10). There were also numerous workshops in Muslim territories producing decorated and undecorated lead-glazed ware.[19]

Some broad conclusions can be drawn from the analysis of distribution patterns. The imported glazed wares from regions such as Italy and Cyprus remained largely the preserve of Frankish sites (castles, ports, larger towns, and places of Christian pilgrimage), and did not penetrate far beyond the coastal regions of Greater Syria. The same can be said for locally produced pottery such as the glazed frying pans. Exceptions to this general rule are large Islamic cities such as Hama in Syria, a market for all the types of high-quality pottery at the time. Cypriot, crusader, and Aegean pottery has also been located at the port of Alexandria. Turning to the periphery of the kingdom of Jerusalem, a rather different picture emerges. The published ceramics from Karak castle in southern Jordan (under crusader control until 1188–9) provide little evidence of the importation of glazed wares from workshops in crusader Palestine, Italy, or Cyprus. This can also be said of the smaller frontier fortress at Wu'ayra (Vaux Moïse) near Petra. Both cases would suggest that the Frankish inhabitants made use of the local ceramics in their everyday lives. Surprisingly enough, the excavated contexts from the last decades of crusader occupation at Wu'ayra also turned up examples of glazed stonepaste wares, probably manufactured in Damascus.[20] Syrian stonepaste wares were also evidently enjoyed by wealthy individuals in crusader territories west of the Jordan river, and their presence at the port of Acre suggests that some were destined for export. Unlike the luxury stonepaste wares, the decorated lead-glazed wares from Muslim-controlled regions of southern Greater Syria do not appear to have circulated extensively in Frankish territories. Thus political borders were indeed porous, but only for the more expensive types of glazed ceramic.

That the Mediterranean was connected into larger trading networks (for instance those of gold, slaves, and ivory from the kingdom of Mali) to the south, the north, and the east can be seen in the archaeological record. The penetration of Islamic goods as far as England can be demonstrated through the recovery of North African glazed ware from the medieval port at Southampton. The famous thirteenth-century enamelled glass beaker known as the 'Luck of Edenhall' (Fig. 8.7) shows how Syrian luxury goods could travel long distances, among the personal possessions of pilgrims and crusaders. Glazed stonepaste jars and alberelli manufactured in Syria and Egypt in the thirteenth and four-teenth centuries were frequently employed for the transportation of expensive commodities such as preserved fruit, ginger, and medicines. The vessels them-selves were evidently much valued in Europe, and records of glazed wares *alla domaschina* (from Damascus) appear in the inventories of noble families in late medieval Florence and elsewhere.[21]

Among the most expensive commodities of Mediterranean trade were the glazed wares produced in south-eastern China during the Sung, Yuan, and Ming dynasties. Arriving into the Mediterranean via land routes through Asia, and in greater volume through ports on the Persian Gulf and Red Sea (see below), these items could be bought in the markets of Cairo, Alexandria, and Damascus. Celadon ('green ware'), qingpai porcelain, and blue and white porcelain were evidently a ubiquitous feature of urban life in the Middle East. Those unable to afford such luxuries could purchase locally produced imita-tions (chapter 5). Additional costs associated with resale in the markets of the Middle East further increased the substantial price tag for purchasers in Europe. The social status of these commodities was emphasised by their conspicuous presence in diplomatic gifts sent by the Mamluk sultans to rulers in Italy, France, and Cyprus. Chinese wares have appeared on excavations of medieval sites in Italy, England, Hungary, and perhaps Greece and Spain, while a handful of complete vessels possesses solid documentary evidence proving that they made their way into Europe before 1500.[22] Chinese ceramics of the thirteenth to the fifteenth century have left a less conspicuous trace in the archaeological record of the Islamic world; for instance small assemblages have been found on a few sites in Greater Syria with the distribution restricted to cities, urban citadels, castles, and ports.[23] It may be that this does not reflect the true nature of the consumption of Chinese glazed ware; such expensive items were often collected – which is clearly demonstrated by the massive group in the Topkapı Palace in Istanbul – and treated as family heirlooms. The remarkable discovery, in the late 1960s, of more than 600 Chinese and Japanese vessels (including Yuan and early Ming pieces) owned by the occupants of the Douma district of Damascus illustrates that the ownership of imported ware was not restricted to the political and economic elite of Syrian society and that these items could remain within individual families for centuries.[24]

Indian Ocean trade

Maritime trade has existed in the Indian Ocean region from ancient times. Archaeological evidence may place the first contacts between the Indus valley and Oman as early as the third millenniumBCE, while from the first century CE we possess a detailed written account of mercantile activity, the *Periplus of the Erythaean Sea*, believed to have been written by an unnamed Egyptian mariner.[25] Two factors are of primary importance in assessing the sea trade pursued in the Indian Ocean. The first is the seasonal pattern of the monsoon winds, which dictate the annual timetable for sailors plying the routes between the western coast of the Indian subcontinent, the coast of Africa between Mozambique and Somalia (sometimes known as the 'Swahili corridor'), and the Middle Eastern ports on the Red Sea, Persian Gulf, and coast of southern Arabia (Fig. 8.9). The second factor is the uneven distribution of natural resources and manufacturing capacity among the landmasses bordering the ocean. From sources such as the *Periplus*, the documents in the Cairo *Geniza*, and the archive excavated at Quseir (see below), we get some idea of the commodities exported from each region. Without entering into great detail, it is apparent that the primary economic importance of East Africa was as a supplier of slaves and raw materials – such as timber, gold, and ivory – and as a recipient for imported manufactured goods. The import and export trade through the Middle Eastern and Indian ports reflected a more even balance between raw materials and manufactured goods, with the ports of southern India and Sri Lanka gaining additional benefit from the resale of spices, silks, glazed ceramics, and other commodities from south-east Asia.[26]

   Siraf is surrounded by arid lands, unsuited for agriculture. The wealth of
this Persian Gulf port was based on maritime trade. Already functioning as a
naval base in the Sasanian period, Siraf enjoyed a status secondary to that of
the great Iraqi port–city of Basra from the seventh to the first half of the tenth
century. With its larger population and vibrant industrial sector, Basra dominated the Persian Gulf trade; but the port was to suffer a series of misfortunes,
starting with the Zanj rebellion of 871 and culminating in destructive raids
launched from Oman in 943 and 952–3. Siraf was one of the Persian Gulf ports
to benefit from the gradual decline of Basra, and written sources indicate that
Siraf was at its most prosperous during the third quarter of the tenth century.
This favoured situation appears to have been relatively short-lived, however. An
earthquake is recorded in 977 (though little evidence of it was detected during
the excavations), and the last dated coin from the mint of Siraf was struck in
382/992. Evidently merchants started to desert the city for Oman, and in the
mid-eleventh century Siraf was largely eclipsed by the island entrepôt of Kish/
Qais, 200 km to the south-east.[27]
   Written sources report that in the ninth and tenth centuries the markets of
Siraf dealt in luxury products such as ivory, pearls, ambergris, gems, and spices.
The elaborately carved stucco decoration (dated to the early eleventh century)
in the wealthier homes of Siraf provides some indication of the wealth generated
by commerce. Excavated ceramics and coins represent, however, the most
consistent archaeological record of trade in the port. The earliest manifestation
of international contacts takes the form of Indian burnished pottery dating from
the first to the third century.[28] Considerable information about long-distance
trading activities in later centuries came from the sequence established in the
excavations of the congregational mosque and Sasanian fort below it (chapter
6). Only one Chinese sherd was detected in an eighth-century context at
Siraf, but the excavations of the congregational mosque suggest a remarkable
upsurge of Chinese pottery in the two phases of the platform fill that have been
dated, with the aid of coin evidence, to between 803–4 and c.815. Among the
most significant imports of this period are the large glazed stoneware storage
jars commonly known as 'Dusun ware' (chapter 3). Two vessels carried Arabic
inscriptions incised under the glaze (that is, before the vessel was fired) with
the names of Yusuf and what may read as Maymun. Presumably these inscriptions were designed to identify the owners of consignments of goods shipped
from China.[29] Ninth and tenth-century excavated contexts contain the types
of white glazed stoneware encountered at Samarra and other Abbasid urban
sites.[30] Through the course of the eleventh century Chinese ceramics became
less common, though the presence of celadon ware and early blue and white
porcelain indicates that Siraf maintained some trading contacts well into the
fourteenth and fifteenth centuries. A hoard of Chinese coins, probably buried in

the fourteenth century but containing issues dating from the period 621–1265, was also recovered from a residential complex.[31]

Other evidence of trade can be inferred from the Islamic pottery excavated at Siraf. Pottery kilns were established in the tenth century to produce the ceramic containers needed for the repackaging of the commodities passing through the port (which invites comparison with the seventh-century amphora kilns in the vicinity of the Jordanian port of Ayla). Much of the decorated glazed ware at Siraf was probably destined for export to other regions bordering the Indian Ocean. From the ninth century on, this included the famous tin-glazed ware from Iraq. The presence of Iraqi glazed ceramics, Siraf-style storage vessels, and 'Dusun' storage jars at Manda, Shanga, and Pate on the Lamu archipelago provides credible evidence for the involvement of the Persian port in maritime trade with East Africa. Similar wares are also reported from excavations at Banbhore in Pakistan. A later phase of export can be identified with the appearance in the early eleventh century of a distinctive style of sgraffito pottery produced in kilns in southern Iran. These decorated wares have been recovered on Kilwa island (Tanzania).[32] This is the last evidence for significant international export trade from Siraf; in later centuries the bulk of this activity moved to sites further east in the Persian Gulf and to the ports of the Red Sea.

Situated on the Egyptian coast of the Red Sea, considerably to the north of the other major ports of 'Aydhab and Suakin, Quseir (also known as Quseir Qadim, or 'old Quseir') was a thriving port in the thirteenth and fourteenth centuries. Like Siraf, Quseir is located in an inhospitably arid stretch of coastal land and derived its *raison d'être* from maritime trade. The excavations of Quseir have revealed abundant evidence of economic contacts both in the Indian Ocean and beyond, to south-east Asia.[33] While one could list other potential similarities with Siraf, it is the differences that are perhaps more important; for they help to explain some of the specific characteristics of the artefacts recovered from Quseir. A cursory examination of Quseir on a map would suggest that the port was better placed than its southern counterpart, 'Aydhab, to connect the urban centres of Egypt with wider maritime trade. Certainly the distance from Quseir to the Nile town of Qus through the Wadi Hammamat is considerably shorter – and carriage of goods by land was much more expensive than by sea – but this advantage was more than offset by the monsoon winds, which would usually carry ships only as far north as 'Aydhab. The winds, currents, and reefs of the northern section of the Red Sea are notoriously difficult to navigate.

Excavations have revealed that Quseir had previously functioned as a port, from the first to the third century CE. The activity of the port (known as Myos Hormos) and of its southern neighbour Berenice in this phase can be connected to the operation of the nearby Roman gold mines and quarries at Mons Claudiana and Mons Porphyritae. At Siraf there was evidence for continuity between the Sasanian and Islamic phases, but Quseir represents the re-establishment of a commercial enterprise after a cessation of activity for just under a millennium. Arabic geographical sources often describe Quseir as the 'port of Qus', and it would seem that the second phase at the port is linked to the Ayyubid revival of Red Sea trade. This correlates well with the earliest dated document (1215/612) found in the archive of fragmentary papers from within the structure dubbed by excavators as 'the Sheikh's house'. The Mamluk author al-Qalqashandi (d. 1418) reports that Quseir was sometimes used by merchants (known as the Karimi) to land cargoes of spices bound for Fustat via Qus, but documents from 'the Sheikh's house' indicate that the inhabitants of the port also relied upon the storage and sale of more mundane commodities – wheat, barley, flour, and rice – to maintain their livelihoods. The main profits from this secondary business were derived from the high prices that could charged to pilgrims making their way to Mecca and Medina. The lucrative spice trade of the Karimi merchants was largely extinguished by the rapacious tax regimes of Mamluk sultans in the early fifteenth century, but it seems likely that Quseir had already ceased to be a major player in international commerce some decades before.[34]

The textual evidence suggests that, during the thirteenth and fourteenth centuries, Quseir was operating in several economic spheres, from the international trade in spices to more localised networks in southern Egypt, the Hijaz, and southern Arabia. Pottery imported to Quseir in this phase included small quantities of unglazed Nubian vessels that, presumably, were utilised by the inhabitants of the port, as well as a diverse assemblage of Chinese ceramics. The latter group – comprising Ting ware, celadon, blue and white porcelain, and 'Martabani' storage jars – was mainly destined for transit to Qus and Cairo, though excavations of 'the Sheikh's house' revealed that the occupants also made use of Chinese celadon vessels in their daily lives.[35] The remainder of the pottery found at Quseir was probably produced in Egypt, perhaps with a few pieces coming from Syrian workshops. Much of this collection consisted of simple glazed and unglazed ware for the storage, cooking, and serving of food, though there are also examples of more expensive underglaze-painted stonepaste wares. Egyptian glazed wares were probably exported from Quseir to Yemen and from sites along the coast of East Africa. Analysis of the glass recovered from Quseir gives another insight into the nature of this export trade in the Ayyubid and early Mamluk periods; comparanda for the glass vessels, bracelets, and beads from Quseir suggest trading links with the Aden region of Yemen, Gedi, Mafia, Manda, and Kilwa on the African coast, and perhaps even with the Persian Gulf and the western coast of India. 'Aydhab was also actively engaged in the export of Egyptian ceramics and glass.[36]

The dry soil conditions in Egypt make it one of the few regions of the world where ancient textiles regularly survive buried beneath the ground. Excavations in Quseir offer an invaluable insight into the trade in cloth, particularly the import of resist-dyed (and mainly block-printed) cottons from India (Fig. 8.8).[37] The recovery of a resist-dyed fragment from an eleventh-century context at Fustat, and the confirmation of this dating through carbon-14 analysis of comparable textiles in museum collections, indicate that the import of these Indian cloths pre-dates the re-establishment of Quseir as a port in the early thirteenth century.[38] It was during the life-span of Quseir that the trade seems to have been at its height, and a wide variety of decorated fabrics (probably mainly from Gujarat) has been catalogued from the site. It is important to recognise, however, that these vividly coloured artefacts did not fetch high prices in Egypt – although, if they can be identified with the 'mahabis' cloth mentioned in the Cairo Geniza, the Indian cotton textiles cost more in the markets of Cairo and Fustat than Egyptian cotton fabrics. The presence of Arabic and pseudo-Arabic inscriptions on some pieces indicates that Indian manufacturers were designing patterns specifically for an export market. It was not until the fifteenth century that Egyptian textile workers employed the same technique of block-printing to mass-produce cheap textiles carrying epigraphic ornament.[39]

Notes

1 Grierson (1959), 129–40.
2 Bonner (2001). Bonner's translation of the saying attributed to caliph 'Umar appears at p. 415.
3 Bass, Steffy and Van Doorninck (1984); Jenkins (1992).
4 Bulliet (1975), 92–110; Crone (1987); Groom (2005).
5 Al-Ansary (1982), 59–126.
6 Petersen (2001). See also Milwright (2008a), 91–2.
7 Mouton et al. (1996).
8 Sauvaget (1941); Milwright (2008a), 90–1.
9 Kiani (1981). On the architecture of the Saljuq caravanserais, see Hillenbrand (1994), 338–50.
10 Al-Rashid (1978), 33; Finster (1978b), 57–9.
11 Finster and Schmidt (1976), 16–24; Al-Dayel, al-Hilwa and MacKenzie (1979); 46–7, pls 30, 32a; Creswell and Allan (1989), 261, 280–4. On the architecture and hydraulic engineering along the road, see also MacKenzie and al-Hilwa (1980); Morgan and al-Hilwa (1981).
12 Al-Rashid (1979); Wilkinson (1980). See also Creswell and Allan (1989), 381–2.
13 Al-Rashid (1986).
14 Lebecq (1997).
15 Goitein (1967–88), 1: 209–20, 301–5.
16 For instance, Chinese (and Persian) ceramics have been located in architectural contexts in Iran, Syria, Oman, and coastal regions of East Africa. See Costa (2001), 223; Chittick (1974), 1: pls 32b, 45a; 2: 306–8, 312; Chittick (1984), 54; Horton (1996), 71, pl. 33.

17 Abulafia (1985). For a catalogue and analysis of the Pisan *bacini*, see Berti and
    Tongiorgi (1981). On the glazed ceramics of North Africa, see also Jenkins (1975).
18 Ellenblum (1998).
19 On the circulation of glazed ceramics in the crusader states and neighbouring Muslim
    polities, see Pringle (1986); Boas (1994); Whitehouse (1997), 4–5; Kubiak (1998);
    Milwright (2003), 85–91.
20 Vannini and Vanni Desideri (1995), 535.
21. Whitehouse (1997); Milwright (1999), 506–7.
22 Whitehouse (1972); Milwright (1999), 513–16; Carswell (2000), 59–77, 127–43,
    170–2.
23 Milwright (2008a), 238–43.
24 Carswell (1972); Carswell (2000), 67–8.
25 Casson (1989); Whitehouse (2001), 411.
26 Goitein (1963); Tampoe (1989), 117–30; Barnes (1997), 1: 95–9.
27 Whitehouse and Williamson (1973), 33–5; Lowick (1974), 319–24; Whitehouse
    (1975), 263–4.
28 Williamson (1972), 99–100, 106; Whitehouse (1973a), 242; Whitehouse and
    Williamson (1973), 38–9, 48–9.
29 Whitehouse (1973a), 244–6, pl. 18.
30 Tampoe (1989), 72–4, fig. 113.
31 Lowick (1985), 6, 57–63.
32 Tampoe (1989), 90–1, 104, 107–11; Whitehouse (1973b); Whitehouse (2001),
    419–21.
33 For reports of the excavations on this site, see Whitcomb and Johnson (1979) and
    (1982); Peacock, Blue and Moser, eds (2002).
34 Whitcomb and Johnson (1979), 4–5; Guo (2004).
35 John Carswell in Whitcomb and Johnson (1982), 193–9; Guo (2004), 63. The
    sheikh's house also contained sherds of Nubian and Yemeni pottery.
36 Meyer (1992), 73–131. On the imported ceramics and glass found at sites in East
    Africa, see Chittick (1974), 2: 302–16, 395–411; Chittick (1984), 65–105, 159–79;
    Horton (1996), 271–322.
37 Vogelsang-Eastwood (1990).
38 Louise Mackie in Kubiak and Scanlon, eds (1989), 88–9, colour pl. 2; Barnes (1997),
    1: 33–42.
39 Goitein (1967–88), 4: 171; Barnes (1997), vol. 1: 92–4; Atil (1981), 239, cat. 122.

9

The 'post-medieval' Islamic world

The archaeological studies discussed in the previous chapters have dealt in the main with material dating before the fifteenth century. Indeed, it is only relatively recently that the material culture of the later centuries has become a focus of interest in the sub-discipline of Islamic archaeology, and in archaeology in general. The relatively small number of published reports dealing with the period from the fifteenth to the early twentieth century limit the scope of synthetic analysis, though the fast pace of developments in this area gives reason for the optimistic view that archaeology will make a genuine contribution to the study of this period. The abundance of archival data and other written sources from these centuries offers rich resources for historians, and their reconstructions of social and political life and of the shifting dynamics of inter-regional and international trade provide a vital framework for the interpretation of archaeological data from excavations and surveys.[1]

While there can be little doubt that the economies and political structures of the Islamic world experienced major transformations between the end of the fifteenth century and the beginning of the twentieth, it would be futile to point to one historical event or socio-economic phenomenon that marked the end of the 'medieval' Islamic world. This was rather the action of many factors occurring at different rates in the Islamic world, and often affecting urban and rural populations in different and sometimes unpredictable ways. Some contributory factors can be traced to earlier centuries, though their full impact was not felt until the sixteenth century or later. Examples include the use of gun-powder and the advances in technology that occurred in Europe in the aftermath of the Black Death. The impact of the former can be seen in changes in the defenses of military sites; for instance the increasing availability of hand-held firearms among the bedouin of Greater Syria is a significant factor in the evolution of the fortifications of the later Ottoman *hajj* forts on the road from Damascus to the Hijaz. New weaponry also necessitated changes to fortifications in other regions, including the Abdullah Khan Kala in Merv and Qal'at Bahrain (see below).[2] Increased investment in new technology in the fourteenth and fifteenth centuries ultimately led to Europe overtaking the manufacturing sectors of Islamic North Africa and the Middle East and reversing the balance of trade in the Mediterranean.

The capture of Constantinople in 1453 by the Ottomans (one of the so-called 'gun-powder empires') sent shockwaves across Europe and represented an early chapter in a much larger territorial expansion, which was to spread into Iraq, North Africa, the Balkans, and Central Europe. Islamic polities suffered reverses with the loss of the last Spanish dominions to the *Reconquista* in 1492, the capture of ports in Morocco by the Portuguese, and the maritime expeditions undertaken by the Holy Roman Emperor Charles V (r. 1519–56) against the coast of North Africa. The defeat of the Ottoman navy at Lepanto in 1571 was a turning point in the balance of maritime power in the Mediterranean. Political and economic considerations are, of course, profoundly interconnected; the twin European maritime achievements of the 'discovery' of the New World and the opening of the route to India via the Cape of Good Hope are cases in point. The economic exploitation of the Americas brought with it new commodities like tobacco, but also a massive influx of gold into the economies of Europe. The voyage of Vasco da Gama to India in 1497–8 had far-reaching consequences for the rulers of the Middle East, for they were no longer able to control and to profit from the long-distance trade in luxury goods from southeast Asia and India to Europe. Commercial relations with the east were not the sole prerogative of nations or city–states: particularly significant, and exercising huge economic power and political influence at their height, were the East India Company (granted royal charter in London in 1600) and the Dutch East India Company (Vereenigde Oost-Indische Compagnie or VOC, founded in 1602). Perhaps the most enduring economic phenomena of the late eighteenth and nineteenth centuries were the industrialisation of western Europe and the increasing scale of exports to other parts of the world.

Signs of these political, economic, socio-cultural, and technological changes can be detected in the archaeological record of the Islamic world. It is in the urban environment that they are most visible; for instance the spread of the Ottoman Empire was given a conspicuous visual form in towns and cities through the construction of mosques and other religious institutions, caravanserais, and improvements to the water supplies (chapter 5). Consumers in urban markets were the first to enjoy the benefits of the availability of new imported goods, just as their craft sectors were the first to experience the challenges of competing with European industry. Although standing architecture, architectural decoration (particularly tiles), and the arts of this period (in public and private collections) have all been subjected to detailed analysis, there are relatively few published reports of excavations of Ottoman period urban sites in the Middle East – Saraçhane in Istanbul, the Damascus citadel, Jerusalem, and the port of 'Akko (Acre) being important exceptions (Fig. 9.1).[3]

The archaeological examination of the material culture of villages and small rural towns in the Middle East presents a rather different picture, with, as might be expected, signs of considerable continuity with the practices of earlier centuries. While, again, the coverage of published archaeological projects is not extensive, significant recent studies include Sardis and Aphrodisias in Turkey, Hatara Saghir in north-western Iraq, Malka, Hubras and Umm al-Jimal in northern Jordan, and the Palestinian villages of Ti'innik, Tal Qaymun (ancient Yoqne'am, a site later occupied by a mid-eighteenth-century fort built by the local ruler, Dhahir al-'Umar), and Zir'in.[4] Later occupation phases on rural sites present difficulties, particularly the paucity of coins, dated inscriptions, and other artefacts that might be employed to establish chronological parameters for the excavated strata. The very conservative nature of rural pottery production (chapter 7) contrasts with the faster pace of change in urban areas.

Perhaps the most important point to be drawn from these examples is that the precise characteristics of the ceramic assemblages are contingent upon the function of the site itself and upon its location in relation to larger towns and cities, centres for craft production, and major trade routes. Thus the Ottoman period ceramics from the remote settlement of Umm al-Jimal were dominated by coarse handmade pottery, a late manifestation of a tradition of village manufacture in Jordan stretching back to the twelfth century. Handmade wares are present at Malka and Hubras to the west and in the Palestinian sites, though all reported more diverse assemblages, including wheelthrown and glazed pottery from urban manufacturing centres in the south of Greater Syria and further afield.[5] Villagers in Iraq and Anatolia were also able to draw upon locally made and imported pottery, the small town of Sardis reporting a surprisingly rich array of glazed pottery, including 'Miletus ware', Iznik and Kütahya wares, and Chinese blue and white porcelain.[6]

The remainder of this chapter examines the archaeological evidence from two perspectives. The first section considers the consumption of two commodities – tobacco and coffee. While the commodities themselves have left little trace in the excavated record, the ceramic items associated with their consumption, particularly tobacco pipes and coffee cups, are crucial to understanding the widespread social and economic changes experienced in the Islamic world from the sixteenth to the early twentieth century. The second case study considers the role of archaeology in the study of colonial occupation – western European and Ottoman – in Morocco, Bahrain, and Greece.

Tobacco, coffee and the importation of glazed pottery into Islamic lands

The origins of tobacco smoking in Europe and in the Islamic world can be pinpointed with reasonable accuracy; the first tobacco plant was brought to Spain from the Americas in 1518. By the first decade of the seventeenth century pipe smoking was already well established in Egypt and Turkey, and, despite periodic attempts at prohibition, it continued to thrive all over the Islamic world. Although other modes of smoking were introduced later – notably the water pipe or *narghile* – the clay pipe was the most widely used. In the Islamic world this took the form of the *chibouk* (or *çibuk*), a three-part arrangement of a clay pipe bowl (other materials such as wood, metal, and meerschaum, a silicate of magnesium, were also employed) attached to a hollow reed or wooden tube with a mouthpiece, commonly made of amber or some other resilient material (Fig. 9.2). A guild of pipe-makers was established in Sofia in 1604, and during the seventeenth century many other production centres sprang up in Greece and Turkey: Istanbul, Varna, Thebes, and Yiannitsa were all celebrated for their pipes.[7]

The significance of this historical information is that it provides a *terminus post quem* of c.1600 for all clay tobacco pipes found on excavations in the Islamic world (the suggestion that such pipes were used in earlier periods for the smoking of hashish is now discredited). The geographical distribution of clay pipes found on excavations and surveys is impressive, covering the Islamic world from Central Asia to North Africa. Excavations have also uncovered ceramic sections from *narghiles*, which indicates that this mode of smoking remained popular in towns and cities. Basic typological distinctions formulated by John Hayes in his study of the Ottoman period ceramics from the Saraçhane excavations in Istanbul have proved useful in establishing the chronological development of pipes in the Middle East.[8] Leaving aside the wealth of stamped, moulded, and incised decoration, two variables should be noted: the colour of the ceramic and the internal volume of the pipe bowl. Dating to the first half of the seventeenth century, the earliest pipes tend to be pale grey, with a small bowl and a long shank (the limited internal volume being probably a reflection of the high cost of tobacco at the time). From the mid-seventeenth century on there is a tendency for these grey pipes to possess larger bowls and shorter shanks. The size of the pipe bowl increases further in the eighteenth century, and this period is also notable for the common use of a burnished red slip applied over the pipe. The technique of red-burnishing remained popular into the nineteenth century.

The ongoing publication of excavated assemblages of tobacco pipes in the Middle East and elsewhere will doubtlessly result in more refined typologies. The likelihood of distinct regional variations in terms of ceramic fabric, pipe shape, and decorative modes present a significant challenge in this respect, as does the possibility that high-quality pipes were traded over considerable distances within the Islamic world. Istanbul was a major centre for pipe production, and it is likely that the inhabitants of Saraçhane mainly relied upon the local indus-tries. Nevertheless, even here there are Bulgarian pipes in the later nineteenth century.[9] Assemblages from provincial sites in Anatolia, Greater Syria, Iraq, or Egypt can be expected to comprise pipes from a wider variety of manufacturing sites. By the eighteenth century many Middle Eastern cities and towns possessed their own workshops. The crudely hand-modelled and undecorated examples recovered from excavations of rural settlements in southern Jordan suggest that, lacking access to the fine clay pipes from Palestine and Syria, some villagers and bedouin improvised their own smoking equipment.[10]

This last point highlights the socio-economic dimensions of tobacco smoking. Widespread cultivation of tobacco in Anatolia and around the eastern Mediterranean during seventeenth century eliminated the initial reliance upon imports from the New World, thus reducing the cost of the habit. This drop in the price of tobacco broadened its accessibility to all groups in society (the widespread distribution of pipes on urban and rural sites confirms this general observation). Social status could, however, be signalled both through the quality of the tobacco and through the materials employed in the *chibouk* itself. While the stems and mouthpieces seldom survive, written descriptions and representa-tions of *chibouks* from the eighteenth and nineteenth centuries attest to the use of amber, gilding, silver inlay, and precious stones. Ceramic pipe bowls could also be very elaborate; a good example is the hefty specimen allegedly owned by 'Ali Pasha (d. 1822), the Ottoman ruler of Ioannina in north-west Greece.[11] Changing social preferences in the last decades of the nineteenth century were to spell the gradual demise of pipe smoking. Although archaeology does not yet provide the means to track this phenomenon, it is clear from textual sources that town and city dwellers across the Ottoman Empire abandoned the pipe in favour of smoking cigarettes.[12] An important social divide opened up at this time, however, with continued pipe smoking in rural areas, and particularly among bedouin. While traditional pipe smoking largely disappeared from the Islamic world, the *narghile* has maintained a social niche in tea houses and public baths to the present day.

The consumption of coffee (*qahwa* in Arabic) can be traced back to Ethiopia in the thirteenth or fourteenth century, and from there it spread to Yemen. By the late fifteenth century coffee was being consumed by Yemeni students in Cairo, and the first reference to the drinking of coffee in Damascus was made in 1534. Despite periodic bans instigated by religious authorities, the practice of drinking coffee soon gained popularity all over the Ottoman Empire and elsewhere in the Islamic world. Coffee was prepared in the homes of the wealthy, but larger quantities were consumed in the coffee houses that proliferated in cities and towns.[13] The cultivation of coffee was initially restricted to the Horn of Africa and Yemen. In the late seventeenth and early eighteenth centuries coffee plantations were established by European merchants in Java, Sri Lanka, Surinam, and Jamaica. The pre-eminent status of coffee as the social drink of the Islamic Middle East was, however, challenged in the eighteenth and nineteenth centuries by tea. Like the transition from pipe smoking to cigarettes, the switch from coffee to tea – at least among educated urbanites – probably reflected a general desire to emulate more 'modern' and 'western' modes of consumption.

Economic historians have provided a detailed picture of the coffee trade from the sixteenth to the early twentieth century, and individual ports such as Mukha (from which the term Mocca derives) in Yemen and Tur in the Sinai peninsula of Egypt have been subjected to detailed study.[14] The product itself has left little trace in the archaeological record. More important in archaeological terms are the objects that were associated with the preparation and serving of coffee, because these items can be used to assess the extent of the geographical and social distribution of coffee drinking. In particular, one may focus on the small glazed pottery cups (known in Arabic as *finjan* and in Turkish as *finçan*), which were used for serving coffee both in coffee houses and in the domestic environment.

Three areas of coffee cup production are particularly significant in the period from the sixteenth to the nineteenth century: south-east China; Kütahya in Anatolia; and the European factories – particularly those in southern France around Marseilles and the Meissen workshop in Dresden – responsible for the manufacture of tin-glazed earthenware and soft-paste and hard-paste porcelain. The seaborne transport of Chinese ceramics to the Islamic world is extensively documented in historical and archaeological sources (chapters 3 and 8). The vigorous trade in porcelain and celadon to the Middle East during the Yuan (1271–1368) and Ming dynasties (1368–1644) also stimulated the production of local imitations in regions such as Turkey, Iran, Syria, Egypt, and Central Asia. Evidently there was no slackening in the volume of imports arriving at Middle Eastern ports in later centuries; for instance a trader for the Dutch East India Company managed to sell 85,165 pieces at the the port of Mukha in 1640. Porcelain coffee cups were transported from the Arabian peninsula to Egypt, Greater Syria, and Turkey by merchants, and in the personal baggage of pilgrims returning from the *hajj* to Mecca and Medina.[15]

Analysis of the Chinese, Thai, and Vietnamese glazed wares at the port of Tur on the coast of the Sinai revealed that the largest concentrations occurred in the sixteenth and seventeenth centuries and consisted mainly of small cups designed for the consumption of coffee or tea. Excavation of a wreck off the coast of Sadana Island in the Red Sea uncovered a cargo comprising Chinese blue and white porcelain (including small cups), spices, and products from Yemen such as coffee and incense. An inscribed copper vessel provided a *terminus post quem* of 1764 for the wreck, while the absence of cannon led the excavators to believe that the boat plied the coastal routes in the Red Sea and did not venture further east into the Indian Ocean.[16] Chinese porcelain coffee cups have also been located on excavations in Greater Syria, though the number of published finds is limited. These vessels tend to occur on ports or urban sites such as the citadel in Damascus, but are very rare in provincial towns and villages. This distribution indicates that Chinese imports retailed for a relatively high price throughout the Ottoman period (but see the example of the porcelain collections in the houses of Douma discussed in chapter 8).[17]

If one reviews archaeological data from other Islamic sites in the Middle East and the Mediterranean, a similar picture emerges of increasing international trade with south-east Asia from the sixteenth to the nineteenth century. Imported bowls and cups from China, Thailand, and Vietnam appear at Julfar, a port abandoned in 1633 as commercial activities moved to Ras al-Khaimah.[18] Along with unglazed wares from East Africa, the Islamic imported wares included imitations of Chinese ceramics produced by Persian potters. Probably produced in the southern province of Kirman and shipped across the Gulf, comparable seventeenth-century Iranian stonepaste wares (some with copies of Chinese characters inscribed on their bases) have been recovered from Qal'at Bahrain. This site also reported a cache of Chinese pottery sherds dating from the thirteenth to the sixteenth century. The Dutch East India company also commissioned Persian potters to produce imitations of Chinese blue and white porcelain, exporting these wares via its trading station in Bandar 'Abbas (known in sources of the time as Gomron or Gombroon) between 1652 and c.1682.[19] In Istanbul, the excavations at Saraçhane brought to light a small assemblage of Chinese wares, mainly dating from the sixteenth and seventeenth centuries. Chinese ceramics are rare in Ottoman Greece, the potteries of Kütahya largely satisfying the demand for high-quality decorative glazed ware.[20] A rather different aesthetic preference can be detected in the Maghrib; the bulk of the surviving Far East imports (principally from private collections rather than recovered during excavations) consists in polychromatic Imari wares, either from the Japanese workshops of Arita or from kilns in China.[21]

With the decline of Iznik in the seventeenth century, Kütahya emerged as the dominant manufacturer in Anatolia. Less sophisticated than Iznik wares in artistic and technical terms, the glazed stonepaste wares of Kütahya remained popular for their bright colours and relatively low cost (Fig. 9.3). Kütahya was particularly active in the export of its wares in the eighteenth century (standards of manufacture slipped noticeably in the nineteenth century). Coffee cups and saucers formed a large part of Kütahya's output, and these had a wide distribution in the eastern Mediterranean, including in Greece, the Balkans, Turkey, Syria, Palestine, and Egypt.[22] What is striking about the potteries of Kütahya is their willingness to adapt to changing tastes even to the extent of plagiarising designs such as the crossed swords motif, used on the bases of Meissen cups during the 'Marcolini' period (1756–73). Meissen coffee cups and Kütahya 'imitations' have been recovered (singly or together) on excavations in urban sites such as Saraçhane, the Damascus citadel, and Acre, as well as in the abandoned village located at Horvet 'Eleq in Israel.[23] In the nineteenth century, the vibrant but rather coarsely made glazed wares from Çanakkale were also exported to Greece, the Balkans, and Greater Syria. Another production centre exporting glazed ware around the eastern Mediterranean was Didymoteichon in northern Greece.[24]

The later export of glazed pottery from Europe to the Middle East can be divided into two main phases. Lasting from the fifteenth to the seventeenth century, the first phase is dominated by glazed earthenware from Italy (largely Maiolica and sgraffito) and lustre-painted vessels from Spain. More significant in the present context is the second phase, dating from the second half of the eighteenth to the early twentieth century. While tin-glazed earthenwares formed part of the export market (particularly from southern France), the major change is the introduction of soft-paste and hard-paste porcelains able to compete in technical and aesthetic terms with Chinese export wares. Industrialised production practices allowed European manufacturers to offer high quality glazed porcelains at relatively low prices (being aided from the 1830s on by the introduction of steam-ships into the Mediterranean). Meissen is the most famous of these ceramic factories, but many others were engaging in this lucrative trade. Recent excavations in the Damascus citadel afford an insight into the volume of French, Italian, German, and British glazed pottery entering the Middle East in the late eighteenth and nineteenth century. Equally important is the fact that these glazed wares were evidently being bought and used by less wealthy individuals: European porcelain cups and other vessels have been located in small towns and villages in Greater Syria, Anatolia, and Greece. The assemblage at Horvet 'Eleq, though unfortunately recovered from unstratified contexts, does point to changing patterns of consumption in the transition from a traditional Palestinian village to an early twentieth-century Zionist settlement populated by European Jews.[25]

As decorated ceramic cups and coffee pots (even those from China) retailed for significantly lower prices than their metalwork counterparts, caution should be exercised in assessing the economic significance of the trade in glazed wares. Nevertheless, their very affordability to a wide spectrum of Islamic society greatly increased their visibility in Islamic society. These items were bought both by private individuals for use at home, but large numbers must have been needed for the coffee houses that became the main source of entertainment for men in cities, small towns, and even villages. This is an issue that has not been considered in specifically archaeological terms, though the spatial distribution of coffee houses in Damascus has been recovered through the analysis of written sources. That the coffee house was also an important social institution in rural areas has been demonstrated by research conducted in Anatolia.[26] The widespread distribution of decorative coffee cups – Turkish, European, and Chinese – can also be attributed, in part, to their use in provincial coffee or tea houses. Bowls, plates, jugs, and other types of imported vessel also played a conspicuous role in domestic environments, being displayed in reception rooms and for the serving of meals. The nineteenth-century English traveller Mary Rogers even records the practice of affixing English 'willow-pattern' plates into the façade of a house owned by a merchant in Nazareth, a decorative mode recalling the *bacini* of medieval churches in Italy and Greece (chapter 8).[27]

The increasing volumes of imports from Europe during the nineteenth century were to have profound implications for the Islamic Middle East. Native industries often struggled to compete with cheap mass-produced imports, and the economies of many regions were reduced to the status of exporters of raw materials, with their own markets increasingly dominated by imported textiles, glass, metalwork, and glazed pottery. Where earlier phases of imported ceramics from China had actually stimulated the creativity of Islamic potters (who were also able to undercut the high prices of imported stonewares and porcelains), the low unit cost of European porcelains created an entirely different challenge. Many indigenous traditions of glazed pottery production were eradicated in the second half of the nineteenth century. It would be a mistake, however, to assert that this was a uniform phenomenon; some regions continued to support vigorous local manufacturing traditions, not just in glazed wares but also in a wide range of other crafts (many of which endure to the present).[28] A distinction should also be drawn between the production of glazed and unglazed ceramics, the latter clearly being more successful in weathering the economic challenges of the late nineteenth and twentieth century. For instance while the glazed pottery workshops of Greater Syria seem to have largely disappeared, centres on the Palestine coast such as Gaza – specialising in a type of reduction-fired (that is, grey bodied) unglazed ceramic – prospered. Recent excavations of late Ottoman contexts in Jordan and Israel illustrate the existence of considerable inter-regional trade of 'Gaza ware' jars (Fig. 9.4).[29]

The archaeology of colonisation

The period from the fifteenth to the nineteenth century is interesting for the evidence it provides on two types of colonisation: first, the drive by European countries to establish territories in Islamic lands; and, second, the western expansion of the Ottoman Empire into Greece, the Balkans, Hungary, and Austria.[30] The former theme is explored in relation to the Portuguese colonial expansion of the fifteenth and sixteenth century, and the latter through an examination of 'post-Byzantine' archaeology in Greece. Although the historical circumstances differ, the two phenomena are linked by the fact that, for the affected regions, they represent a radical reorientation in socio-cultural and economic life. In each case there is a shift in the religious affiliation of the political elite, though this need not have any long-term impact upon the confessional allegiances of the subject population. As with the transition from late antiquity to early Islam (chapter 2), the changing architecture, urban topography, practices of land exploitation, and material culture can all be examined archaeologically. It is to be hoped that future work will examine the most recent (and, in archaeological terms, the most neglected) phases of history in the Islamic world. To take Greater Syria as an example, the remains of Napoleonic trenches have been recovered from 'Akko (Acre), and a few sites such as Ti'innik, Kabri, 'Ayn Karim, Malka and Hubras uncovered material spanning the end of Ottoman rule and the British Mandate in Palestine and Transjordan (1920/22–48). As yet, very little archaeological work has been undertaken on the transition from the Mandate to the states of Jordan and Israel in 1946 and 1948 respectively.[31]

The growth of Portugal as a maritime power can be traced from the fifteenth century. The first colonial incursions were to the south, along the coast of Morocco; under the joint command of King John I (r. 1385–1433) and of Prince Henry the Navigator, the Portuguese succeeded in capturing the important coastal settlement of Sebta (Ceuta) in 1415. After a failed attempt to take Tangier in 1437, the next military expedition led to the capture of Qasr al-Saghir in 1458. The new Portuguese force in the fortified settlement endured a heavy siege conducted by the Marinid ruler of Morocco in 1459. The Portuguese governor of Qasr al-Saghir, Dom Duarte, launched raids into the interior in later years, and later naval expeditions led to the capture of the Atlantic port of Arzila and of the nearby city of Tangier in 1471. This colonial phase in North Africa was of relatively short duration, however; despite the investment by Manuel I (r. 1495–1521), the increasingly heavy cost of defending these colonies persuaded his son, John III (r. 1521–54), to abandon the project. Qasr al-Saghir was evacuated by Portuguese civilians and troops in 1550.[32]

The systematic excavation of the fortifications and settlement of Qasr al-Saghir permits an insight into the changing material culture of a site as it passed from Islamic to Portuguese occupation (it was not reoccupied after 1550). This change of ownership had profound repercussions on all aspects of the site. Relevant to the present discussion are the last phase of Islamic occupation (c.1100–1458) and the Portuguese phase (1458–1550). The archaeology suggests further divisions, the most prosperous part of the Islamic phase lasting from c.1350 to the time of the Portuguese conquest of Ceuta in 1415. The Portuguese phase can be divided into two, the first part representing the use of the site largely as a military outpost (1458-c.1495) and the second (c.1495–1550) the growth of Qasr al-Saghir as a functioning colony. Like Qal'at Bahrain (see below), the Portuguese presence is immediately obvious in the design of the fortifications. The new military force adapted the existing walls and gates, closing off the south-west (Fez) gate and strengthening the other two. The north-west (sea) gate was provided with a citadel and a covered passage (couraca), which allowed access to the sea in times of siege. Inside the walls, the most obvious transformations occurred in the centre, with the replacement of the congregational mosque by the Church of Santa Maria da Misericordia (a second church, dedicated to St Sebastian, was located on the main street leading to the Ceuta gate). Other municipal structures were established in this central zone around the main plaza: an assembly hall directly south of the citadel, and what may be a prison or arsenal replacing the Islamic bathhouse (Fig. 9.5 a and b).

More subtle, but equally significant changes are apparent in the public spaces and houses. The emphasis of the houses of Qasr al-Saghir, in common with that of many Islamic cities in North Africa, was internal: houses were centered around a porticoed courtyard. In the absence of windows on the exterior walls (at least at street level), the notion of privacy was manifested in the bent entranceway that led from the street to the courtyard. While the houses varied in their architectural ambition, many were notable for the quality of their details (such as the tiled floors) and for the presence of latrines and effective drainage. After the Portuguese occupation, the Islamic houses were gradually replaced by a vernacular architecture reflecting the social values of the new inhabitants. The internal planning of the houses changed: an axial arrangement was now leading from the main entrance into public rooms, more private areas being located at the back. Important, too, was the stress upon the façade, and particularly upon the monumental doorways. The excavators also noted a greater concern with public space including the central plaza, and the decorative paving of the main streets. Commercial and industrial premises coexisted with dwellings (a feature seen in contemporary European towns). Both Islamic and Portuguese phases presented relatively diverse assemblages, though it is clear that the inhabitants of the Portuguese phase (particularly after c.1495) were better connected to international markets. While the majority of the objects from Islamic Qasr al-Saghir came from manufacturing centres in Morocco or southern Spain, the assemblages from the Portuguese occupation comprise decorated Maiolica and lustre from Spain, as well as glazed jars from northern Europe (perhaps Germany). The few pieces of Chinese porcelain probably found their way to Qasr al-Saghir in the years following the establishment of mercantile contacts between Portugal and China in 1514.[33]

In 1507 the Portuguese claimed overlordship of Hormuz, requiring the amir to pay an annual tribute. Although the precise sequence of events is uncertain, it would appear that the Portuguese, in an attempt to recover revenues owed to Hormuz by Badr al-Din, governor of Bahrain, launched unsuccessful attacks against Qal'at Bahrain in 1521 and 1529. In 1559, a later governor of Bahrain, Murad Shah, allied himself with the amirate of Hormuz and with the Portuguese in order to repel an Ottoman attack. Two years later, Murad ordered the delivery of stone from the quarries of Jidda Island for the reconstruction of the fort (a task undertaken in 1586 by the Portuguese engineer Inofre de Carvalho). The exca-vation of the site (known in published reports as the 'Hormuzi-Portuguese fort') revealed three phases of construction. It is likely that the first fort on the site is the one described in historical sources of c.1518, and that the second represents adaptations made by Badr al-Din in preparation for the Portuguese attack in 1529. The first phase consisted of an irregular pentagonal plan, with a curtain wall supplemented by a dry moat. This simple enclosure was supplemented in the second phase by an enlargement of the fort to the east. Wide boulevards were constructed inside the walls to facilitate the use of artillery (these features also provided extra buttressing for the curtain wall and corner towers against enemy cannon fire).[34]

The construction techniques employed in the second phase were Persian in character and contrast with the European techniques employed in the third phase (Fig. 9.6). Making use of Genoese military technology, this massive construction encased the earlier fort, retaining the basic plan established in the second phase. The gap between the older curtain wall and the new outer wall allowed for the construction of casemates, and massive bastions were added to the north-west, south-west and south corners of the plan. The loopholes in the walls were calculated to provide complete coverage of musket fire over the areas surrounding the fort. Additional work was done to widen the boulevards, presumably for the large Portuguese cannon. Impressive though all of this work undoubtedly is, the Portuguese did not benefit greatly from their new fort; the Safavid rulers of Iran took Bahrain in 1602 and erected a new fort at Arad, on the nearby island of Muharraq. The Portuguese also appear to have committed a tactical blunder in renovating the fort at Qal'at Bahrain, because the silting up of the channel prevented access for the deep-draft European ships (which had to rely upon the older site of Manama to the west).

If one is to assess the portable artefacts from the settlements of Qal'at Bahrain, a different picture emerges from that presented by Qasr al-Saghir. Prior to the construction of the sixteenth-century fort, the earlier phase of occupation can be attributed to the establishment of a trading station c.1250 by a petty dynasty from the Iranian region of Fars. Originally reusing the third/fourth-century *qasr* as a warehouse, the settlement expanded to form a town (part of which lies underneath the Hormuzi–Portuguese fort, the remainder being razed to eliminate cover which could have been exploited by a hostile force). The contrast between the material culture from this earlier port and the sixteenth-century occupation of the fort is striking. The coins from the earlier phase included Persian issues of the second half of the thirteenth century and twenty-three copper coins of the Tang and Sung dynasties. The ceramics also confirmed the existence of active commercial links with China, India, and Iran during the thirteenth and fourteenth centuries.[35] While some porcelain and Persian stonepaste wares of the sixteenth century were reported, the material record from this second phase, and particularly from the excavated contexts inside the fort, was relatively sparse. Another site associated with Portuguese military and economic expansion, Kilwa Island on the East African coast, also registered little evidence of European presence among the excavated finds (though the presence of Chinese wares of the sixteenth century and later periods indicates a continued participation in long-distance maritime trade).[36] The situation at Qal'at Bahrain is plausibly explained by the changing function of the site, from hosting a largely civilian population engaged in trade to hosting one primarily focused on defence. Also significant is the relocation of commercial activity away from the silted port of Qal'at Bahrain to sites better suited to receive European maritime traffic.

The Ottoman sultans were already wielding their authority in mainland Greece prior to the fall of Constantinople in 1453 and of the despotate of the Morea (Peloponnese) in 1461. Full-scale colonial expansion occurred, however, from the second half of the fifteenth century, and the Ottomans held their Greek territories for most of the period up to the Greek war of independence in the 1820s (Fig. 9.7). Their main competitor for the control of southern Greece was the Republic of Venice, and both Turks and Venetians signalled their authority through the construction of fortifications and monumental architecture (as can be seen today in coastal towns such as Nafplio, Monemvasia, Methoni, Koroni, and Navarino on the Peloponnese, and Nafpaktos on the northern shore of the Gulf of Corinth). Venice reasserted its control of southern Greece in the 1680s, but was forced to relinquish these territories to the Turks after 1699. Within the towns themselves, Ottoman authority was given its most conspicuous form through the construction of the characteristic mosques, with their domed prayer halls and tall, pencil-like minarets. Many of these survive to the present (usually without their minarets), though only the mosques of Thrace in the north-east of Greece retain their original function as places of Muslim worship. An unobtrusive but equally important contribution to the urban infrastructure was the installation of fountains and bathhouses fed by spring water. In the case of Nafpaktos (chapter 5), the springs were located in the walled town, but in other places such as Nafplio and the Ottoman citadel of Navarino (Anavarin-i Cedid) the springs were more distant and required the construction of aqueducts and channels.[37]

The Ottoman occupation of Greece brought with it demographic changes; a Turkish administrative elite established itself in the towns, castles and country estates (*çiftliks*) and was supported by a military contingent. In addition to Sunni Islam, one also finds traces of less orthodox practices, particularly of the Bekhtashi Order, which was much favoured by the Janissary corps; for instance two eighteenth-century fountains in Nafplio contain inscriptions with Bekhtashi connotations suggesting that the town once contained dervish lodges (*tekkes*) run by the order (Fig. 9.8).[38] The Ottoman authorities also settled populations of Albanians and Turkomans into regions of Greece, though in some ways this practice only continued the policies adopted in mainland Greece by the Byzantine Empire. Thus, in common with the situation of the preceding centuries of Byzantine, Frankish, and Venetian rule, Ottoman Greece would have been ethnically, linguistically, and confessionally heterogenous. Ottoman cadastral records and the evidence provided by travellers to Greece suggest that the agrarian environment was made up of relatively 'mono-cultural' – Greek, Albanian (*Arvanites*), or Turkish – villages. It has proved difficult, however, to distinguish these different cultural/ethnic groups in the material record recovered from regional surveys in Greece. Another significant change to the countryside of Ottoman Greece was the introduction of new crops, principally cotton, maize, and tobacco.[39]

In the countryside, the 'post-Byzantine' phase (which encompassed Venetian and Ottoman rule as well as the transition to the modern state of Greece) has been approached through regional surveys – particularly in Cyprus and the Peloponnese – and through the study of ceramics. Recent archaeological work is challenging long-held notions of demographic decline during the Ottoman period and of Greek peasantry leaving the land. For instance the correlation of textual evidence (from *daftars*) and field surveys in the southwest Peloponnese indicates a long-term stability of non-Muslim population levels, except during the Ottoman–Venetian wars of the late seventeenth and early eighteenth centuries. The cause of depopulation at that time may have been economic, as the new practice of tax-farming placed undue hardship upon those who cultivated the land. In the Argolid (north-west Peloponnese) the Ottoman–Venetian wars also seem to have resulted in the neglect of the agricultural sector, although written sources indicate that there was a demographic upsurge from the mid-eighteenth until the early nineteenth century. That this is not reflected in the field surveys may reflect problems in identifying the diagnostic ceramics of this period.

Archaeologically, the most obvious transformation of rural areas during Ottoman rule was the creation of çiftliks. These agricultural estates represented an important component of the landscape of fertile regions such as the plains of Thessaly in central Greece, and many of these structures endured into the early twentieth century. The çiftlik of Hasan Aga near Navarino in south-west Morea provides relatively plentiful textual and archaeological information on this phenomenon. The estate of Hasan Aga appears in Venetian and Ottoman cadastral records of c.1700 and 1716 respectively, as well as in the account of the traveller William Gell (d. 1836) and in the French Expédition scientifique de Morée (started in 1829). This general dating was confirmed by the ceramics gathered from the site. Reconnaissance of the hilltop site revealed a retaining wall surrounding an area of about four hectares and having other walls and buildings within. The most important building in the enclosure was a two-storey tower (possibly equipped with gun slits), which invites comparisons with the much grander tower, of the late eighteenth-century 'Hasan Pasha tower', of a çiftlik on the plain of Troy in Turkey.[40]

An increasing cultural orientation towards Istanbul and Anatolia is also suggested by the Ottoman period ceramics gathered in surveys and excavations in southern Greece. Leaving aside the continuation of earlier, local ceramic traditions, glazed and unglazed, the Ottoman period is notable for the introduction of tobacco pipes, of Anatolian glazed wares from Iznik, Kütahya and Çanakkale, and of the pottery of Didymoteichon in the northern Greek province of Thrace. By the early nineteenth century European porcelains, including transfer-printed 'willow-pattern' ware, made their appearance in mainland Greece. Areas under Venetian control or with stronger commercial links with the west also made use of Italian Maiolica and sgraffito wares. This latter phenomenon has been noted in excavations and surveys conducted in Cyprus, Crete, and Butrint in Albania. As a general rule, the extent and range of imported ware in a rural area depended upon environmental factors and proximity to major centres of commerce. For instance the mountainous region of Aetolia appears to have enjoyed little access to imported glazed ware, even though Ottoman daftars clearly indicate that the area was settled with numerous villages.[41]

To conclude this section, one can question the extent to which the 'colonial' archaeology presented above is significantly different from the archaeology of earlier phases of occupation (best exemplified by the Frankish settlement of the crusader states of the Middle East – though one could also consider the Norman conquest of Sicily or the Spanish Reconquista). Certainly there are aspects of the Portuguese and Ottoman examples that are peculiar to their times. The defensive architecture of the settlements in Morocco and Bahrain exhibit obvious adaptations to the use of cannon and hand-held firearms. Secondly, the material culture manifested with Qasr al-Saghir, particularly in the second 'Portuguese' phase, represents the incorporation of this site into a new network of international trade, which encompassed northern Europe and China. While international trade had obviously been a feature of the economies both of the Islamic world and of Europe in earlier periods, changes from the late fifteenth century in maritime routes, ship design, and navigation clearly affected the volume of traffic and the nationalities of the principal actors. Most important was the ability of European mariners and merchants to bypass the Middle Eastern mediators of trade with south-east Asia. As one turns to post-Byzantine Greece, there is evidence for a reorientation of trade in luxury goods, first towards Italy and then towards the Ottoman heartland of Anatolia. This consumption of imported manufactured goods is, in part, the reciprocal dimension of the flow of cash crops – particularly cotton and tobacco – from rural Greece. The archaeology of the eighteenth and nineteenth centuries in the eastern Mediterranean also points to the increasing role of European industry in the economies and cultural life of the Ottoman regions.

Conversely, the archaeological evidence exhibits areas of continuity with earlier practices. The evidence for international trade at sites such as Qasr al-Saghir or Qal'at Bahrain is hardly new (and indeed, in the latter case, the most active economic phase preceded the Hormuzi–Portuguese fort). The situation in Greece prompts similar questions, as the Ottoman occupation was part of a series of colonial periods, including the Venetian administration and the Frankish takeover in the aftermath of the Fourth Crusade in 1204. Like the Frankish and Venetian lords, the Ottomans constructed or renovated castles in their Greek provinces. Their approach to the urban environment finds considerable parallels to the Venetian occupation in their construction of monumental religious architecture, though the Turkish authorities probably devoted greater attention to the provision of water. This latter point may be partly explained by the Muslim requirement for ritual cleanliness (a point emphasised by the ubiquitous presence of Ottoman bathhouses in Greek towns).

Taking a broader perspective, the establishment of the çiftliks in Greece and elsewhere in the Ottoman Empire can be compared to that of the eighth-century qusur of Greater Syria and Iraq, in that they functioned as elite residences controlling areas of cultivated land. Other fruitful comparisons might be drawn with the munya of Umayyad Spain (chapter 5), in that they represent the imposition of a Muslim elite onto a largely Christian agrarian landscape.[42] If one looks to the Frankish colonial settlement of the crusader kingdom of Jerusalem, points of similarity and difference emerge. While the major urban centres and the large castles were the strongholds of crusader power, recent research indicates that Frankish settlers established villages equipped with churches in rural Palestine. Just as the churches retain Romanesque or Gothic characteristics of their European counterparts, so the wealthier colonists also brought with them the practice of constructing 'manor houses'. Examples of these substantial residential buildings have been identified at sites such as Khirbat al-Lawza and Khirbat Salman.[43] Where the *çiftliks* of Greece transplanted an Anatolian model into a predominantly Christian rural environment, the pattern of Frankish settlement in the kingdom of Jerusalem appeared to follow a different course. Franks seem to have avoided areas occupied by Muslim villages, favouring those populated by Syrian Christians (even though the indigenous Christians were not of the Latin church). In other words, where the Ottomans imposed themselves into a Christian setting, the picture gained from the kingdom of Jerusalem suggests a degree of interaction between western and eastern Christians, the Muslim population being segregated from this process of assimilation.

Notes

1 For general surveys of the archaeology of this period, see Lynda Carroll in Orser, ed. (2002), 406–7; Baram and Carroll, eds (2000); Yenisehiroglu (2005).
2 Petersen (2001); Brun (2005), 619–24.
3 Hayes (1992), 233–395; François (2002) and (2008); Edelstein and Avissar (1997).
4 Crane (1987) and (1988); François (2001); Simpson (1997); De Vries (1998); Ziadeh (1995); Walker (2005). See also Milwright (2000), 191–3, table 1; McQuitty (2001).
5 De Vries (1998), 215–18 and notes; Walker (2005), 82–3.
6 Crane (1987), 49–56; François (2002); Simpson (1997).
7 Robinson (1985), 149–57; Simpson (1995b).
8 Hayes (1992), 233–395.
9 Hayes (1980). Also Hayes (1992), 391–5.
10 Milwright (2000), 199–200.
11 Robinson (1985), 55–6, pls 39, 44c, 45a and b.
12 Baram (2000), 152. For an eye-witness account of the decline of pipe-manufacturing in late nineteenth-century Damascus, see Qasimi, Qasimi and al-Azem (1960), 330.
13 Van Arendonk (1973); Marino (1995); Rafeq (2001), 127–32.
14 Brouwer (2001); Kawatoko (2001). Also other contributions in Tuchscherer, ed. (2001).
15 Brouwer (2001), 282–3; Establet and Pascual (2001), 147–9.
16 Kawatoko (2001), 55–7, figs 5 and 6; Kawatoko (2005), 853–4; Ward (2000), 186, figs 7.1 and 7.2. Chinese wares were also found on an early eighteenth-century wreck near Sharm al-Shaykh; see Raban (1971).
17 Milwright (2000), 197, table 1. See also Carswell (1972); Carswell (2000), 67–8.
18 Hansmann (1985), 25–47.
19 Volker (1971), 113–16, pl. 25; Carswell (2000), 150; Frifelt (2001), 131–40.
20 Hayes (1992), 261–4; Vroom (2003), 176.

21 Erzini and Vernoit, forthcoming.
22 Milwright (2000), 198; Vroom (2007), 84–6.
23 Hayes (1992), pl. 44b; Boas (2000), 554, fig. 6; François (2002); Edelstein and Avissar (1997), colour pl. III.4; Milwright (2008b). For a survey of the ceramics of Kütahya, see Altun, Carswell and Öney (1991).
24 On these production centres, see Altun, Carswell and Öney (1991), 103–43; Bakirtzis (1980). See also Hayes (1992), 268–92; Vroom (2003), 180–4.
25 Boas (2000); Milwright (2008b); François (2002).
26 Beeley (1970). These results are also discussed in Vroom (2007), 86–9.
27 Quoted in Milwright (2003), 102–3.
28 For historical perspectives on manufacturing in Turkey in this period, see Quataert, ed. (1994), 87–121.
29 Walker (2005), 83–4. Also Milwright (2000), 196. The fundamental work on pottery production at Gaza remains Gatt (1885).
30 The study of the material culture of the Ottoman period in the Balkans has, until recently, largely focused on monumental architecture – on which see Kiel (1990) – and the traditional vernacular building and crafts. For a survey of archaeological research in Bulgaria, see Guionova (2005).
31 For references, see Milwright (2000), 192–6; Walker (2005). For the excavation of military trenching employed in 1948, see Toombs (1985), 6–14.
32 Redman (1986). For a brief summary of the results, see Orser, ed. (2002), 396–8.
33 Redman (1986), 102–36, 190–216.
34 Kervran, Hiebert and Rouguelle (2005), 345–412; also Frifelt (2001). On the archaeology of the *Gereza* on Kilwa island (thought to be the site of the early sixteenth-century Portuguese fort of Sant'Iago), see Chittick (1974), 1: 219–23, pls 90–6.
35 Frifelt (2001), 62–141, 166–7; Kervran, Hiebert and Rouguelle (2005), 297–328, 378–88.
36 Chittick (1974), 2: 312–13. See also Chittick (1984), 70–1.
37 Zarinebaf, Bennet and Davis (2005), 241–57.
38 Milwright and Baboula (2009), 232–4.
39 Jameson, Runnels, and van Andel (1994), 404–14; Stedman (1996); Davis, ed. (1998), 245–61; Sutton, ed. (2000); Zarinebaf, Bennet and Davis (2005). On the agricultural practices in Ottoman Cyprus, see Given (2000).
40 Susan Alcock in Davis (1998), 262–66. Also Zarinebaf, Bennet and Davis (2005), 193–209.
41 Vroom (2003), 164–227; Vroom (2007), 88.
42 Sauvaget (1967); Anderson (2007).
43 Ellenblum (1998). See also Ellenblum (2007), 103–86.

10

Conclusion

It should be known that many weak-minded persons in cities hope to discover property under the surface of the earth and to make some profit from it. They believe that all the property of the nations of the past was stored underground and sealed with magic talismans. These seals, they believe, can be broken only by those who chance upon the [necessary] knowledge and can offer the proper incense, prayers, and sacrifices to break them.[1]

This admonition forms part of a chapter entitled 'Trying to make money from buried and other treasures is not a natural way of making a living', in Ibn Khaldun's famous sociological treatise al-Muqaddima (The Prolegomenon). There is no mistaking Ibn Khaldun's disdain for the superstitious practices of treasure hunters. Although his own reconstruction of the past relied upon texts – chronicles, biographies, geographical encyclopaedias, religious and legal scholarship, and archival sources – he was not insensitive to the material world around him and to the ways in which the human environment had shaped the course of history. Thus he interests himself in the diverse characteristics of settlements, the rise and fall of civilisations, and the crafts practised by the inhabitants of urban and rural areas. Given the extraordinary range of his interests, it is tempting to speculate upon how he might have viewed the activities of modern archaeologists. Would he have judged archaeology to be a legitimate avenue of research into earlier centuries, or would he have dismissed it as little more than treasure hunting conducted by the 'weak-minded'?

If such speculation appears frivolous, it is intended to introduce a more serious question: to what extent has Islamic archaeology established itself as an independent form of historical inquiry? Just as Ibn Khaldun expressed his low opinion of those who sought out buried property, some modern historians have doubted the usefulness of archaeology as a tool in the study of the Islamic past. One does not have to search far to find reasons for supporting this position. Apart from the substantial number of incompletely published projects, one must also contend with the sometimes lamentable quality of the excavations of Islamic occupation levels and of their subsequent publication. This is particularly a feature of the late nineteenth and early twentieth century, although even today there are excavation directors who pay little attention to the upper layers of sites, in their eagerness to recover material from more ancient phases. As noted in the introduction, the highly variable quality of the published data clearly hampers attempts to draw out wider temporal or spatial phenomena that might be of value for Islamic historians and art historians, as well as for archaeologists working in other periods and regions. Another significant limitation in this respect is the uneven geographical coverage of the excavations and surveys across the Islamic world. Lastly, criticism has been leveled at archaeologists for their sometimes uncritical employment of primary written sources and for their habit of drawing unwarranted or overly ambitious inferences from methodologically contentious fieldwork.[2]

These problems should not be minimised, and for the foreseeable future there is no likelihood that archaeology will rival the geographical scope and sheer detail of the account provided by modern historians working with the textual record of the Islamic world. Furthermore, even when conducted to the highest standards, excavations and field surveys are never going to replace certain types of information available in the written sources. For instance, discussing the important recovery of the eighth-century residence of the Abbasid family at Humayma in southern Jordan, Chase Robinson observes that the buildings and portable artefacts are unlikely to provide new evidence concerning the crucial events leading up to the coup of 749–50, which toppled the Umayyad caliphate and brought the Abbasids to power.[3] In other words, allowing for a few exceptional finds, archaeology is not a suitable method for the study of short-term actions and individual decisions. These issues continue to be the domain of the political historian. That said, there are many ways in which archaeology can contribute to the study of the Islamic past by addressing lacunae in the primary written sources, by complementing conclusions formulated by historians, and by elaborating new interpretive models.[4] Many examples have been discussed in this book, and in the following paragraphs I will highlight some of the principal themes.

One of the most important contributions of archaeology is its ability to identify processes that occur over extended time periods. For instance, it is now apparent that cities and towns of the Middle East and North Africa underwent significant changes – cultural, administrative, economic, demographic, and architectural – in the two centuries prior to the Islamic conquests. Of course, some aspects of these changes can be recovered from the textual record, but archaeology is able to lend a tangible quality to this question by demonstrating such things as the precise evolution of the street plans, the emergence of new ceramic wares, or the changing roles performed by individual buildings. As one charts these developments from site to site, it becomes evident that the erosion of the orthogonally planned 'classical' cities occurred at different rates and that, even under Islamic rule, Hellenistic principles of urban design could be revived (though with limited long-term success). Archaeology also adds to our understanding of the diversity of urban forms in late antiquity, from the fortified cities of the Sasanian Empire to the looser 'organic' configurations of smaller towns in regions as diverse as Greater Syria, the Arabian peninsula, and North Africa.

Long-term processes have also been tracked in rural environments. Allowing for methodological problems related to the dating of domestic architecture, hydraulic features, and unglazed ceramics, regional surveys still represent the best means to assess fluctuations in population and land use. Increasingly scholars are finding evidence for continuity between the late antique and the early Islamic centuries, both in terms of settlement patterns and in terms of practices of cultivation. In some cases canal systems declined after the ninth century, while in others (for instance in Andalus) the introduction of new forms of irrigation technology after the Islamic conquest benefited the rural economy for centuries after. By reviewing the evidence for settlement in later periods, it becomes evident that rural prosperity was contingent upon a range of factors, some having short-term impact (for instance political instability, wars, or periods of disease and famine), and others more lasting effects (for instance environmental change, or proximity to major roads or urban centres).[5] Conversely, the cultivation and processing of expensive commodities like sugar were particularly vulnerable to external factors and could be extinguished by a reduction in state investment or by competition from more efficient producers. In general, the paucity of textual sources dealing with the economic and social life of villages makes it fertile ground for archaeological study. Irrigation networks, field systems, crop use, animal husbandry, domestic life, rural crafts, diet, disease, and burial practices are some of the areas which have been illuminated by excavations and surveys.

Turning to the urban environment after the tenth century, excavations have provided some vital clues concerning the everyday lives of town and city dwellers. While some historians have sought to recover information concerning the activities and beliefs of the poorer classes of pre-modern Islamic urban society, the inevitable reliance upon the writings of the educated, literate elite places constraints upon this field of inquiry.[6] In this context it is easy to appreciate the value of excavations in less affluent areas of towns and cities. For instance the houses of 'Fustat-C' stand in contrast to the richer domestic architecture exposed elsewhere in the city. Nevertheless, the finds from 'Fustat-C' were notable for the presence of imported ceramics and relatively expensive embroidered textiles and ornamented leather. One could hardly say that the day-to-day lives of the wealthier city dwellers are exhaustively documented in the available written records (with a few exceptions such as the Jewish community of the Egyptian capital), and many questions are best approached through archaeology. Excavations are an excellent means to study the water supply and sanitation systems both in urban environments and in palatial complexes.

It would be unwise, however, to emphasise the independence of archaeology from the text-based historical record. As suggested above, archaeology often functions as a complementary discipline contributing to a more nuanced picture of the Islamic past. To return to the question of the transition to Islamic rule, the archaeological record from the seventh century provides intriguing evidence that the Muslim community took some time to find appropriate ways to express its core values both in the public sphere, through monumental inscriptions, coins, papyri, and buildings, and in the private sphere, for example through inscribed grave markers and portable artefacts. Equally important in this respect is the much larger body of archaeological data illustrating the relatively limited impact which the imposition of the new Muslim elite had on the everyday lives of the indigenous religious communities of the nascent Islamic Empire. Thus archaeology does not overturn the historical account of the seventh century, but it does add significant perspectives, which can aid in the evaluation of this formative phase of Islamic history.

The study of religious practice has also benefited from archaeological research. While the earliest history of the mosque in the seventh century still relies upon written descriptions, the relative abundance of surviving structures from the eighth and ninth centuries allows for a deeper consideration of questions of morphology, materials of construction, and integration of the congregational mosque (and of the *dar al-imara*) into the urban environment. Equally significant is the way in which archaeological techniques can be employed in the study of the evolution of a mosque over the course of decades or centuries, as it adapted to the changing requirements of the Muslim community it served. These issues are also pertinent to the study of places of worship constructed by non-Muslim populations within the Islamic world. For instance the study of the churches and synagogues of Greater Syria illustrates the continued expenditure of Christian and Jewish communities upon construction work, repairs, and the laying of elegant mosaic pavements. Just as the church mosaics can reveal divergences from orthodox Christian opinion (for example in the placing of crosses on a floor mosaic), the examination of Muslim cemeteries demonstrates the gulf which often existed between the strictures of Islamic law and local practice. In addition to displays above ground – gravemarkers and mausolea – excavators have noted less conspicuous deviations occurring beneath the ground; these include the presence of grave goods, unusual orientations of the body, and even secondary burial.

Economic historians have employed a wide range of textual sources in the analysis of international trading systems; for instance impressive results have come from the correlation of mercantile archives in Italy, the Cairo *Geniza*, and the more sparse group of Islamic official records. While archaeology is less equipped to recover the sheer variety of traded commodities mentioned in these sources – organic items being especially prone to decay – excavations of ship-wrecks, ports, towns, and cities provide many avenues of interpretation. Exca-vations of ports on the Persian Gulf, Red Sea, and East African coast illustrate the contribution of maritime trade to the economic development of the Islamic world. Commerce with China is, of course, the most famous aspect of this activity, though extensive contacts with the Indian subcontinent are apparent from ceramics excavated in the Persian Gulf and from resist-dyed fabrics recovered from Quseir and Fustat. Other bodies of data such as the coin hoards of western Russia, of the Baltic states, and of Scandinavia illuminate long-term economic contacts that are only minimally addressed in contemporary written sources. It might be thought that the relative abundance of archival data and of other written sources after the sixteenth century would negate the value of excavations and surveys, but this is contradicted by recent advances in the field of Ottoman archaeology. Perhaps most interesting is the increasing presence of new commodities – principally tobacco, coffee, and tea – and the glazed porce-lains and clay pipes used to consume them in the Middle East, North Africa, and the Balkans. Archaeology provides an important confirmation of the degree to which industrially manufactured goods from Europe dominated the markets of much of the Islamic world in the nineteenth and early twentieth centuries.

Similar points can be made concerning the archaeological study of crafts and industry. Excavations of industrial areas allow for a consideration of the totality of manufacturing rather than privileging the most aesthetically engaging artefacts (as often happens in museum displays devoted to Islamic art). As might be expected, artisans often had to direct much of their energy to the production of mundane but essential items such as tools, storage vessels, cooking pots, lamps, or drainage pipes. Analysis of the wider environment helps to identify the critical natural resources (clay deposits, metal ores, fuel, and so on) and the transport infrastructure employed to supply bulk commodities to the workshops of these industrial zones. Where urban manufacturing tended to be male-oriented, highly specialised, and commercially driven, different dynamics are apparent in rural crafts. Models drawn from ethnographic research suggest localised craft traditions often passed through families from mother to daughter, most of this activity probably being centred upon their own domestic require-ments rather than upon the market place.

Already responsible for many remarkable discoveries, Islamic archaeology is still in its relatively early stages of development. Its true potential has yet to be realised. Clearly one requirement is the need for further fieldwork; many parts of the Islamic world are sparsely covered by existing archaeological research, while much remains to be done in even relatively well trodden regions like Greater

Syria and the Iberian peninsula. New analytical techniques – often developed in other fields of research – allow archaeologists to ask fresh questions about their material, and thus to expand upon our understanding of past societies in the Islamic world. Each new publication represents another tessera within a larger mosaic, and it is worth noting in this context just how much research time (and monetary expense) is often distilled into a few pages of a book or scholarly journal. This is not, however, a question of simply adding more site reports and catalogues of finds to the existing assemblage of publications; Islamic archaeology must also engage in a fuller dialogue with other historical disciplines. Archaeologists need to draw together the existing data from specific regions and periods in order to write synthetic accounts that are accessible to the lay reader. Projects should continue the existing trend towards collaboration among specialists, both on site and in post-excavation analysis. The recent advances in the field of historical archaeology show how much can be gained from the careful correlation of material evidence with primary written sources. Given that most archaeologists do not possess the linguistic skills to exploit fully the Arabic, Persian, Turkish, and other textual traditions of the pre-modern Islamic world, it would be fruitful to encourage greater involvement from Islamic historians in the setting of initial research goals and in the subsequent interpretation of the evidence. Lastly, archaeology also represents a collaboration between archaeologists and the inhabitants of the countries in which the excavated sites are located. Fostering links both at an institutional and at a human level, archaeology has the potential to enrich the lives of all those involved in it – though the archaeologists themselves should remain ever mindful of the responsibility they owe to the cultural heritage of the countries in which they are privileged to work.

Notes

1 Ibn Khaldun (1958), 2: 319.
2 For instance, see comments in Morony (1994) and Johns (2003), 411–12.
3 Robinson (2003b), 53. For the finds from Humayma, see Foote (1999).
4 A spirited call for medieval archaeology to free itself from the 'tyranny' of the textual record is given in Champion (1990).
5 The plain of Balqa' in Jordan has been productively approached from the perspective of the 'food systems' operating in different periods of its history. See LaBianca (1990).
6 An excellent example of this approach to the written record is Shoshan (1993).

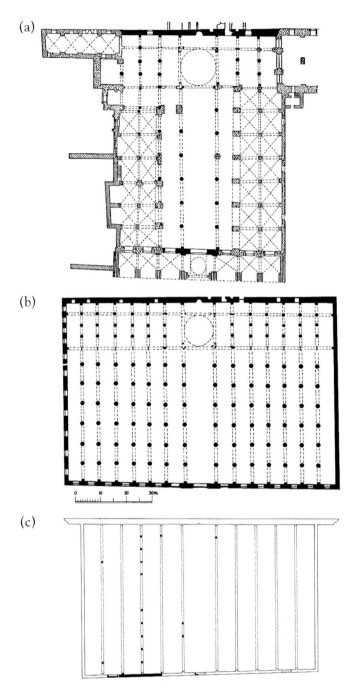

Figure 6.1 (a) Plan of the Aqsa mosque, Jerusalem (after Hamilton 1949);
(b) Reconstruction of 'Aqsa II' (after Creswell 1989); (c) Reconstruction of
'Aqsa I' (after Johns 1999). Images courtesy of Oxford University Press.

198

SHANGA

Development of Mosques

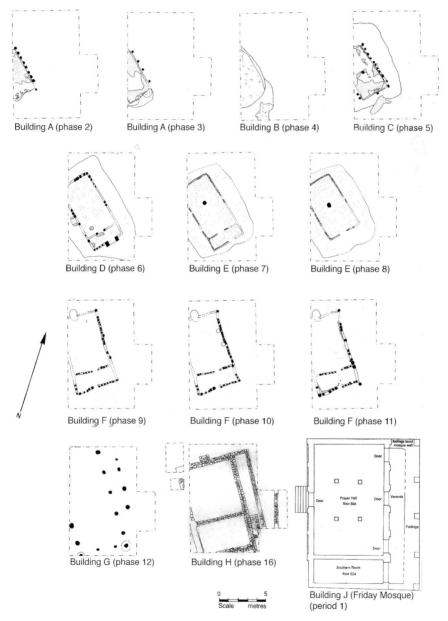

Building A (phase 2)   Building A (phase 3)   Building B (phase 4)   Building C (phase 5)

Building D (phase 6)   Building E (phase 7)   Building E (phase 8)

Building F (phase 9)   Building F (phase 10)   Building F (phase 11)

Building G (phase 12)   Building H (phase 16)   Building J (Friday Mosque)
(period 1)

N

Figure 6.2 The mosque of c.1000 excavated at Shanga and the building phases recovered beneath it. Drawn by Sue Grice. Courtesy of Mark Horton.

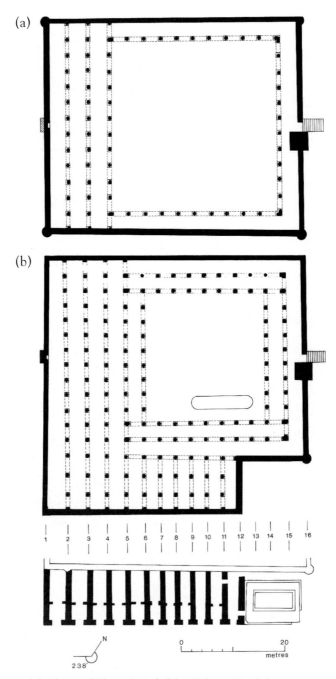

Figure 6.3 (a) Plans of Phase I and (b) of Phase II of the congregational mosque at Siraf, Iran. Drawn by David Whitehouse. Courtesy of the British Institute of Persian Studies.

Figure 6.4 Modern pressed clay pilgrim tokens in the Pa Minar Mosque, Zavareh, Iran. Photograph: Marcus Milwright.

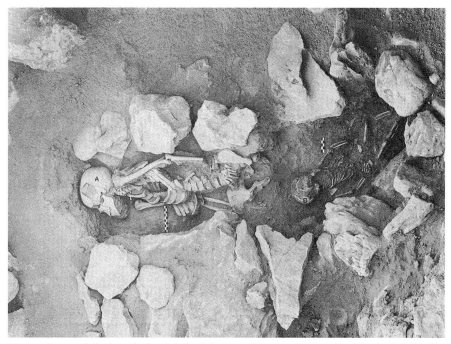

Figure 6.5 Adult female burial, looking south-west. Lower limbs of adult body removed on the occasion of the burial of an infant. Tal al-Hasi, Israel. Photo: T. Rosen. After Toombs (1985). Courtesy of Wilfrid Laurier University Press.

Figure 6.6 Detail of the mosaic pavement at the east end of the naos of the church of St Stephen, Umm al-Rasas, Jordan (719 and 756). Photograph: Marcus Milwright.

Figure 6.7 Mosaic from the church of the Acropolis, Ma'in, Jordan. Seventh century. Madaba Mosaic Museum, Jordan. Photograph: Marcus Milwright.

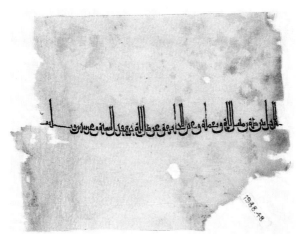

Figure 7.1 Linen tabby textile with *tiraz* embroidered in dark blue silk. Inscription dated 932/320. Ashmolean Museum, University of Oxford (EA 1988.48). Gift of Professor Percy Newberry.

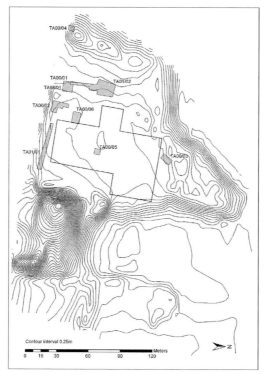

Figure 7.2 Distribution of late eighth- and early ninth-century kilns, excavated by the Raqqa Ancient Industries Project at Tal Aswad, Raqqa, Syria (1998–2001). Courtesy of Keith Challis.

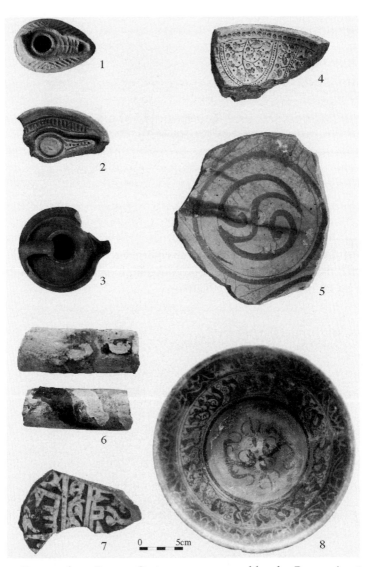

Figure 7.3 Pottery from Raqqa, Syria. 1–7 excavated by the Raqqa Ancient Industries Project; 8: Raqqa Archaeological Museum. (1) and (2) Relief-moulded lamp and mould, late eighth or early ninth century, Tal Aswad; (3) Unglazed lamp, eleventh century, Tal Fukhkhar; (4) Ceramic mould for unglazed jugs, late eighth or early ninth century, Tal Aswad; (5) Sgraffito lead-glazed earthenware bowl, eleventh or twelfth century, Tal Fukhkhar; (6) Kiln rods splashed with green glaze, eleventh or twelfth century, Tal Fukhkhar; (7) Slip-painted lead-glazed bowl, eleventh century, Tal Fukhkhar; (8) Under-glaze-painted turquoise-glazed stonepaste bowl, late twelfth or early thirteenth century. Photographs: Marcus Milwright.

Figure 7.4 Lustre-painted and glazed ceramic jar, Egypt (eleventh century), C.48-1952. By permission of the Board of Trustees of the Victoria and Albert Museum.

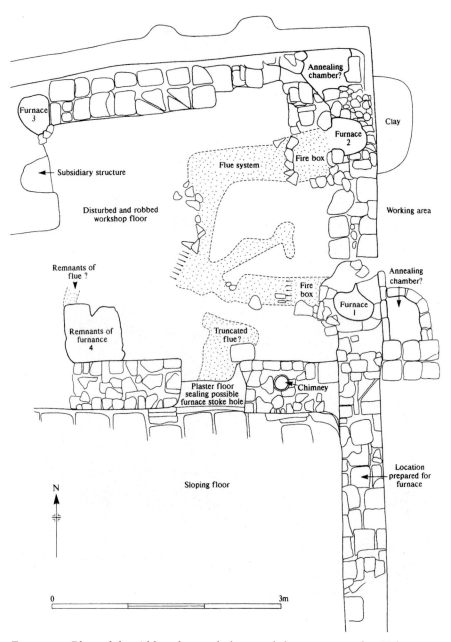

Annealing
chamber?

Furnace
3

Clay

Subsidiary structure

Flue system

Fire box

Furnace
2

Disturbed and robbed
workshop floor

Working area

Remnants of
flue ?

Fire
box

Annealing
chamber?

Remnants of
furnace
4

Furnace
1

Truncated
flue ?

Plaster floor
sealing possible
furnace stoke hole

Chimney

N

Location
prepared for
furnace

Sloping floor

0   3m

Figure 7.5 Plan of the Abbasid period glass workshop excavated at Tal
Zujaj, Raqqa, Syria. Raqqa Ancient Industries Project. Courtesy of Julian
Henderson.

Figure 7.6 Sixth- or seventh-century clay oven (*tabun*) excavated in
Mudaybi', Jordan. Karak Resources Project. Photograph: Marcus Milwright.

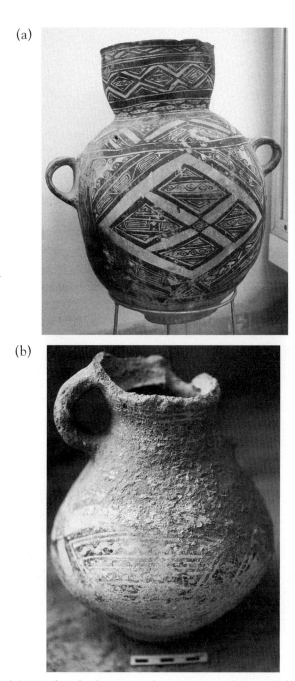

(a)

(b)

Figure 7.7 (a) Handmade slip-painted ceramic jar, thirteenth/fourteenth century. 'Amman Citadel Museum, Jordan; (b) Handmade slip-painted jug, thirteenth/fourteenth century. Karak Castle Museum, Jordan. Photographs: Marcus Milwright.

Figure 8.1 View of Ribat-i Sharaf, Iran. Early twelfth century. Photograph: Marcus Milwright.

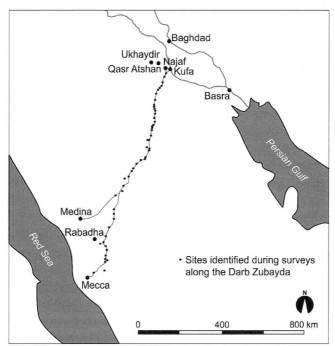

Figure 8.2 Route of Darb Zubayda from Kufa to the Hijaz. After al-Rashid (1986)

Figure 8.3 Tin-glazed bowl with cobalt decoration. Probably Basra, Iraq. Early ninth century (6.3 x 20.6cm). Arthur M. Sackler Gallery, Smithsonian Institution, Washington DC. Gift of Victor and Takako Hauge, S2004.64.

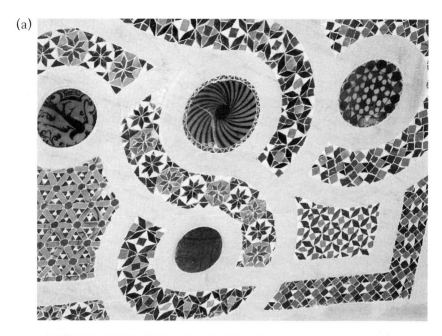

Figure 8.4 (a) Detail of the Bove pulpit in San Giovanni del Toro, Ravello, Italy. Early thirteenth century. The roundels are made from underglaze-painted and lustre-painted stonepaste bowls, probably Syrian. Photograph: Robert Mason; (b) Detail of the north side of the church of San Piero a Grado, Pisa, Italy. Late tenth to eleventh century. The glazed plates on the façade were removed and replaced with modern reproductions in 1976. Photograph: Cristina Tonghini.

Figure 8.5 Mihrab in al-Shawadhina mosque, 'Aqr, Oman. Dated 1530/936.
Carved stucco with inset porcelain bowls and plates. Photograph: Ruba
Kana'an.

Figure 8.6 Map of Greater Syria showing major cities, towns and castles of the crusader states. Adapted from Hugh Kennedy, *Crusader Castles* (Cambridge, 1994). The borders of the crusader, Armenian and Muslim polities are approximate.

213

Figure 8.7 The 'Luck of Edenhall'. Thirteenth-century Syrian enamelled glass beaker and decorated leather case (probably fourteenth century, French). By permission of the Board of Trustees of the Victoria and Albert Museum.

Figure 8.8 Dark and light blue dyed cotton tabby textile fragment with block-printed resist pattern, tenth century, India. Ashmolean Museum, Oxford (EA 1990.250). Gift of Professor Percy Newberry.

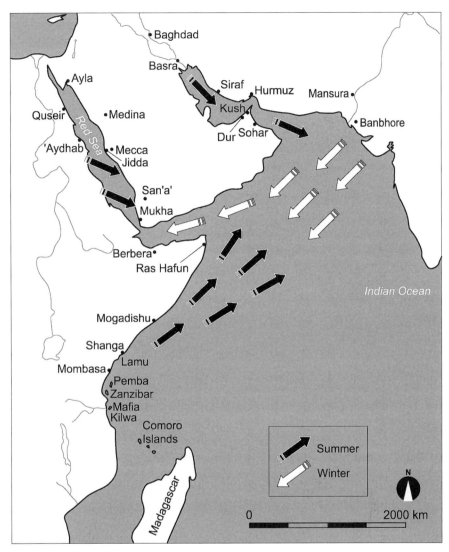

Figure 8.9 Major ports around the Indian Ocean operating during the mediaeval period. Arrows indicate the prevailing winds.

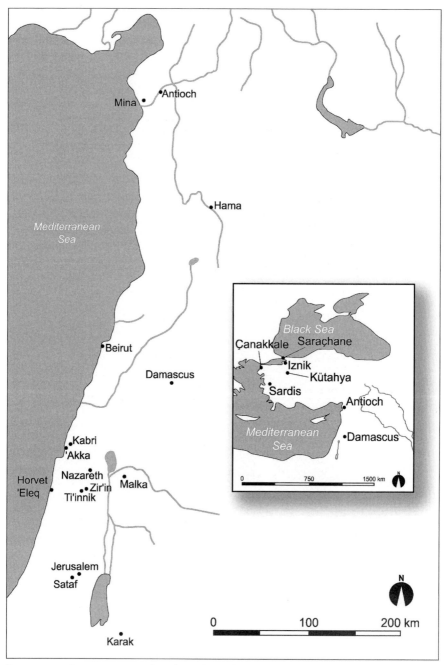

Figure 9.1 Ottoman period archaeological sites in Greater Syria and Anatolia.

Figure 9.2 Clay tobacco pipes recovered during French excavations in Jerusalem. (1) and (2) Grey-bodied pipes, eighteenth century; (3) Red-bodied pipe, eighteenth century. Photographs: Kay Prag.

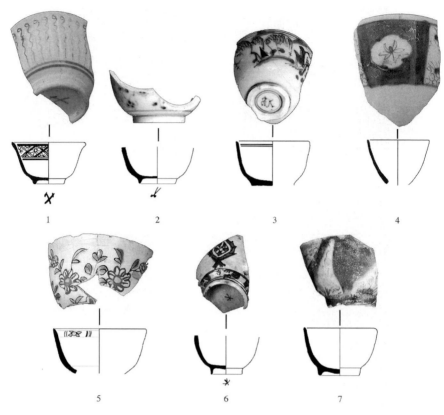

Figure 9.3 Coffee cups found during Franco-Syrian excavations in the citadel of Damascus directed by Sophie Berthier. (1) and (2) Meissen porcelain, eighteenth century; (3) Chinese porcelain, late seventeenth or early eighteenth century; (4) Chinese Imari porcelain, 1725–45; (5) Polychrome glazed stonepaste, Kütahya, eighteenth century; (7) Blue and white stonepaste, Kütahya, eighteenth century, with mark possibly imitating Meissen (after 1733); (7) Cobalt and lustre painted stonepaste, Iran, seventeenth century. Photographs and drawings courtesy of Véronique François.

Figure 9.4 Reduction-fired storage vessel, late nineteenth or early twentieth century, Jordan. Private collection. Photograph: Marcus Milwright.

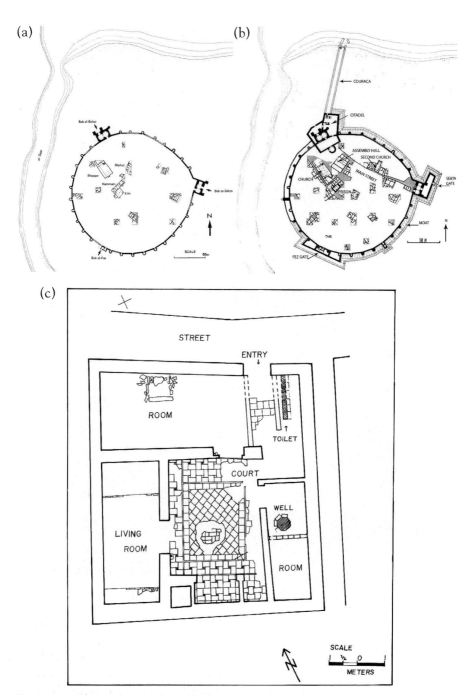

Figure 9.5 Plans of Qasr al-Saghir, Morocco: (a) During the Islamic phase;
(b) During the Portuguese period. (c) Excavated house from the Islamic
phase. Courtesy of Charles Redman.

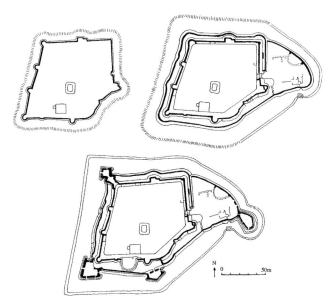

Figure 9.6 Reconstructed plans of the three phases of the 'Hormuzi-Portuguese fort' at Qal'at Bahrain, Bahrain. After Kervran, Hiebert and Rouguelle (2005).

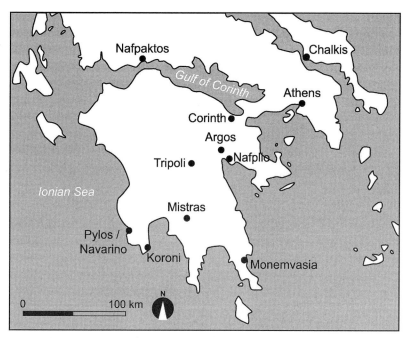

Figure 9.7 Main towns and ports in southern Greece during the Ottoman period.

Figure 9.8 Eighteenth-century fountain on Kapadistriou street, Nafplio, Greece. Photo: Marcus Milwright.

Glossary

The italicised terms and geographical regions listed in the glossary are Arabic (unless stated otherwise). For more detailed definitions of many of the terms given below, see the relevant entries in the *Encyclopaedia of Islam. New Edition* (Leiden 1960–2005). For a more detailed discussion of the archaeological terminology, see Bahn and Renfrew (2000).

Andalus	Term used to describe the Islamic regions of the Iberian peninsula.
Bacini (Italian)	Glazed ceramic vessels set into the façades of churches and other buildings.
Bayt (pl. *buyut*)	Complex of interconnected rooms in a palace or other residential building.
Bazar (English bazaar)	Market place. See also *suq*.
Bedouin (sg. *badu*)	Pastoral nomads in the Middle East.
Birka	Cistern.
Caliph (Anglicised form of *khalifa*)	Leader of the Sunni Muslim community.
Cardo (Latin)	Principal street, running north–south in a classical city (*polis*).
Carbon-14	Radioactive isotope of carbon, the decay of which is employed to date organic artefacts recovered from excavations.
Çiftlik (Turkish)	Country estate.
Daftar (Turkish)	Document recording a cadastral survey in a region of the Ottoman Empire.
Dar al-imara	Urban residence of a caliph or regional governor in the early Islamic Empire; usually located on the *qibla* side of the mosque.
Decapolis (ancient Greek)	Name given to ten urban centres in late antique Palestine and Jordan; it includes Pella and Scythopolis/Bet Shean.

Decumanus (Latin)	Principal street, running east–west in a classical city (*polis*).
Dinar	(Arabic, derived from Latin *denarius*) Islamic gold coin.
Dirham	(derived from Ancient Greek *drachme*, employed in Sasanian Iran) Islamic silver coin.
Falaj (pl. *aflaj*)	Collective term for the water transport systems in Oman.
Flux	Compound used to lower the temperature at which silica vitrifies; pre-modern fluxes in the Islamic world usually contain high concentrations of lead or alkalis (sodium and/or potassium compounds).
Geniza (Hebrew)	A storeroom attached to a synagogue into which documents and scraps of paper were placed.
Greater Syria (in Arabic *Bilad al-Sham*)	Geographical area comprising the modern states of Syria, Jordan, Lebanon, Israel, the Palestine Authority, and south-eastern Turkey.
Hadith	Sayings attributed to the Prophet Muhammad and companions of the Prophet.
Hajj	Annual pilgrimage to Mecca and Medina; one of the 'five pillars' (*rukn*) of Islam.
Hijra	Migration undertaken by the Muslim community from Mecca to Medina in 622.
Huerta (Spanish)	Collective term for the water transport systems on the Iberian peninsula.
Hypostyle mosque	Common form of the mosque in the early Islamic world: a one-storey building in which the roof is supported by columns or piers.
Ifriqiya	Historical region centred on the modern state of Tunisia and encompassing parts of Morocco and Algeria.
Khirbat	Abandoned settlement.
Khurasan	Historical region in the eastern Islamic world encompassing north-eastern Iran and parts of Afghanistan, Tajikistan, Pakistan, Uzbekistan, and Turkmenistan.
Limes (Latin: 'boundary')	System of forts built along the frontiers of the Roman Empire.
Lustre	Technique of firing a reflective metallic coating (a mixture of silver and copper) onto glass or the glazed surface of a ceramic vessel.
Madina	Town or city.
Madrasa	Religious school.

Maqsura	Royal enclosure within the prayer hall of a congregational mosque; it encloses the *mihrab* and *minbar* at the centre of the *qibla* wall.
Masjid al-jami'	Congregational mosque (also known as a 'Friday mosque' or 'great mosque', and in Persian as *masjid-i jami'*): mosque employed for communal prayer on Fridays.
Mihrab	Niche or plaque placed in the *qibla* wall; mosques may have more than one *mihrab*.
Minbar	Pulpit located next to the *mihrab* on the *qibla* wall and used for the delivery of the weekly sermon (*khutba*).
Misr (pl. *amsar*)	City; name given to the garrison settlements established during the Islamic conquests of the seventh and eighth centuries.
Munya	Agricultural estate in Muslim Spain (*Andalus*).
Nisba	Final component of a personal name that usually identifies one's place of birth.
Polis (pl. *poleis*; ancient Greek)	City.
Qal'a	Castle or fort.
Qanat (pl. *qanawat*; Persian)	Underground canal, probably originating in Iran and used elsewhere in the Islamic world.
Qasr (pl. *qusur*)	Palace or country residence.
Qibla	The direction of prayer in Muslim worship, i.e. towards the black stone in the eastern corner of the Ka'ba in Mecca.
Qur'an	Holy book of Islam, believed by Muslims to be the revealed word of God (Allah) transmitted to His Prophet, Muhammad.
Reconquista (Spanish)	Name given to the Christian campaigns between the eighth century and 1492, of 'reconquering' the Muslim territories of the Iberian peninsula.
Settlement pattern	Distribution of permanent or semi-permanent settlements within a rural area in a given time period.
Sgraffito (Italian)	A decorative technique employed on glazed ceramics whereby the slip is incised or carved away prior to the application of the glaze; also known as *sgraffiato* or slip-incising.
Shahada	Muslim profession of faith, and one of the 'pillars' (*rukn*) of Islam; it testifies to the oneness of God and to the status of Muhammad as the Prophet of Allah.

Stonepaste	Artificial ceramic made from a mixture of pale coloured clay, ground quartz, and ground glass (also frit ware or frit paste).
Stratigraphy	Analysis of the stratification, i.e. of the distinct layers (strata) recovered during an excavation. This study aims to establish the temporal sequence of architectural construction and of the deposition of artefacts.
Suq	Market place.
Sura	Chapter in the holy *Qur'an*.
Survey	Also field survey, surface survey or regional survey: the technique of recording artefacts and surface features within a specified area of land. This is done in order to establish the changing settlement patterns over centuries or millennia.
Tal	(often given as *tell*, *tel*, and *tall* in archaeological publications) An artificial mound created through human occupation over an extended period of time.
Tepe (Persian)	See *tal*.
Tin glaze	A glaze made opaque white through the addition of tin oxide.
Tiraz	Textile band embroidered with an inscription, usually naming the caliph and/or the secular ruler of an Islamic region.
Waqf (also *waqfiyya*)	Charitable bequest, usually established for the benefit of a religious institution.

Dynasties and periods

For further details on the Muslim dynasties listed below, see Bosworth (1996).

Abbasid   Sunni caliphate, 749–1517. Based in Iraq (749–1258) and, as puppet rulers of the Mamluk sultans, in Cairo (1261–1517). Successors to the Umayyads, the Abbasids presided over most of the early Islamic Empire in the eighth and ninth centuries.

Aghlabid   Governors of Ifriqiya (Tunisia), Algeria, and Sicily, 800–909.

Ayyubid   Sunni Muslim Kurdish dynasty controlling, at various times, Egypt, Greater Syria, Yemen, the Hijaz, and north-western Mesopotamia: 1171–1250 (Egypt); 1174–1260s (Greater Syria).

Byzantine   Period which continues the history of the Roman Empire in the east after the splitting of the empire in the third century and the official adoption of Christian doctrine in the early fourth century; it terminates with the capture of Constantinople (Istanbul) in 1453. In the archaeological study of the Middle East (excluding Anatolia) and North Africa, the 'Byzantine period' lasts from the fourth to the early seventh century.

Crusades   Military expeditions sanctioned by the papacy. The Crusades in the Middle East led to the creation of the crusader states of the kingdom of Jerusalem, the county of Tripoli, the principality of Antioch, and the county of Edessa between 1098 and 1291, and the Latin Empire of Constantinople between 1204 and 1261.

Fatimid   Shi'a dynasty controlling, at times, North Africa, Sicily, Egypt, and Greater Syria, 909–1171.

Ghassanid   Pre-Islamic Arab dynasty operating in eastern Syria from the third century to 638.

Ghaznavid   Turkish sultanate controlling Afghanistan, north-western India, and parts of Iran and Turkmenistan, 977–1186.

Ilkhanid   Mongol khanate comprising Iran, Iraq, and parts of Anatolia and the Caucasus, 1256–1353. The mass conversion of the Ikhanate to Islam occurred in 1295.

Lakhmid   Pre-Islamic Arab dynasty operating in western Iraq, with its
                  capital located at Hira on the western bank of the Euphrates,
                  c. 266–638.

Late antiquity   Period usually defined as lasting from the mid-third century
                  roughly until the eighth century.

Mamluk   Turkish and Circassian sultanate in Egypt, Greater Syria, and
                  the Hijaz, 1250–1517.

Ottoman   Turkish sultanate (also Osmanlis) rising to political prominence
                  in late thirteenth-century Anatolia and terminating in 1924.
                  At its height in the sixteenth and seventeenth centuries, the
                  empire comprised Anatolia, the Balkans, North Africa, and
                  much of the Middle East.

Rashidun   The period of the first four ('Rightly Guided') caliphs: Abu Bakr,
                  'Umar, 'Uthman, and 'Ali – 632–61.

Roman   In archaeological publications dealing with the eastern Mediter-
                  ranean and North Africa, 'Roman' refers to the phase of Roman
                  (Republican and Imperial) dominion prior to the adoption of
                  Christianity in the early fourth century (the Byzantine period).

Saljuq   Turkish dynasty controlling, at various times, Iran, Iraq, Syria,
                  and Anatolia. 'Great Saljuq' period: 1040–1154; in control of
                  much of Anatolia ('Saljuqs of Rum'): 1081–1307.

Samanid   Rulers of Transoxania and Khurasan, 819–1005.

Sasanian   Pre-Islamic Persian dynasty, c.223–651.

Umayyad   First dynasty of Islam, 661–750. A branch of the Umayyad family
                  retained control of much of the Iberian peninsula (*Andalus*),
                  756–1031.

Zirid   Rulers of Tunisia and eastern Algeria, 972–1152.

Bibliography

'Abd al-Raziq, Ahmad (1967), 'Documents sur la poterie d'époque mamlouke, Šaraf al-Abwani', *Annales Islamologiques* 7: 21–32.

Abdul Jabbar Beg, Muhammad (1972), 'A contribution to the economic history of the caliphate: A study of the cost of living and economic status of artisans in Abbasid Iraq', *Islamic Quarterly* 16: 139–67.

Abulafia, David (1985), 'The Pisan *bacini* and the mediaeval Mediterranean: A historian's perspective', in Caroline Malone and Simon Stoddart, eds, *The Cambridge Conference. Part IV: Classical and Medieval Archaeology*, Papers in Italian Archaeology 4, BAR International Series 246, Oxford, pp. 287–302.

Abu-Lughod, Janet (1987), 'The Islamic city – historic myth, Islamic essence, and contemporary relevance', *International Journal of Middle East Studies* 19: 155–76.

Adams, Robert (1965), *Land behind Baghdad: A History of Settlement on the Diyala Plains*, Chicago and London.

— (1970), 'Tell Abu Sarifa: A Sassanian – Islamic ceramic sequence from south central Iraq', *Ars Orientalis* 8: 87–119.

— (1981), *The Heartland of Cities: Surveys of Ancient Settlement and Land Use on the Central Flood Plain of the Euphrates*, Chicago.

Adams, William (1996), *Qasr Ibrîm, the Late Medieval Period*, London.

Akbar, Jamal (1989), '*Khatta* and the territorial structure of early Muslim towns', *Muqarnas* 6: 22–32.

Al-Ansary, Abdul Rahman (1982), *Qaryat al-Fau: A Portrait of Pre-Islamic Civilisation in Saudi Arabia*, London.

Al-As'ad, Khaled and Franciszek Stepniowski (1989), 'The Umayyad suq in Palmyra', *Damaszner Mitteilungen* 4: 205–23.

Album, Steve and Tony Goodwin (2002), *The Pre-Reform Coinage of the Early Islamic Period*, Sylloge of Islamic coins in the Ashmolean 1, London.

Al-Dayel, K., Salah al-Hilwa and Neil MacKenzie (1979), 'Preliminary report on the third season of Darb Zubaydah Survey, 1978', *Atlal* 3: 43–54.

Allan, James (1973), 'Abu'l-Qasim's treatise on ceramics', *Iran* 11: 111–20.

— (1974), 'Incised wares of Iran and Anatolia in the 11th and 12th centuries', *Keramos* 64: 15–22.

— (1982), *Nishapur: Metalwork of the Early Islamic Period*, New York.

Allan, James and Brian Gilmour (2000), *Persian Steel: The Tanavoli Collection*, OSIA15, Oxford and New York.

Allan, James, L. Llewellyn and F. Schweizer (1973), 'The history of so-called Egyptian faience in Islamic Persia: Investigations into Abu'l-Qasim's treatise', *Archaeometry* 15.2: 165–73.

Allan, James and Caroline Roberts, eds (1987), *Syria and Iran: Three Studies in Medieval Ceramics*, OSIA 4, Oxford.

Allen, Terry (1982), '*Siraf III*: Review', *Ars Orientalis* 13: 188–9.

— (1986), *A Revival of Classical Antiquity in Syria*, Wiesbaden.

Almagro, Antonio and Pedro Jiménez (2000), 'The Umayyad mosque of the citadel of Amman', *Annual of the Department of Antiquities in Jordan* 44: 459–75.

Almagro, Antonio, Pedro Jiménez and Julio Navarro (2000), *El Palacio Omeya de Amman III. Investigación Arqueológica y Restauración, 1989–1997*, Granada.

Al-Rashid, Sa'ad (1978), 'Darb Zubaydah in the 'Abbasid period: Historical and archaeological aspects', *PSAS* 11: 33–45.

— (1979), 'Ancient water-tanks on the haj route from Iraq to Mecca and their parallels in other Arab countries', *Atlal* 3: 55–62.

— (1986), *Al-Rabadhah: A Portrait of Early Islamic Civilisation in Saudi Arabia*, Harlow.

Altun, A. John Carswell and G. Öney (1991), *Turkish Tiles and Ceramics*, Istanbul.

Anderson, Glaire (2007), 'Villa (*munya*) architecture in Umayyad Córdoba: Preliminary considerations', in Anderson and Rosser-Owen, eds, pp. 53–77.

Anderson, Glaire and Mariam Rosser-Owen, eds (2007), *Revisiting Al-Andalus: Perspectives on the Material Culture of Islamic Iberia and Beyond*, Medieval and Early Modern Iberian World 34, Leiden and Boston.

Anon. (1968), 'Mansura', *Pakistan Archaeology* 5: 186–202.

Anon. (1992), *Terres secrètes de Samarcande, céramique du VIIIe au XIIIe siècle*, Paris.

Anon. (1989), *The Periplus Maris Erythraei*, trans. by Lionel Casson, Princeton.

Anon. (1993), *The Art of Medieval Spain*, AD 500–1200, New York.

Anon. (2000), *L'Art copte en Egypte : 2000 ans de christianisme*, Paris.

Arce, Ignacio (2004), 'The Umayyad hydraulic system at Amman citadel – collection, storage, distribution, use and sewage', in Hans-Dieter Bienert and Jutta Häser, eds, *Men of Dykes and Canals: The Archeology of Water in the Middle East*, Rahden, pp. 243–60.

— (2006), 'Qasr Hallabat (Jordan) revisited: Reassessment of the material evidence', in Kennedy, ed. , pp. 26–44.

Ashfaque, S. (1969), 'The Grand Mosque of Banbhore', *Pakistan Archaeology* 6: 182–209.

Ashtor, Eliyahu (1981), 'Levantine sugar industry in the later Middle Ages: A case of technological decline', in A. Udovitch, ed., *The Islamic Middle East, 700–1900: Studies in Economic and Social History*, Princeton, NJ, pp. 91–132.

Aslanapa, Oktay, Serare Yetkin and Ara Altun (1989), *The Iznik Tile Kiln Excavations (The Second Round: 1981–1988)*, Istanbul.

Atasoy, Nurhan and Julian Raby (1994), *Iznik: The Pottery of Ottoman Turkey*, 2nd edn, London.

Atil, Esin (1981), *Renaissance of Islam: Art of the Mamluks*, Washington, DC.

Avner, Rina (2003), 'The recovery of the Kathisma church and its influence on octagonal buildings', in Bottini, Di Segni and Chrupcala, eds, pp. 173–86.

Avni, G. (2004), 'Early mosques in the Negev highlands: New archaeological evidence on Islamic penetration of southern Palestine', *BASOR* 294: 83–100.

Bacharach, Jere (1996), 'Marwanid Umayyad building activities: Speculations on patronage', *Muqarnas* 13: 27–44.

Badawy, Alexander (1978), *Coptic Art and Archaeology: The Art of the Christian Egyptians from the Late Antique to the Middle Ages*, Cambridge, MA and London.

Bahgat, Aly and Félix Massoul (1930), *La Céramique musulmane de l'Egypte*, Cairo.

Bahn, Paul and Colin Renfrew (2000), *Archaeology: Theories, Methods and Practice*, 3rd edn, London and New York.

Bakhit, M. Adnan and Robert Schick, eds (1989), *The History of Bilad al-Sham during the Umayyad Period. Proceedings of the Third Symposium*, vol. 2, Amman.

Bakirtzis, C. (1980), 'Didymoteichon: Un centre de céramique post-byzantine', *Balkan Studies* 21.1: 147–53.

Balfet, Hélène (1965), 'Ethnographic observations in North Africa and archaeological interpretation: The pottery of the Maghreb', in Frederick Matson, ed., *Ceramics and Man*, London, pp. 161–77.

Ball, Warwick (1976), 'Two aspects of Iranian Buddhism', *Bulletin of the Asia Institute of Pahlavi University* 1–4: 103–63.

Baram, Uzi (2000), 'Entangled objects from the Palestinian past: Archaeological perspectives for the Ottoman period, 1500–1900', in Baram and Carroll, eds, pp. 137–59.

Baram, Uzi and Lynda Carroll, eds (2000), *A Historical Archaeology of the Ottoman Empire: Breaking new Ground*, Contributions to Global Historical Archaeology, New York and Boston.

Barnes, Ruth (1997), *Indian Block-Printed Textiles in Egypt: The Newberry Collection in the Ashmolean Museum, Oxford*, Oxford.

Bartl, Karin and Stefan Hauser, eds (1996), *Continuity and Change in Northern Mesopotamia from the Hellenistic to the Early Islamic Period*, Berliner Beiträge zum vorderen Orient 17, Berlin.

Bar-Yosef, Ofer and Anatoly Khazanov (1992), *Pastoralism in the Levant: Archaeological Materials and Anthropological Perspectives*, Monographs in World Archaeology 10, Madison.

Bass, George, J. Steffy and F. van Doorninck (1984), 'Excavation of an 11th-century shipwreck at Serce Limani, Turkey', *National Geographic Society Research Reports* 17: 161–82.

Bazzana, André (1998), 'Le *hisn*: Modèle d'organisation du peuplement rural dans l'Andalus', in Gayraud, ed., pp. 217–44.

— (1999), '"Al-Djubb": Le stockage de l'eau dans les édifices castraux et les habitats d'al-Andalus', in Bazzana, ed., pp. 371–95.

—, ed. (1999), *Archéologie et espaces agraires méditerranéens au Moyen Age*, Castrum 5, Collection de l'Ecole de Rome 105, Madrid, Rome and Murcia.

Beeley, Brian (1970), 'The Turkish village coffeehouse as a social institution', *Geographical Review* 60.4: 475–93.

Benco, Nancy (1987), *The Early Medieval Pottery Industry at al-Basra, Morocco*, BAR International Series 341, Oxford.

Ben-Dov, Meir (1985), *In the Shadow of the Temple: The Discovery of Ancient Jerusalem*, Jerusalem.

Benoist, Anne, Michel Mouton and Jeremie Schiettecatte (2003), 'The artefacts from the fort of Mleiha: Distribution, origins, trade and dating', *PSAS* 33: 59–76.

Benvenisti, Meron (1970), *The Crusaders in the Holy Land*, New York.

Bernsted, Anne-Marie (2003), *Early Islamic Pottery, Materials and Techniques*, London.

Berthier, Paul (1966), *Un épisode de l'histoire de la canne à sucre. Les anciennes sucreries du Maroc et leurs réseaux hydrauliques. Etude archéologique et d'histoire économique*, 2 vols, Rabat.

Berti, Graziella and Liana Tongiorgi (1981), *I bacini ceramici medievali delle chiese di Pisa*, Rome.

Bianquis, Thierry, George Scanlon and Andrew Watson (1974), 'Numismatics and the dating of early Islamic pottery in Egypt', in Kouymjian, ed., pp. 163–73.

Bier, Lionel (1986), *Sarvistan: A Study in Early Iranian Architecture*, University Park, PA and London.

Bierman, Irene, ed. (1995), *Identity and Material Culture in the Early Islamic World*, UCLA Near East Center Colloquium Series, Los Angeles.

Bisheh, Ghazi (1993), 'From *castellum* to *palatium*: Umayyad mosaic pavements from Qasr al-Hallabat in Jordan', *Muqarnas* 10: 49–56.

Blackburn, M. and D. M. Metcalf, eds (1981), *Viking-Age Coinage in Northern Lands: The Sixth Oxford Symposium on Coinage and Monetary History*, BAR International Series 122, Oxford.

Blair, Sheila (1992), 'What is the date of the Dome of the Rock?', in Raby and Johns, eds, pp. 59–87.

— (1997), Inscriptions on medieval Islamic textiles, *Riggisberger Berichte* 5: 195–217.

— (2006), *Islamic Calligraphy*, Edinburgh.

Blair, Sheila and Jonathan Bloom (1994), *The Art and Architecture of Islam, 1250–1800*, New Haven and London.

Bliss, Frederick and Robert Macalister (1902), *Excavations in Palestine during the Years, 1898–1900*, London.

Bloom, Jonathan (1989), *Minaret, Symbol of Islam*, OSIA 7, Oxford.

— (1996), 'Islamic Art. X: Historiography', in Jane Turner, ed, *Grove Dictionary of Art*, vol. 16, London and New York: 546–51.

— (2001), *Paper before Print: The History and Impact of Paper in the Islamic World*, New Haven and London.

Boas, Adrian (1994), 'The import of western ceramics to the Latin Kingdom of Jerusalem', *Israel Exploration Journal* 44: 102–20.

— (1999), *Crusader Archaeology: The Material Culture of the Latin East*, London and New York.

— (2000), 'Pottery and small finds from the Late Ottoman village and the early Zionist settlement', in Yizhar Hirschfeld, *Ramat Hanadiv Excavations: Final Report of the 1994–1998 Seasons*, Jerusalem, pp. 554–80.

Bonner, Michael (2001), 'The *Kitab al-Kasb* attributed to al-Shaybani: Poverty, surplus, and the circulation of wealth', *Journal of the American Oriental Society* 121.3: 410–27.

Bosworth, Clifford (1996), *The New Islamic Dynasties: A Chronological and Genea-logical Manual*, Edinburgh.

Bottini, G. Claudio, Leah Di Segni and L. Daniel Chrupcala, eds (2003), *One Land – Many Cultures. Archaeological Studies in Honour of Stanislao Loffreda* OFM, Jerusalem.

Boucharlat, Rémy and Michel Mouton (1994), 'Mleiha (Emirate of Sharjah, UAE) at the beginning of the Christian era', *PSAS* 24: 13–26.

Boucharlat, Rémy, Audran Labrousse and Monique Kervran (1979), 'Une sucrerie d'époque islamique sur la rive droîte de Chaour à Suse', *Cahiers de la Délégation Archéologique Française en Iran* 10: 155–237.

Boucharlat, Rémy, E. Haerinck, O. Lecomte, Dan Potts and K. Stevens (1989), 'The European archaeological expedition to Ed-Dur, Umm al-Qaiwayn (UAE): An interim report on the 1987 and 1989 seasons', *Mesopotamia* 24: 7–72.

Bowersock, Glen, Peter Brown and Oleg Grabar, eds (2001), *Interpreting Late Antiquity: Essays on the Postclassical World*, Cambridge, MA and London.

Bozdogan, Sibel and Gülru Neçipoglu (2007), 'Entangled discourses: Scrutinizing orientalist and nationalist legacies in the architectural history of the "lands of Rum"', *Muqarnas* 24: 1–6.

Brisch, Klaus (1965), 'Das omayyadische Schloss in Usais (II)', *Mitteilungen des Deutschen Archäologischen Instituts Abteilung Kairo* 20: 138–77.

Brouwer, C. (2001), 'Al-Mukha as a coffee port in the early decades of the seven-teenth century according to Dutch sources', in Tuchscherer, ed. (2001), pp. 271–95.

Brown, Robin (2000), 'The distribution of thirteenth- to fifteenth-century glazed wares in Transjordan: A case study from the Kerak plateau', in Lawrence Stager, Joseph Greene, and Martin Coogan, eds, *The Archaeology of Jordan and Beyond: Essays in Honor of James A. Sauer*, Winona Lake, pp. 84–99.

Brun, Pierre (2005), 'From arrows to bullets: The fortifications of Abdullah Khan Kala (Merv, Turkmenistan)', *Antiquity* 79: 616–24.

Bujard, Jacques and Denis Genequand (2001), 'Umm al-Walid et Khan Zabib, deux établissements Omeyyades en limite du désert Jordanien', in B. Geyer, ed., *Conquête de la steppe et appropriation des terres sur les marges arides du Croissant Fertile*, Lyon, pp. 189–218.

Bulliet, Richard (1975), *The Camel and the Wheel*, Cambridge, MA.

— (1979), *Conversion to Islam in the Medieval Period: An Essay in Quantitative History*, Cambridge, MA and London.

— (1992), 'Pottery styles and social status in in medieval Khurasan', in Knapp, ed., pp. 75–82.

Butzer, Karl, Juan Mateu, Elizabeth Butzer and Pavel Kraus (1985), 'Irrigation agro-systems in eastern Spain: Roman or Islamic origins', *Annals of the Association of American Geographers* 75.4: 479–509.

Caiger-Smith, Alan (1985), *Lustre Pottery: Technique, Tradition, and Innovation in Islam and the Western World*, London and New York.

Canaan, Tawfiq (1927), *Mohammedan Saints and Sanctuaries in Palestine*, London.

Canby, Sheila (2000), 'Islamic archaeology: By accident or design?', in Vernoit, ed. (2000), pp. 128–37.

Carlier, Patricia (1989), 'Qastal al-Balqa': An Umayyad site in Jordan', in Bakhit and Schick, eds, pp. 104–39.
Carswell, John (1972), 'China and the Near East: The recent discovery of Chinese porcelain in Syria', in William Watson, ed., *The Westward Influence of the Chinese Arts from the Fourteenth to the Eighteenth Century*, Colloquies on the Art and Archaeology of Asia, London: 20–5.
— (1979), 'Sin in Syria', *Iran* 17: 15–24.
— (2000), *Blue and White: Chinese Porcelain around the World*, London.
Challis, Keith, Gary Priestnall, Adam Gardner, Julian Henderson and Sara O'Hara (2004), 'Corona remotely-sensed imagery in dryland archaeology: The Islamic city of al-Raqqa, Syria', *Journal of Field Archaeology* 29: 139–53.
Champion, Timothy (1990), 'Medieval archaeology and the tyranny of the historical record', in D. Austin and L. Alcock, eds, *From the Baltic to the Black Sea: Studies in Medieval Archaeology*. London: 79–95.
Charles, Michael. C. Hoppé, G. Jones, A. Bogaard and J. D. Hodgson (2003), 'Using weed functional attributes for the identification of irrigation regimes in Jordan', *Journal of Archaeological Science* 30: 1429–41.
Chiat, Marilyn (1982), *Handbook of Synagogue Architecture*, Chico.
Chittick, Neville (1974), *Kilwa: An Islamic Trading City on the East African Coast*, The British Institute in Eastern Africa Memoir Series 5, Nairobi.
— (1984), *Manda: Excavations at an Island Port on the Kenya Coast*, The British Institute in Eastern Africa Memoir Series 9, Nairobi.
Contadini, Anna (1998), *Fatimid Art at the Victoria and Albert Museum*, London.
Costa, Paolo (2001), *Historic Mosques and Shrines of Oman*, BAR International Series 938, Oxford.
— (2002), 'Notes on tradition hydraulics and agriculture in Oman', in Morony, ed., pp. 303–25 (reprinted from *World Archaeology* 14, 1983: 273–95).
Crane, Howard (1987), 'Some notes on Turkish Sardis', *Muqarnas* 4: 43–58.
— (1988), 'Traditional pottery making in the Sardis region of western Turkey', *Muqarnas* 5: 9–20.
Cressier, Patrice (1996), 'A propos des apports orientaux dans l'hydraulique agraire d'al-Andalus: Observations sur le barrage', *Madrider Beiträge* 24: *Spanien under der Orient im frühen under hohen Mittelalter*: 142–56.
— (1999), 'Châteaux et terroirs irrigués dans la province d'Almería (Xe–XVe siècles)', in Bazzana, ed., pp. 439–54.
Creswell, Keppel (1952), *The Muslim Architecture of Egypt*, Oxford.
— (1969), *Early Muslim Architecture*, vol. 1, rev. edn, Oxford.
Creswell, Keppel and James Allan (1989), *A Short Account of Early Muslim Architecture*, rev. and suppl. by James Allan, Aldershot.
Crone, Patricia (1987), *Meccan Trade and the Rise of Islam*, Oxford.
Crowfoot, Grace (1932), 'Pots, ancient and modern', *Palestine Exploration Fund Quarterly Statement*: 179–87.
Daiber, Verena and Andrea Becker, eds (2004), *Raqqa III: Baudenkmäler und Paläste I*, Mainz am Rhein.
Danti, Michael (2004), *The Ilkhanid Heartland: Hasanlu Tepe (Iran), Period I*, Hasanlu

Excavation Reports II, Philadelphia.

Daryaee, Touraj (2003), 'The Persian Gulf in Late Antiquity', *Journal of World History*, 14.1: 1–16.

Davies, Siriol and Jack Davis, eds (2007), *Between Venice and Istanbul: Colonial Landscapes in Early Modern Greece*, Hesperia Supplements 40, Princeton, NJ.

Davis, Jack, ed. (1998), *Sandy Pylos: An Archaeological History from Nestor to Navarino*, Austin.

Denon, Vivant (1802), *Voyage dans la basse et la Haute Egypte pendant les compagnes du général Bonaparte*, Paris.

Déroche, François (1992), *The Abbasid Tradition: Qur'ans of the Eighth to the Tenth Centuries AD*, Nasser D. Khalili Collection of Islamic Art 1, London.

De Vries, Bert (1998), *Umm el-Jimal: A Frontier Town and its Landscape in Northern Jordan, Volume 1: Fieldwork 1972–1981*, JRA Supplementary Series 26, Portsmouth, Rhode Island.

— (2000), 'Continuity and change in the urban character of the southern Hauran from the fifth to the ninth century: The archaeological evidence at Umm al-Jimal', *Mediterranean Archaeology* 13: 39–45.

Dien, Albert (2004), 'Western exotica in China during the Six Dynasties period', in Xiaoneng Yang, ed., *New Perspectives on China's Past. Chinese Archaeology in the Twentieth Century*, New Haven and London, pp. 362–79.

Dodds, Jerrilyn, ed. (1992), *Al-Andalus: The Art of Islamic Spain*, New York.

Dunn, Archibald (1999), 'From *polis* to *kastron* in southern Macedonia: Amphipolis, Khyrsoupolis, and the Strymon delta', in Bazzana, ed., pp. 399–413.

Eakins, J. Kenneth (1993), *Tell el Hesi: The Muslim Cemetery in Fields V and VI/X (Stratum II). The Joint Archaeological Expedition to Tell el-Hesi, Volume 5*, ASOR Excavation Reports, Winona Lake.

Edelstein, G. and Miriam Avissar (1997), 'A sounding in old Acre', *'Atiqot* 31: 129–36.

Einsler, Lydia (1914), 'Das Töpferhandwerk bei den Bauernfrauen von Ramallah und Umgegend', *Zeitschrift des Deutschen Palästina-Vereins* 37: 249–60.

Elders, Joseph (2001), 'The lost churches of the Arabian Gulf: Recent discoveries on the islands of Sir bani Yas and Marawah, Abu Dhabi Emirate, United Arab Emirates', *PSAS* 31: 47–57.

Ellenblum, Ronnie (1998), *Frankish rural Settlement in the Latin Kingdom of Jerusalem*, Cambridge.

— (2007), *Crusader Castles and Modern Histories*, Cambridge and New York.

Erzini, Nadia (2000), 'Cultural administration in French North Africa and the growth of Islamic art history', in Vernoit, ed. (2000), pp. 71–84.

Erzini, Nadia and Stephen Vernoit (forthcoming), 'Imari ware in Morocco', *Muqarnas*.

Establet, Colette and Jean-Paul Pascual (2001), 'Café et objets du café dans les inventaires de pèlerins musulmans vers 1700', in Tuchscherer, ed. (2001), pp. 143–51.

Ettinghausen, Richard (1952), 'The "Beveled style" in the post-Samarra period', in George Miles, ed., *Archaeologica Orientalia in Memoriam Ernst Herzfeld*. Locust Valley, pp. 72–83.

Ettinghausen, Richard, Oleg Grabar and Marilyn Jenkins-Madina (2001), *Islamic Art and Architecture, 650–1250*, New Haven and London.

Ewert, Christian and Jens-Peter Wisshak (1981), *Forschungen zur almohadischen Moscheen I*, Mainz.

Farooq, Abdul Aziz (1974–86), 'Excavations at Mansurah (13th season)', *Pakistan Archaeology* 10–12: 3–35.

Faucherre, Nicholas (2004), 'La Forteresse de Shawbak (Crac de Montréal), une des premières forteresses franques sous son corset mamelouk', in Nicholas Faucherre, Jean Mesqui and Nicholas Prouteau, eds, *La Fortification au temps des Croisades*, Rennes, pp. 43–66.

Fayolle, Véronique (1992), *La Poterie modelée du Maghreb oriental. De ses origines au XXe siècle: Technologie, morpologie, fonction*, Paris.

Finster, Barbara (1978a), Die Reiseroute Kufa – Sa'udi-Arabien in frühislamischer Zeit: Bericht über den Survey vom 8.-14. Mai 1976 auf dem westeuphratischen Wüstenstreifen', *Baghdader Mitteilungen* 9: 53–91.

— (1978b), 'Die Freitagsmoschee von San'a'. Vorläufiger Bericht 1', *Baghdader Mitteilungen* 9: 92–133.

— (1994), *Frühe iranische Moscheen: Vom Beginn des Islam bis zur Zeit Salguqischer Herrschaft*, Berlin.

Finster, Barbara and Jürgen Schmidt (1976), 'Sasanidische und frühislamische Ruinen im Iraq', *Baghdader Mitteilungen* 8: 57–150.

— (1979), 'Die Freitagsmoschee von San'a'. Vorläufiger Bericht 2. Teil der Ostriwaq', *Baghdader Mitteilungen* 10: 179–92.

— (2005), 'The origin of "desert castles": Qasr Bani Muqatil near Karbala, Iraq', *Antiquity* 79: 339–49.

Flanagan, James, David McCreery and Khair Yassine (1994), 'Tell Nimrin: Preliminary report of the 1993 season', *ADAJ* 38: 204–44.

Flood, Finbarr (2001), *The Great Mosque of Damascus: Studies on the Makings of an Umayyad Visual Culture*, Islamic Civilization, Studies and Texts 33, Leiden and Boston.

— (2003), 'Pillars, palimpsests, and princely practices: Translating the past in Sultanate Dehli', *Res* 43: 95–116.

Foote, Rebecca (1999), 'Frescoes and carved ivory from the Abbasid family homestead at Humeima', *JRA* 12.1: 423–28.

— (2000), 'Commerce, industrial expansion, and orthogonal planning: Mutually compatible terms in settlements of Bilad al-Sham during the Umayyad period', *Mediterranean Archaeology* 13: 25–38.

Foss, Clive (2002), 'Life in city and country', in Cyril Mango, ed., *The Oxford History of Byzantium*, Oxford and New York, pp. 71–95.

Fowden, Garth (2001), 'Varieties of religious community', in Bowersock, Brown and Grabar, eds, pp. 82–106.

— (2004), *Qusayr 'Amra: Art and the Umayyad Elite in Late Antique Syria*, Berkeley and London.

François, Véronique (2001), 'Eléments pour l'histoire ottomane d'Aphrodisias: La vaisselle de terre', *Anatolia Antiqua* 9: 147–90.

— (2002), 'Production et consommation de vaisselle à Damas, l'époque ottomane', *Bulletin d'Etudes Orientales* 53–54: 157–74.

— (2008), *Céramique de la citadelle de Damas. Epoques mamelouke et ottomane*, CDRom, Aix-en-Provence.

Frifelt, Karen (2001), with contributions by Pernille Bangsgaard and Venetia Porter, *Islamic Remains in Bahrain*, The Carlsberg Foundation's Gulf Project, Gylling.

Frye, Richard (2005), *Ibn Fadlan's Journey to Russia: A Tenth-Century Traveler from Baghdad to the Volga River*, Princeton.

Funari, Paolo, M. Hall and Sian Jones, eds (1999), *Historical Archaeology: Back from the Edge*, London and New York.

Galdieri, Eugenio, ed. (1972–84), *Isfahan: Masgid-i Gum'a*, Rome.

Gatt, G. (1885), 'Industrielles aus Gaza', *Zeitschrift des Deutschen Palästina-Vereins* 8: 69–79.

Gaube, Heinz (1974), 'An examination of the ruins of Qasr Burqu'', *Annual of the Department of the Antiquities of Jordan* 19: 93–100.

Gayraud, Roland-Pierre (1998), 'Fostat: Evolution d'une capitale arabe du VIIe au XIIe siècle d'après les fouilles d'Istabl 'Antar', in Gayraud ed., pp. 435–60.

Gayraud, Roland-Pierre, ed. (1998), *Colloque international d'archéologie islamique, IFAO, Le Caire, 3–7 février 1993*, Textes arabes et études islamiques 36, Cairo.

Gelichi, Sauro and Marco Milanese (1998), 'Problems in the transition toward the medieval in Ifriqiya: First results from the archaeological excavations at Uchi Maius (Teboursouk, Béja)', in Khanoussi, Ruggieri and Vismara, eds, pp. 457–84.

— (2002), 'The transformation of the ancient towns in central Tunisia during the Islamic period: The example of Uchi Maius', *Al-Masaq* 14.1: 33–45.

Genequand, Denis (2003), 'Ma'an, an early Islamic settlement in southern Jordan: Preliminary report on the survey in 2002', *ADAJ* 47: 25–35.

— (2004a), 'Al-Bakhra' (Avatha), from Tetrarchic fort to Umayyad castle', *Levant* 36: 225–42.

— (2004b), Châteaux omeyyades de Palmyrène', *Annales Islamologiques* 38: 3–44.

— (2005), 'From "desert castle" to medieval town: Qasr al-Hayr al-Sharqi (Syria)', *Antiquity* 79: 350–61.

— (2006a), 'Umayyad castles: The shift from late antique military architecture to early Islamic palatial building', in Kennedy, ed., pp. 3–25.

— (2006b), 'Some thoughts on Qasr al-Hayr al-Gharbi, its dam, its monastery and the Ghassanids', *Levant* 38: 63–83.

Given, Michael (2000), 'Agriculture, settlement and landscape in Ottoman Cyprus', *Levant* 32: 209–30.

Gichon, Mordechai and Robert Linden (1984), 'Muslim oil lamps from Emmaus', *Israel Exploration Journal* 34: 156–65, pls 21, 22.

Glick, Thomas (1970), *Irrigation and Society in Medieval Valencia*, Cambridge, MA.

— (2002), 'Hydraulic technology in al-Andalus', in Morony, ed., pp. 327–39 (reprinted from S. Jayyusi, ed., *The Legacy of Muslim Spain*, Leiden 1992, pp. 974–86).

Golombek, Lisa (1988), 'The draped universe of Islam', in Priscilla Soucek, ed.,

Content and Context of the visual Arts of the Islamic World, University Park, PA and London, pp. 25–38.

Goitein, Shlomo (1963), 'Letters and documents on the Indian trade', *Islamic Culture* 37: 188–205.

— (1967–88), *A Mediterranean Society: The Jewish Communities of the Arab World as Portrayed in the Documents of the Cairo Geniza*, Berkeley and Los Angeles, vol. 1: *Economic Foundations* (1967); vol. 2: *The Community* (1971); vol. 3: *The Family* (1978); vol. 4: *Daily Life* (1983); vol. 5: *The Individual* (1988).

Golvin, Lucien (1957), *Le Magrib central à l'époque des Zirides. Recherches d'archéologie et d'histoire*, Paris.

Grabar, Oleg (1966), 'The earliest Islamic commemorative structures. Notes and documents', *Ars Orientalis* 6: 7–46.

— (1973), *The Formation of Islamic Art*, New Haven and London.

— (1990), *The Great Mosque of Isfahan*, New York.

— (1996), *The Shape of the Holy: Early Islamic Jerusalem*, Princeton.

Grabar, Oleg, Renata Holod, James Knustad and William Trousdale (1978), *City in the Desert: Qasr al-Hayr East*, Harvard Middle Eastern Monographs 23/24, Cambridge, MA.

Grafman, Rafi and Myriam Rosen-Ayalon (1999), 'Two great Syrian Umayyad mosques: Jerusalem and Damascus', *Muqarnas* 16: 1–15.

Gratuze, B. and J.-N. Barrandon (1990), 'Islamic glass weights and stamps', *Archaeometry* 32: 155–62.

Grenet, Frantz and Claude Rapin (1998), 'De la Samarkand antique à la Samarkand islamique: continuités et ruptures', in Gayraud, ed., pp. 387–402.

Grierson, Philip (1959), 'Commerce in the Dark Ages: A critique of the evidence', *Transactions of the Royal Historical Society*, 5th series, 9: 123–40.

Groom, Nigel (2005), 'Trade, incense and perfume', in Gunther, ed., pp. 104–13.

Grube, Ernst, ed. (1994), *Cobalt and Lustre. The First Centuries of Islamic Pottery*, The Nasser D. Khalili Collection of Islamic Art 9, Oxford and New York.

Guichard, Pierre (1999), 'Le paysage rural du *Shark* al-Andalus vu à travers la documentation chrétienne de l'époque de la Reconquête', in Bazzana, ed., pp. 129–36.

Guionova, Guergana (2005), 'Etat de la recherche archéologique concernant la période ottomane en Bulgarie', *Turcica* 37: 267–79.

Gunther, Ann, ed. (2005), *Caravan Kingdoms: Yemen and the Ancient Incense Trade*, Washington, DC.

Guo, Li (2004), *Commerce, Culture, and Community in a Red Sea Port in the Thirteenth Century: The Arabic Documents from Quseir*, Islamic History and Civilization: Studies and Texts 52, Leiden and Boston.

Hagen, Norbert, Mustafa al-Hassoun and Michael Meinecke (2004), 'Die Grosse Moschee von ar-Rafiqa', in Daiber and Becker, eds, pp. 25–39.

Hamarneh, Salih (1977–8), 'Zir'at qasab al-sukkar wa sina'atuhu 'inda al-'Arab al-Muslimin' (Sugar cane cultivation and refining under the Arab Muslim during the Middle Ages)', *ADAJ* 22: 12–19 (Arabic section).

Hamdani, Hasan ibn Ahmad (1931 and 1938), *Kitab al-iklil*, Book 8, ed. by A. al-Karmali. Baghdad (1931); translated by Nabih Amin Faris as *The Antiquities of South Arabia*, Princeton Oriental Texts 3 Princeton NJ and Oxford (1938).

Hamilton, Robert (1959), *Khirbat al-Mafjar, an Arabian Mansion in the Jordan Valley*, Oxford.

— (1949), *The Stuctural History of the Aqsa Mosque: A Record of Archaeological Gleanings from Repairs of 1938–1942*, London and Jerusalem.

— (1992), 'Once again the Aqsa', in Raby and Johns, eds, pp. 141–4.

Hansman, John (1985), *Julfar, an Arabian Port, Its Settlement and Far Eastern Ceramic Trade from the 14th to the 18th Centuries*, London.

Hauptmann, Andreas (2000), *Zur frühen Metallurgie des Kupfers in Fenan/Jordanien*, Der Anschnitt. Zeitschrift für Kunst und Kultur Bergbau 11, Bochum.

Hauptmann, Andreas and W. Weisberger (1987), 'Archaeometallurgical and mining-archaeological investigations in the area of Feinan, Wadi 'Arabah (Jordan)', *ADAJ* 31: 419–37.

Hayes, John (1980), 'Turkish clay pipes: A provisional typology', in P. Davey, ed., *The Archaeology of the Clay Tobacco Pipe, No.4*, BAR International Series 92, Oxford, pp. 3–10.

— (1992), *Excavations at Saraçhane in Istanbul. Volume 2: The Pottery*, Princeton and London.

Heidemann, Stefan (2003), 'Die Geschichte von ar-Raqqa/ar-Rafiqa – ein Überblick', in Heidemann and Becker, eds, pp. 9–56.

— (2006), 'The history of the industrial and commercial area of 'Abbasid Al-Raqqa, called *Al-Raqqa al-Muhtariqa*', *BSOAS* 69.1: 33–52.

Heidemann, Stefan and Andrea Becker, eds (2003), *Raqqa II. Die islamische Stadt*, Mainz am Rhein.

Helms, Svend (1990), with contributions by A. Betts, W. and F. Lancaster, and C. Lenzen, *Early Islamic Architecture of the Desert: A Bedouin Station in Eastern Jordan*, Edinburgh.

Henderson, Julian (1999), 'Archaeological investigations of an Islamic industrial complex at Raqqa, Syria', *Damaszener Mitteilungen*, 11: 243–65.

— (2000), *The Science and Archaeology of Materials: An Investigation of Inorganic Materials*, London and New York.

Henderson, Julian, Keith Challis, Sara O'Hara, Sean McLoughlin, Adam Gardner and Gary Priestnall (2005), 'Experiment and innovation: Early Islamic industry at al-Raqqa, Syria', *Antiquity* 79: 130–45.

Herrmann, Georgina, K. Kurbansakhatov, St John Simpson, Vladimir Zavyalov, Gabriele Puschnigg, Dan Hall, Barbara Cerasetti, Eleana Leoni, Pierre Brun, Akmohammed Annaev, David Gilbert, Jens Kröger and Robert Hillenbrand (2001), 'The international Merv project: Preliminary report on the ninth year (2000)', *Iran* 39: 9–52.

Herzfeld, Ernst (1923–48), *Die Ausgrabungen von Samarra*, Berlin, Vol. 1: *Der Wandschmuck der Bauten von Samarra und seine Ornamentik* (1923); vol. 3: *Die Malereien von Samarra* (1927); vol. 5: *Die vorgeschichtliche Töpfereien* (1930); vol. 6: *Geschichte der Stadt Samarra* (1948).

Hillenbrand, Robert (1981), 'Islamic art at the crossroads: East versus west at Mshatta', in Abbas Daneshvari, ed., *Essays in Islamic Art and Architecture in*

Honor of Katharina Otto-Dorn, Malibu, pp. 63–86.

— (1982), "'*La dolce vita*" in early Islamic Syria: The evidence of later Umayyad palaces', *Art History* 5.1: 1–35.

— (1986), 'Archaeology vi: Islamic Iran', *Encyclopaedia Iranica* 2.3: 317–22.

— (1994), *Islamic Architecture: Form, Function and Meaning*, Edinburgh and New York.

— (1999), "Anjar and Early Islamic urbanism', in G. Brogiolo and Bryan Ward-Perkins, eds, *The Idea and Ideal of the Town between Late Antiquity and the Early Middle Ages*, The Transformation of the Roman World 4, Leiden and Boston: 60–98.

Hirschfeld, Yizhar (2001), 'Habitat', in Bowersock, Brown and Grabar, eds, pp. 258–72.

Hodder, Ian (1989), 'Writing archaeology: Site reports in context', *Antiquity* 63: 268–74.

Hodder, Ian,Michael Shanks, Alexandra Alexandri, Victor Buchli, John Carman, Jonathan Last and Gavin Lucas, eds (1995), *Interpreting Archaeology: Finding Meaning in the Past*, London and New York.

Hodges, Richard and David Whitehouse (1983), *Mohammed, Charlemagne and the Origins of Europe: Archaeology and the Pirenne Thesis*, London.

Horton, Mark (1996), *Shanga: The Archaeology of a Muslim Trading Community on the Coast of East Africa*, Memoirs of the British Institute in Eastern Africa 14, London.

— (2004), 'Islam, archaeology, and Swahili identity', in Whitcomb, ed., pp. 67–88.

Hourani, Albert and Samuel Stern, eds (1970), *The Islamic City: A Colloquium*, Oxford.

Hovén, Bengt (1981), 'On oriental coins in Scandinavia', in Blackburn and Metcalf, eds, pp. 119–28.

Howard-Johnston, James (1995), 'The two great powers in late antiquity: A comparison', in Averil Cameron, ed., *The Byzantine and Early Islamic Near East. III: States, Resources and Armies*, Princeton, NJ, pp. 157–226.

Hoyland, Robert (1997), *Seeing Islam as Others Saw It. A Survey and Evaluation of Christian, Jewish and Zoroastrian Writing on Islam*, Studies in Late Antiquity and Islam 13, Princeton, NJ.

— (2001), *Arabia and the Arabs: From the Bronze Age to the Coming of Islam*, London and New York.

— (2006), 'New documentary texts and the early Islamic state', *BSOAS* 69.3: 395–416.

Humphreys, John (1980), *Excavations in Carthage 1977 Conducted by the University of Michigan*, vol. 5, New Dehli.

Ibn al-Kalbi, Hisham (1969), *Kitab al-Asnam*, ed. and trans. by Wahib Atallah, Paris.

Ibn Khaldun, 'Abd al-Rahman b. Muhammad (1958), *The Muqaddimah: An Introduction to History*, trans. by Franz Rosenthal, New York.

Insoll, Timothy (1999), *The Archaeology of Islam*, Oxford.

— (2003), *The Archaeology of Islam in Sub-Saharan Africa*, Cambridge.

— (2004), *Archaeology, Ritual, Religion*, Themes in Archaeology, London and New York.

—, ed. (2001), *Archaeology and World Religion*, London and New York.

Jalloul, Néji (1998), 'Permanences antiques et mutations médiévales: Agriculture et produits du sol en Ifriqiya au haut Moyen Age (IXe–XIIe s.)', in Khanoussi, Ruggieri and Vismara, eds, pp. 485–511.

Jameson, Michael, Curtis Runnels, and Tjeerd van Andel (1994), *A Greek Countryside: The Southern Argolid from Prehistory to the Present Day*, Stanford.

Jansson, Ingmar (1988), 'Wikingerzeitlicher orientalischer Import in Skandinavien. Oldenburg – Wolin – Staraja Ladoga – Novgorod – Kiev', *Bericht der Römisch-Germanischen Kommission* 69: 564–647.

Jenkins, Marilyn (1975), 'Western Islamic influences on Fatimid Egyptian iconography', *Kunst des Orients* 10: 91–107.

— (1984), 'Mamluk underglaze-painted pottery: Foundations for future study', *Muqarnas* 2, 95–114.

— (1992), 'Early medieval Islamic pottery: The eleventh century reconsidered', *Muqarnas* 9: 56–66.

Jenkins-Madina, Marilyn (2006), *Raqqa Revisited: Ceramics of Ayyubid Syria*, New Haven and London.

Jiayao, An (1991), 'Dated Islamic glass in China', *Bulletin of the Asia Institute* New Series 5: 123–37.

Johns, Cedric (1935), 'Excavations at Pilgrim's Castle, 'Athlit (1932–1933): Stables at the south-west of the suburb', *Quarterly of the Department of Antiquities of Palestine* 5: 31–60.

Johns, Jeremy (1995a) 'The *longue durée*: State and settlement strategies in southern Transjordan across the Islamic centuries', in Eugene Rogan and Tariq Tell, eds, *Village, Steppe and State. The Social Origins of Modern Jordan*, London and New York: 1–31.

— (1995b), 'The Greek church and the conversion of Muslims in Norman Sicily?', *Byzantinische Forschungen* 21: 133–57.

— (1998), 'The rise of Middle Islamic hand-made geometrically-painted ware in Bilad al-Sham (11th–13th centuries AD)', in Gayraud, ed., pp. 65–93.

— (1999), 'The "House of the Prophet" and the concept of the mosque', in Jeremy Johns, ed., *Bayt al-Maqdis: Jerusalem and Early Islam*, OSIA 9.2, Oxford, pp. 59–112.

— (2003), 'Archaeology and the history of early Islam: The first seventy years', *JESHO* 46.4: 411–36.

Jones, Alan (1998), 'The dotting of a script and the dating of an era: The strange neglect of PERF 558', *Islamic Culture* 72.4: 95–103.

Jones, R., G. Tompsett, K. Politis and E. Photos-Jones (2000), 'The Tawahin as-Sukkar and Khirbat ash-Shaykh 'Isa project. Phase I: the surveys', *ADAJ* 34: 523–34.

Kafadar, Cemal (2007), 'A Rome of one's own: Reflections on cultural geography and identity in the lands of Rum', *Muqarnas* 24: 7–25.

Kareem, Jum'a (2000), *The Settlement Patterns in the Jordan Valley in the Mid- to Late Islamic Period*, BAR International Series 877, Oxford.

Karev, Yury (2004), 'Samarqand in the eighth century: The evidence of transformation', in Whitcomb, ed., pp. 51–66.

Kawatoko, Mutsuo (2001), 'Coffee trade in the al-Tur port, south Sinai', in Tuchscherer, ed., pp. 51–66.

— (2005), 'Multi-disciplinary approaches to the Islamic period in Egypt and the Red Sea coast', *Antiquity* 79: 844–57.

Kennedy, Hugh (1985a), 'From *polis* to *madina*: Urban change in late antique and early Islamic Syria', *Past and Present* 106: 3–27.

— (1985b), 'The last century of Byzantine Syria: A reinterpretation', *Byzantinische Forschungen* 10: 141–83.

— (2001), *The Armies of the Caliphs: Military and Society in the Early Islamic State*, Warfare and History, London and New York.

—, ed. (2006), *Muslim Military Architecture in Greater Syria. From the Coming of Islam to the Ottoman Period*, History of Warfare 35, Leiden and Boston.

Kennet, Derek (2001), 'The form of the military cantonments at Samarra. The organisation of the Abbasid army', in Robinson, ed., pp. 157–82.

— (2004), *Sasanian and Islamic Pottery from Ras al-Khaimah. Classification, Chronology and Analysis of Trade in the Western Indian Ocean*, Society for Arabian Studies Monographs 1, Oxford.

— (2005), 'On the eve of Islam: Archaeological evidence from Eastern Arabia', *Antiquity* 79: 107–18.

Kervran, Monique and Axelle Rouguelle (1984), 'Recherche sur les niveaux islamiques de la Ville des Artisans, Suse, 1976–1978', *Cahiers de la Délégation Archéologique Française en Iran* 14: 7–120.

Kervran, Monique, Fredrik Hiebert and Axelle Rouguelle (2005), *Qal'at Bahrain, a Trading and Military Outpost: 3rd Millennium BC– 17th Century AD*, Indicopleustoi Archaeologies of the Indian Ocean 4, Turnhout.

Khamis, Elias (2001), 'Two wall mosaic inscriptions from the Umayyad market place in Bet Shean/Baysan', *BSOAS* 64: 159–76.

Khan, Ahmad Nabi (1990), *Al-Mansurah: A Forgotten Arab Metropolis in Pakistan*, Museums and Monuments Series 2, Karachi.

— (1991), *Development of Mosque Architecture in Pakistan*, Islamabad.

Khan, F. (1976), *Banbhore: A Preliminary Report on the Recent Archaeological Excavations at Banbhore*, 4th edn, Karachi.

Khan, Sir Sayyid Ahmad (1979), *Monuments of Delhi: Historical Study (Asar al-Sanadid)*, trans. by R. Nath, New Delhi.

Khanoussi, Mustapha, Paola Ruggieri and Cinzia Vismara, eds (1998), *L'Africa romana. Atti del XII convegno di studio Olbia, 12–15 dicembre 1996*, Sassari.

Kiani, Muhammad Yusuf (1981), *Yadgar'ha-yi Rubat-i Sharaf* (English title: *Discoveries from Robat-e Sharaf*), Tehran.

Kiel, Machiel (1990), *Studies on the Ottoman Architecture of the Balkans*, Aldershot.

King, Geoffrey (1985), 'Islam, Iconoclasm and the declaration of doctrine', *BSOAS* 48: 267–77.

— (1987), 'The distribution of sites and routes in the Jordanian and Syrian deserts', *PSAS* 20: 91–105.

— (1989), 'The Umayyad qusur and related settlements in Jordan', in Bakhit and Schick, eds, pp. 71–80.

— (1997), 'A Nestorian monastic settlement on the island of Sir bani Yas, Abu Dhabi: A preliminary report', *BSOAS* 60.2: 221–235.

King, Geoffrey and Averil Cameron, eds (1994), *The Byzantine and Early Islamic Near East II: Land Use and Settlement Patterns*, Princeton, NJ.

Kouymjian, Dickran, ed. (1974), *Near Eastern Numismatics, Iconography, Epigraphy and History. Studies in Honor of George C. Miles*. Beirut.

Knapp, A. Bernard, ed. (1992), *Archaeology, Annales, and Ethnohistory*, New Directions in Archaeology, Cambridge and New York.

Koechlin, Raymond (1928), *Les Céramiques musulmanes de Suse au Musée du Louvre*, Paris.

Kohl, Philip, Mara Kozelsky and Nachman Ben-Yehuda, eds (2007), *Selective Remembrances: Archaeology in the Construction, Commemoration, and Consecration of National Pasts*, Chicago and London.

Krautheimer, Richard (1986), *Early Christian and Byzantine Architecture*, 4th edn, Harmondsworth.

Kröger, Jens (1995), *Nishapur: Glass of the Early Islamic Period*, New York.

Kromann, Anne and Else Roesdahl (1996), 'The Vikings and the Islamic lands', in Kjeld von Folsach, Torben Lundbaek, Peder Mortensen and Lise Funder, eds, *The Arabian Journey: Danish Connections with the Islamic World over a Thousand Years*, Århus: 9–17.

Kubiak, Wladislaw (1998), 'Pottery from the north-eastern Mediterranean countries found in Fustat', in Gayraud, ed., pp. 335–46.

Kubiak, Wladislaw and George Scanlon (1973), 'Fustat: Re-dating Bahgat's houses and the aqueduct', *Art and Archaeology Research Papers* 4: 138–48.

—, eds (1989), *Fustat Expedition Final report. Vol. 2; Fustat-C*, American Research Center in Egypt Reports 2, Winona Lake.

Küchler, M. (1991), 'Moschee und Kalifenpaläste Jerusalems nach den Aphrodito-Papyri', *Zeitschrift des Deutschen Palästina-Vereins* 107: 120–43.

LaBianca, Øystein (1990), *Sedenterization and Nomadization: Food System Cycles at Hesban and Vicinity in Transjordan*, Hesban I, Berriens Springs.

LaGro, H. Eduard and Hubert de Haas (1989–90), 'Sugar pots, a preliminary study of technical aspects of a class of medieval pottery from Tell Abu Sarbut, Jordan', *Newsletter of the Department of Pottery Technology* 7–8: 7–20.

Laing, Ellen (1991), 'A report on the western Asian glassware in the Far East', *Bulletin of the Asia Institute* New Series 5: 109–21.

Lambert, Phyllis, ed. (2001), *Fortifications and the Synagogue: The Fortress of Babylon and the Ben Ezra Synagogue*, 2nd edn, Montréal.

Lambourn, Elizabeth (2008), 'Tombstones, texts, and typologies: Seeing sources for the early history of Islam in southeast Asia', *JESHO* 51: 252–86.

Lamm, Carl (1928), *Ausgrabungen von Samarra IV: Das Glas von Samarra*, Berlin.

Lane, Arthur (1957), *Early Islamic Pottery: Mesopotamia, Egypt, Persia*, London.

Lassner, Jacob (1970), *The Topography of Baghdad in the Early Middle Ages: Texts and Studies*, Detroit.

Lebecq, Stéphane (1997), 'Routes of change: Production and distribution in the West (5th–8th century)', in Leslie Webster and Michelle Brown, eds, *The Transformation of the Roman World*, AD 400–900, London, pp. 67–78.

Leisten, Thomas (2003), *Excavations in Samarra. Volume 1: Architecture. Final Report of the first Campaign*, 1910–1912, Baghdader Forschungen 20, Manz am Rhein.

Lemeunier, Guy (1999), 'L'Irrigation à Murcia au début de l'époque moderne', in Bazzana, ed., pp. 91–100.

Leone, Anna (2003), 'Late antique North Africa: Production and changing use of buildings in urban areas', *al-Masaq*, 15.1: 21–33.

Levine, Lee (2005a), *The Ancient Synagogue: The First Thousand Years*, 2nd edn, New Haven and London.

— (2005b), 'Figural art in ancient Judaism', *Ars Judaica* 1: 9–26.

Lézine, Alexandre (1965), *Mahdiya: Recherches d'archéologie islamique*, Archéologie Méditerranéene 1, Paris.

— (1966), *Architecture de l'Ifriqiya*, Paris.

— (1967), 'Notes d'archéologie ifriqiyenne', *Revue des Etudes Islamiques* 35: 52–101.

Lopez, Robert (1943), 'Mohammed and Charlemagne: A revision', *Speculum* 18.1: 14–38.

Lopez, Robert and Irving Raymond (2001), *Medieval Trade in the Mediterranean World*, new edn, New York.

Lowick, Nicholas (1974), 'Trade patterns on the Persian Gulf in the light of recent coin evidence', in Kouymjian, ed., pp. 319–33.

— (1985), *The Coins and Monumental Inscriptions*, Siraf 15, London.

Luz, Nimrod (1997), 'The construction of an Islamic city in Palestine. The case of Umayyad al-Ramla', *Journal of the Royal Asiatic Society* Series 3, 7.1: 27–54.

MacDonald, Burton, Russell Adams and Piotr Bienkowski, eds (2001), *The Archaeology of Jordan*, Sheffield.

MacKenzie, Neil and Salah al-Hilwa (1980), 'Darb Zubayda architectural documentation program. A. Darb Zubayda-1979: A preliminary report', *Atlal* 4: 37–50.

McQuitty, Alison (2001), 'The Ottoman period', in MacDonald, Adams and Bienkowski, eds, pp. 561–93.

Magness, Jodi (2003), *The Archaeology of the Early Islamic Settlement in Palestine*, Winona Lake.

Maier, F. and M.-L. Wartburg (1983), 'Excavations at Kouklia (Palaeopaphos). Twelfth preliminary report: Seasons 1981 and 1982', *Report of the Department of Antiquities of Cyprus*: 300–14, pls XLVIII–LII.

Malik ibn Anas (1989), *Al-Muwatta of Imam Malik ibn Anas. The First Formulation of Islamic Law*, trans. by A. Bewley, London and New York.

Mango, Marlia (1996), 'Byzantine maritime trade with the East (fourth–seventh centuries)', *Aram* 8: 139–63.

Mann, Vivian, Thomas Glick and Jerrilyn Dodds, eds (1992), *Convivencia: Jews, Muslims and Christians in Medieval Spain*, New York.

Maqrizi, Ahmad ibn 'Ali Taqi al-Din (1934–72), *Kitab al-Suluk li-ma'rifat duwal al-muluk*, ed. by M. Ziada and S. Ashour, Cairo.

Marçais, Georges (1928), *Les Faïences à reflets métalliques de la Grande Mosquée de Kairouan*, Paris.

Marino, Brigitte (1995), 'Cafés et cafetiers de Damas aux XVIIIe et XIXe siècles', *Revue du Monde Musulman et de la Mediterranée* 75–6: 275–94.

Mason, Robert (2004), *Shine like the Sun: Lustre-Painted and Associated Pottery from the Medieval Middle East*, Bibliotheca Iranica: Islamic Art and Architecture Series 12, Toronto and Costa Mesa.

Mason, Robert and Edward Keall (1991), 'The 'Abbasid glazed wares of Siraf and the Basra connection: Petrographic analysis', *Iran*, 29: 51–66.

Mason, Robert and Michael Tite (1994), 'The beginnings of Islamic stonepaste technology', *Archaeometry* 36.1: 77–92.

Mason, Robert and Michael Tite (1997), 'The beginnings of tin-opacification of pottery glazes', *Archaeometry* 39: 41–58.

Matson, Frederick (1948), 'The manufacture of eighth-century Egyptian glass weights and stamps', in George Miles, ed., *Early Arabic Glass Weights and Stamps*, Numismatic Notes and Monographs 111, New York, pp. 31–69.

McNicoll, Anthony (1983), with contribution by Roland Fletcher, *Taşkun Kale: Keban Rescue Excavations in Eastern Anatolia*, British Institute of Archaeology at Ankara, Monograph 6, BAR International Series 168, Oxford.

McNicoll, Anthony, P. Edwards, J. Hanbury-Tenison, J. Hennessy, T. Potts, R. Smith, A. Walmsley and P. Watson (1992), *Pella in Jordan 2: The Second Interim Report of the Joint University of Sydney and College of Wooster Excavations at Pella, 1982–1985*, Mediterranean Archaeology Supplement 2, Sydney.

McQuitty, Alison (1995), 'Watermills in Jordan: Technology, typology, dating and development', *Studies in the History and Archaeology of Jordan* 5: 745–51.

McQuitty, Alison, M. Sarley-Pontin, M. Khoury, M. Charles and C. Hoppé (1997–8), 'Mamluk Khirbat Faris', *Aram* 9–10: 181–226.

Meinecke, Michael (1992), 'Early Abbasid stucco decoration in Bilad al-Sham', in Muhammad Bakhit and Robert Schick, eds, *Bilad al-Sham during the Abbasid Period, 132 AH/750 AD– 451 AH/1059 AD*, Amman.

Meri, Josef (2002), *The Cult of Saints among Muslims and Jews in Medieval Syria*, Oxford.

Mershen, Birgit (1985), 'Recent handmade pottery from north Jordan', *Berytus* 33, 1985: 75–87.

Meyer, Carol (1992), *Glass from Quseir al-Qadim and the Indian Ocean Trade*, Studies in Ancient Oriental Civilization 53, Chicago.

Michel, Anne (2001), *Les églises d'époque byzantine et umayyade de la Jordanie, Ve–VIIIe siècle. Typologie architecturale et aménagements liturgiques*, Bibliothèque de l'Antiquité Tardive 2, Turnhout.

Miglus, Peter, ed. (1999), *Ar-Raqqa I. Die frühislamische Keramik von Tall Aswad*, Mainz am Rhein.

Miles, George (1951), *Early Arabic Glass Weights and Stamps: A Supplement*, Numismatic Notes and Monographs 120, New York.

Milson, David (2007), *Art and Architecture of the Synagogue in Late Antique Palestine: In the Shadow of the Church*, Ancient Judaism and Early Christianity 65, Leiden and Boston.

Milwright, Marcus (1999), 'Pottery in the written sources of the Ayyubid-Mamluk period (c. 567–923/1171–1517)', *BSOAS* 62.3: 504–19.

— (2000), 'Pottery of Bilad al-Sham in the Ottoman period: A review of the published archaeological evidence', *Levant* 32: 189–208.

— (2001a), 'Gazetteer of archaeological sites in the Levant reporting pottery of the Middle Islamic period (ca. 1100–1600)', *Islamic Art* 5: 3–39.

— (2001b), 'Fixtures and fittings: The role of decoration in Abbasid palace design', in Robinson, ed. (2001), pp. 79–110.

— (2003), 'Modest luxuries: Decorated lead-glazed pottery in the south of Bilad al-Sham (thirteenth and fourteenth centuries)', *Muqarnas* 20: 85–111.

— (2008a), *The Fortress of the Raven: Karak in the Middle Islamic Period (1100–1650)*, Islamic History and Civilization 72, Leiden and Boston.

— (2008b), 'Imported pottery in Ottoman Bilad al-Sham', *Turcica* 40: 121–52.

Milwright, Marcus and Evanthia Baboula (2009), 'Water on the ground: Water systems in two Ottoman Greek port cities', in Sheila Blair and Jonathan Bloom (eds), *Rivers of Paradise: Water in Islamic Culture*, New Haven and London, pp. 213–37.

Mitchell, Piers (2004), 'The palaeopathology of skulls recovered from a medieval cave cemetery near Safed, Israel (thirteenth to seventeenth century)', *Levant* 36: 243–50.

Monneret de Villard, Ugo (1966), with an introduction by Oleg Grabar, *Introduzione allo studio dell'archeologia Islamica. Le origini e il periodo omayyade*, Venice and Rome.

Morgan, Craig and Salah al-Hilwa (1981), 'Preliminary report on the fifth phase of Darb Zubayda reconnaissance, 1400 AH/1980 AD', *Atlal* 5: 85–107.

Morgan, Peter (1994), 'Sgraffiato: Types and distribution', in Grube, ed., pp. 119–23.

Morony, Michael (1994), 'Land use and settlement patterns in late Sasanian and early Islamic Iraq', in King and Cameron, eds, pp. 221–9.

—, ed. (2002), *Production and the Exploitation of Resources*, Formation of the Islamic World 11, Aldershot and Burlington.

Mouton, J.-M., Sami Salih 'Abd al-Malik, Olivier Jaubert and Claudine Piaton (1996), 'La Route de Saladin (*Tariq Sadr wa Ayla*) au Sinaï', *Annales Islamologiques* 30: 41–70.

Mundell Mango, Marlia (1977), 'Monophysite church decoration', in Anthony Bryer and Judith Herrin, eds, *Iconoclasm*, Birmingham: 59–74.

Museum with no Frontiers (2000), *The Umayyads: The Rise of Islamic Art*, Vienna and Amman.

Navarro, Julio and Pedro Jiménez (2007), 'Evolution of Andalusi urban landscape: From the dispersed to the saturated medina', in Anderson and Rosser-Owen, eds, pp. 115–42.

Neely, James (2002), 'Sassanian and early Islamic water-control and irrigation systems on the Deh Luran plain', in Morony, ed., pp. 251–72 (reprinted from T. Downing and McG. Gibson, eds, *Irrigation's Impact on Society*, Tucson, 1974, pp. 21–42).

Noonan, Thomas (1981), 'Ninth-century dirham hoards from European Russia: A preliminary analysis', in Blackburn and Metcalf, eds, pp. 47–117 (reprinted in Noonan (1998)).

— (1986), 'Why the Vikings first came to Russia', *Jahrbücher für Geschichte Osteuropas* 34: pp. 321–48 (reprinted in Noonan (1998)).

— (1998), *The Islamic World, Russia and the Vikings, 750–900: The Numismatic Evidence*, Aldershot.

Northedge, Alastair (1992), *Studies on Roman and Islamic 'Amman. The Excavations of Mrs C.-M. Bennett and Other Investigations.Volume 1: History, Site and Architecture*, British Academy Monographs in Archaeology 3, Oxford and New York.

— (1994), 'Archaeology and the new urban settlement in Early Islamic Syria and Iraq', in King and Cameron, eds, pp. 231–65.

— (1996), 'Friedrich Sarre's *Die Keramik von Samarra* in perspective', in Bartl and Hauser, eds, pp. 229–58.

— (2001), 'Thoughts on the introduction of polychrome glazed pottery in the Middle East', in Villeneuve and Watson, eds, pp. 207–14.

— (2005a), *The Historical Topography of Samarra*, Samarra Studies 1, British School of Archaeology in Iraq and Fondation Max van Berchem, London.

— (2005b), 'Ernst Herzfeld, Samarra, and Islamic archaeology', in Ann Gunter and Stefan Hauser, eds, *Ernst Herzfeld and the Development of Near Eastern Studies, 1900–1950*. Leiden and Boston, pp. 385–403.

Northedge, Alastair and Robin Falkner (1987), 'The 1986 survey season at Samarra", *Iraq* 49: 143–73.

Northedge, Alastair and Derek Kennet (1994), 'The Samarra horizon', in Grube, ed., pp. 21–35.

Ocaña, Manuel Jiménez (1942), 'La basílica de San Vicente', *Al-Andalus* 7: 347–66.

Ochsenschlager, Edward (2004), *Iraq's Marsh Arabs in the Garden of Eden*, Philadelphia.

Oleson, John (2001), 'Water supply in Jordan through the Ages', in MacDonald, Adams and Bienkowski, eds, pp. 603–14.

Oleson, John, K. Amr, R. Foote, J. Logan, B. Reeves and R. Schick (1999), 'Preliminary report of the al-Humayma excavation project, 1995, 1996 and 1998', *ADAJ* 43: 411–50.

Orser, Charles, ed. (2002), *Encyclopedia of Historical Archaeology*, London and New York.

Ørsted, Peter, L. Ladjimi Sebaï, Habib Ben Hassan, Habib Ben Younes, Jamel Zoughlami and Fathi Bejaoui, (1992), 'Town and countryside in Roman Tunisia: A preliminary report on the Tunisio-Danish survey project in the Oued R'mel basin in and around Segermes', *JRA* 5: 69–96.

Pace, James (1996), 'The cisterns of the al-Karak plateau', *ADAJ* 40: 369–74.

Parker, S. Thomas (1986), *Romans and Saracens: A History of the Arabian Frontier*, Philadelphia.

Peacock, David, Lucy Blue and Stephanie Moser, eds (2002), *Myos Hormos: Quseir Qadim. A Roman and Islamic Port on the Red Sea Coast of Egypt. Interim Report, 2002*, Southampton (www.soton.ac.uk/Projects/projects.asp?ProjectID=20).

Peña, Ignacio (1996), *The Christian Art of Byzantine Syria*, London.

Pentz, Peter (1997), *The Medieval Citadel and its Architecture*, Hama: Fouilles et recherches de la Fondation Carlsberg, 1931–1938, IV, Copenhagen.

Petersen, Andrew (2001), 'Ottoman hajj forts', in MacDonald, Adams and Bien-kowski, eds, pp. 685–91.

Piccirillo, Michele (1993), *The Mosaics of Jordan*, Amman.

Pirenne, Henri (1954), *Mohammed and Charlemagne*, London.

Porter, Venetia (2004), 'Glazed pottery from the Great Mosque at ar-Rafiqa', in Daiber and Becker, eds, pp. 41–3.

Porter, Venetia and Oliver Watson (1987), '"Tell Minis" wares', in Allan and Roberts, eds, pp. 175–248.

Pringle, Denys (1986), 'Pottery as evidence for trade in the crusader states', in Gabriella Airaldi and Benjamin Kedar, eds, *I Communi italiani nel regno Crociato di Gerusalemm*, Genoa, pp. 451–75.

Pugachenkova, A. and E. Rtveladze (1986), 'Archaeology vii: Islamic Central Asia', *Encyclopaedia Iranica* 2.3: 322–26.

Qasimi, Muhammad S., Jamal-Din al-Qasimi and Khalil al-Azem (1960), *Diction-naire des métiers damascains*, ed. Zafer al-Qasimi, Le Monde d'Outre-Mer passé et présent. Deuxième série. Documents III, Paris and Le Haye.

Quataert, Donald, ed. (1994), *Manufacturing in the Ottoman Empire and Turkey, 1500–1950*, Albany, NY.

Raban, Avner (1971), 'The shipwreck off Sharm-el-Sheikh', *Archaeology* 24.2: 146–55.

Rabbat, Nasser (2000), 'Al-Maqrizi's *Khitat*, an Egyptian *lieu de mémoire*', in Doris Behrens-Abouseif, ed., *The Cairo Heritage: Essays in Honor of Laila Ali Ibrahim*, Cairo and New York, pp. 17–30.

Raby, Julian and Jeremy Johns, eds (1992), *Bayt al-Maqdis: 'Abd al-Malik's Jerusalem*, OSIA 9.2, Oxford.

Rafeq, Abdul-Karim (2001), 'The socio-economic and political implications of the introduction of coffee into Syria. 16th–18th centuries', in Tuchscherer, ed., pp. 129–42.

Rawson, Jessica, Michael Tite and M. Hughes (1989), 'The export of Tang Sancai wares: Some recent research', *Transactions of the Oriental Ceramic Society*, 1987–1988: 39–61.

Redford, Scott (1990), 'How Islamic is it? The Innsbruck plate and its setting', *Muqarnas* 7: 119–35.

— (1998), *The Archaeology of the Frontier in the Medieval Near East: Excavations at Gritille, Turkey*, with chapters by Gil J. Stein and Naomi Miller and a contri-bution by Denise C. Hodges, Archaeological Institute of America Monographs, New Series 3, Boston.

Redford, Scott and M. James Blackman (1997), 'Luster and fritware production in medieval Syria', *Journal of Field Archaeology* 24: 233–47.

Redman, Charles (1986), *Qsar es-Saghir: An Archaeological View of Medieval Life*, New York and London.

Redman, Charles and Ann Kinzig (2003), 'Resilience of past landscapes: Resilience theory, society and the *longue durée*', *Ecology and Society* 7: 14. (http://www.consecol.org/vol7/iss14/art14).

Rezq, 'Assem Mohammed (1988), 'The Craftsmen of Muslim Egypt and their social and military rank during the mediaeval period', *Islamic Archaeological Studies* 3: 3–31.

Rice, David (1957), 'Inlaid brasses from the workshop of Ahmed al-Dhaki al-Mawsili', *Ars Orientalis* 2: 283–326.

— (1958), 'Deacon or drink: Some paintings from Samarra re-examined', *Arabica* 5: 15–33.

Riis, Poul, Vagn Poulsen and Erling Hammershaimb (1957), *Les Verreries et poteries médiévales*, Hama, fouilles et recherches de la Fondation Carlsberg, 1931–1938, IV.2, Copenhagen.

Robinson, Chase, ed. (2001), *A Medieval City Reconsidered: An Interdisciplinary Approach to Samarra*, OSIA 14, Oxford.

— (2003a), 'Ar-Raqqa in the Syriac historical tradition', in Heidemann and Becker, eds (2003), pp. 81–85.

— (2003b), *Islamic Historiography*, Themes in Islamic History, Cambridge.

Robinson, Rebecca (1985), 'Tobacco pipes of Corinth and the Athenian Agora', *Hesperia* 54: 149–203.

Rogers, J. Michael (1974), *From Antiquarianism to Islamic Archaeology*, Quaderni dell' Istituto Italiano di Cultura per la RAE, Nuova serie 2, Cairo.

Roll, Israel and Etan Ayalon (1987), 'The market street of Apollonia-Arsuf', *BASOR* 267: 61–76.

Rosen-Ayalon, Miriam (1989), *The Early Islamic Monuments of al-Haram al-Sharif. An Iconographic Study*, Qedem 28, Jerusalem.

— (2006), *Islamic Art and Archaeology in Palestine*, Walnut Creek.

Rothenberg, Benno (1999), 'Archaeo-metallurgical researches in the southern 'Arabah. Part 2: Egyptian New Kingdom (Ramesside) to early Islam', *PEQ*, July–December: 149–75.

Rousset, Marie-Odile (1994), 'Quelques précisions sur le matériel de Hira (céramique et verre)', *Archéologie Islamique* 4: 19–55.

Rubin, Rehav (1989), 'The debate over climatic changes in the Negev, fourth-seventh centuries CE', *PEQ*, January–June: 71–78.

Ruggles, Dede (2000), *Gardens, Landscape, and Vision in the Palaces of Islamic Spain*, University Park.

— (forthcoming), 'The stratigraphy of forgetting: The Great Mosque of Cordoba and its contested legacy', in Helaine Silverman, ed., *Contested Heritage*, New York.

Rye, Owen and Clifford Evans (1976), *Traditional Pottery Techniques of Pakistan. Field and Laboratory Studies*, Smithsonian Contributions to Anthropology 21, Washington, DC.

Sack, Dorothée (1996), *Die Grosse Moschee von Resafa – Rusafat Hisam*, Resafa 4, Mainz.

Safar, Fuad (1945), *Wasit: The Sixth Season's Excavations*, Cairo.

Sarre, Friedrich (1925), *Ausgrabungen von Samarra II: Die Keramik von Samarra*, Berlin.

Sauvaget, Jean (1934), 'Le plan de Laodicée-sur-Mer', *Bulletin d'Etudes Orientales* 4: 81–114.

— (1941), *La Poste aux chevaux dans l'empire des mamelouks*, Paris.

— (1947), *La Mosquée omeyyade de Médine: Etude sur les origines architecturales de la mosquée et de la basilique*, Paris.

— (1949), 'Le plan antique de Damas', *Syria* 26: 316–58.

— (1967), 'Chateaux umayyades de Syrie: Contribution à l'étude de la colonisation arabe aux Ier et IIe siècles de l'Hégire', *Revue d'Etudes Islamiques* 36: 1–52.

Sayre, Edward (1965), 'Summary of the Brookhaven program of analysis of ancient glass', in his *Application of Science in the Examination of Works of Art*, Boston, pp. 145–55.

Scanlon, George (1970), 'Housing and sanitation; Some aspects of medieval Islamic public service', in Hourani and Stern, eds, pp. 179–94.

— (1984), 'Mamluk pottery: More evidence from Fustat', *Muqarnas* 2: 115–26.

— (1986), *Fustat Expedition Final Reports, Vol. 1: Catalogue of Filters*, American Research Center in Egypt Reports 8, Winona Lake.

Scanlon, George and Ralph Pinder-Wilson (2001), *Fustat Glass of the Early Islamic Period. Finds Excavated by the American Research Center in Egypt, 1964–1980*, London.

Schaefer, Jerome (1986), 'An Umayyad potters' complex in the north theatre, Jerash', in Fawzi Zayadine, ed., *Jerash Archaeological Project, 1981–1983*, Amman, pp. 411–59.

Schick, Robert (1995), *The Christian Communities of Palestine from Byzantine to Islamic Rule: A Historical and Archaeological Study*, Studies in Late Antiquity and Early Islam 2, Princeton, NJ.

Schlumberger, Daniel (1939), 'Les Fouilles de Qasr el-Heir el-Gharbi (1936–1938). Rapport préliminaire', *Syria* 20: 195–238.

— (1978), *Lashkari Bazar: Une résidence royale ghaznévide et ghoride*, Mémoires de la Délégation Française en Afghanistan 18, Paris.

Segal, Arthur (1985), 'Shivta – A Byzantine town in the Negev desert', *Journal of the Society of Architectural Historians* 44.4: 317–28.

Shahid, Irfan (1992), 'Ghassanid and Umayyad structures: A case of *Byzance après Byzance*', in P. Canivet and J.-P. Rey-Coquais, eds, *La Syrie de Byzance à l'Islam, VIIe–VIIIe siècles*, Damascus, pp. 299–307.

Shani, Raya (1989), 'On the stylistic idiosyncracies of a Saljuq stucco workshop from the region of Kashan', *Iran* 27: 67–74.

Sherratt, Andrew (1992), 'What can archaeologists learn from *Annalistes*?', in Knapp, ed., pp. 135–42.

Shoshan, Boas (1993), *Popular Culture in Medieval Cairo*, Cambridge Studies in Islamic Civilization, Cambridge.

Silberman, Neil (1982), *Digging for God and Country: Exploration, Archaeology and the Secret Struggle for the Holy Land, 1799–1917*, New York.

— (1989), *Between Past and Present: Archaeology, Ideology, and Nationalism in the Modern Middle East*, New York and London.

Simpson, St John (1995a), 'Death and burial in the late Islamic Near East: Some insights from archaeology and ethnography', in Stuart Campbell and Anthony Green, eds, *The Archaeology of Death in the Ancient Near East*, Oxbow Monographs 51, Oxford, pp. 240–51.

— (1995b), 'An ordeal with a pipe: Changing attitudes to smoking in the Near East during the seventeenth and eighteenth centuries', *Society of Clay Pipe Research Newsletter* 47: 17–22.

— (1996), 'From Tekrit to Jaghjagh: Sasanian sites, settlement patterns and material culture in Northern Mesopotamia', in Bartl and Hauser, eds, pp. 87–126.

— (1997), 'A Late Islamic ceramic group from Hatara Saghir', *Mesopotamia* 32: 87–129.

— (2000), 'Mesopotamia in the Sasanian period: Settlement patterns, arts and crafts', in John Curtis, ed., *Mesopotamia and Iran in the Parthian and Sasanian Periods: Rejection and Revival, c.238 BC–AD 642*, London, pp. 57–66.

Sims, Eleanor (2002), with Boris Marshak and Ernst Grube, *Peerless Images: Persian Painting and Its Sources*, New Haven and London.

Small, David, ed. (1995), *Methods in the Mediterranean: Historical and Archaeological Views on Texts and Archaeology*, Leiden and New York.

Smith, Michael (1992), 'Braudel's temporal rhythms and chronology theory in archaeology', in Knapp, ed., pp. 23–34.

Sodini, Jean-Pierre, Georges Tate, Bernard Bavant, Swantje Bavant, Jean-Luc Biscop, Dominique Orssaud, Cécile Morrisson and François Poplin, (1980), 'Déhès (Syrie du Nord), Campagnes I–III (1976–1978): Recherches sur l'habitat rural', *Syria* 57: 1–303.

Solignac, M.-J. (1964), 'Remarques de méthode sur l'étude des installations hydrauliques ifriquiyennes au Haut Moyen-Age', *Les Cahiers de Tunisie* 47–48: 25–36.

Stedman, Nancy (1996), 'Land use and settlement in post-medieval central Greece: An interim discussion', in Peter Lock and G. Sanders, eds, *The Archaeology of Medieval Greece*, Oxbow Monograph 59, Oxford, pp. 179–92.

Stern, Henri (1963), 'Recherches sur la mosquée al-Aqsa et sur ses mosaïques', *Ars Orientalis* 5: 27–47.

Stevens, Susan, Angela Kalinowski and Hans van der Leest, eds (2005), *Bir Ftouha: A Pilgrimage Church Complex at Carthage*, JRA Supplementary Series 59, Portsmouth, RI.

Sutton, Susan, ed. (2000), *Contingent Countryside: Settlement, Economy, and Land Use in the Southern Argolid since 1700*, Stanford.

Syon, D. (2003), 'A church from the early Islamic period at Khirbet el-Shubeika', in Bottini, Di Segna and Chrupcala, eds, pp. 74–82.

Tabbaa, Yasser (1997), *Constructions of Power and Piety in Medieval Aleppo*, University Park, PA.

Tamari, Vera (1995), 'Abbasid blue-on-white ware', in James Allan, ed., *Islamic Art in the Ashmolean Museum, Part Two*, OSIA 10.2, Oxford and New York, pp. 117–45.

Tampoe, Moira (1989), *Maritime Trade between China and the West: An Archaeological Study of the Ceramics from Siraf (Persian Gulf) 8th to 15th Centuries AD*, BAR International Series 555 Oxford.

Tate, Georges (1992), *Les Campagnes de la Syrie du Nord du IIe au VIIe siècle*, Tome Ier, Paris.

Tite, Michael (1989), 'Iznik pottery: An investigation of the methods of production', *Archaeometry* 31.2: 115–32.

Tite, Michael, I. Freestone, R. Mason, J. Molera, M. Vendrell-Saz and N. Wood (1998), 'Lead glazes in antiquity – methods of production and reasons for use', *Archaeometry* 40.2: 241–60.

Tonghini, Cristina and Ernst Grube (1989), 'Towards a history of Syrian Islamic pottery before 1500', *Islamic Art* 3: 59–93.

Tonghini, Cristina and Julian Henderson (1998), 'An eleventh-century pottery production workshop at al-Raqqa. Preliminary report', *Levant* 30: 113–27.

Toombs, Lawrence (1985), *Tell el Hesi: Modern Military Trenching and Muslim Cemetery in Field I, Strata I–II. The Joint Archaeological Expedition to Tell el-Hesi, Volume 2*, American Schools of Oriental Research Excavation Reports, Waterloo.

Trauth, Norbert (1996), 'Les produits métallurgiques du site médiéval de Saltés (Huelva – Andalousie)', *Archéologie Islamique* 6: 77–88.

Treptow, Tanya (2007), with Donald Whitcomb, *Daily Life Ornamented: The Medieval Persian City of Rayy*, Oriental Institute Museum Publications 26, Chicago.

Trümpelmann, Leo (1965), 'Die Skulpturen von Mschatta', *Archäologische Anzeiger* 2, cols 235–70.

Tsafrir, Yoram and Gideon Foerster (1992), 'The dating of the "earthquake of the sabbatical year" of 749 CE in Palestine', *BSOAS* 55: 231–35.

— (1994), 'From Scythopolis to Baysan – changing concepts of urbanism', in King and Cameron, eds, pp. 95–115.

— (1997), 'Urbanism at Scythopolis–Bet Shean in the fourth to seventh centuries', *DOP* 51: 85–146.

Tuchscherer, Michel, ed. (2001), *Le Commerce du café avant l'ère des plantations coloniales: Espaces, réseaux, sociétés (Xve–XIXe siècle)*, Cahiers des Annales Islamologiques 20, Cairo.

Tushingham, A. Douglas (1985), *Excavations in Jerusalem, 1961–1967*, vol. 1, Toronto.

Tzaferis, Vassilios (2003), 'The Greek inscriptions from the church of Khirbet el-Shubeika', in Bottini, Di Segna and Chrupcala, eds, pp. 83–6.

Urice, Stephen (1987), *Qasr Kharana in Transjordan*, Durham.

Vallejo, Antonio Triano (2007), 'Madinat al-Zahra': Transformation of a caliphal city', in Anderson and Rosser-Owen, eds, pp. 3–26.

Van Arendonk, C. (1973), 'Kahwa', in E. van Donzel, Bernard Lewis and Charles Pellat, eds, *Encyclopaedia of Islam*, new edn, vol. 4, Leiden: 449–53.

Vannini, Guido and Andrea Vanni Desideri (1995), 'Archaeological research on medieval Petra: A preliminary report', *ADAJ* 39: 509–40.

Van Reenan, Dan (1990), 'The *Bilderverbot*, a new survey', *Der Islam* 67: 27–77.

Vasiliev, A. (1956), 'The iconoclastic edict of the caliph Yazid II, AD 721', *DOP* 10: 25–47.

Vernoit, Stephen (1997), 'The rise of Islamic archaeology', *Muqarnas* 14: 1–10.

—, ed. (2000), *Discovering Islamic Art: Scholars, Collectors and Collections, 1850–1950*, London and New York.

Villeneuve, E. and Pamela Watson, eds (2001), *La Céramique byzantine et proto-islamique en Syrie–Jordanie (IVe–VIIIe siècles apr. J.-C.)*, Bibliothèque Archéologique et Historique 159, Beirut.

Vitelli, Giovanna (1981), *Islamic Carthage: The archaeological, historical and ceramic evidence*, Carthage.

Vitelli, Giovanna and Denys Pringle (1978), 'A bibliography of North African medieval pottery', *Medieval Ceramics* 2: 53–58.

Vogelsang-Eastwood, G. (1990), *Resist Dyed Textiles from Quseir Qadim, Egypt*, Paris.

Vogt, Burkhard (2005), 'The Great Marib dam: New research by the German Archaeological Institute in 2002', in Gunther, ed., pp. 119–22.

Vogt, Christine, Guy Bourgeois, Max Schvoerer, Philippe Gouin, Michel Girard and Stéphanie Thiébault (2002), 'Notes on some of the Abbasid amphorae of Istabl 'Antar-Fustat (Egypt)', *BASOR* 326: 65–80.

Volker, T. (1971), *Porcelain and the Dutch East India Company*, Leiden.

Vroom, Joanita (2003), *After Antiquity: Ceramics and Society in the Aegean from the 7th to the 20th Century*AC. *A Case Study from Boeotia, Central Greece*, Leiden.

— (2007), 'Kütahya between the lines: Post-medieval ceramics as historical information', in Davies and Davis, eds, pp. 71–93.

Wade, Rosalind (1979), 'Archaeological observations around Marib, 1976', *PSAS* 9: 114–23.

Walker, Bethany (2004), 'Mamluk investment in Transjordan: A "boom and bust" economy', *Mamluk Studies Review* 8.2: 119–47.

— (2005), 'The Northern Jordan Survey 2003 – Agriculture in late Islamic Malka and Hubras villages: A preliminary report on the first season', *BASOR* 339: 67–111.

Walmsley, Allan (1997–8), 'Settled life in Mamlûk Jordan: Views of the Jordan Valley from Fahl (Pella)', *Aram* 9–10: 129–43.

— (2001), 'Turning east. The appearance of Islamic cream ware in Jordan: The "end of antiquity"?', in Villeneuve and Watson, eds, pp. 305–13.

— (2007), *Early Islamic Syria: An Archaeological Assessment*, London.

Walmsley, Alan and Kristoffer Damgaard (2005), 'The Umayyad congregational mosque of Jarash in Jordan and its relationship to early mosques', *Antiquity* 79: 362–78.

Ward, Cheryl (2000), 'The Sadana island shipwreck: A mid eighteenth-century treasure trove', in Baram and Carroll, eds, pp. 185–202.

Ward, Paul (2002), 'The origin and spread of qanats in the Old World', in Morony, ed., pp. 273–84 (reprinted from *Proceedings of the American Philosophical Society* 112, 1968: 170–81).

Ward, Rachel (1993), *Islamic Metalwork*, London.

— (2004), 'Style versus substance: The Christian iconography on two vessels made for the Ayyubid sultan al-Salih Ayyub', in Bernard O'Kane, ed., *The Iconography of Islamic Art: Studies in Honour of Robert Hillenbrand*, Edinburgh: 309–24.

Watson, Andrew (1983), *Agricultural Innovation in the Early Islamic World: The Diffusion of Crops and Farming Techniques*, Cambridge Studies in Islamic Civilization, Cambridge.

Watson, Oliver (1985), *Persian Lustre Ware*, London.

— (2004), *Ceramics from Islamic Lands*, New York.

Weisgerber, Gerd (1980), 'Patterns of early Islamic metallurgy in Oman', *PSAS* 10: 115–26.

Wenke, Robert (1987), 'Western Iran in the Partho-Sasanian period: The imperial transformation', in Frank Hole, ed., *The Archaeology of Western Iran: Settlement and Society from Prehistory to the Islamic Conquest*, Washington, DC and London, pp. 251–81.

Wheatley, Paul (2001), *The Places where Men Pray Together: Cities in Islamic Lands, Seventh through the Tenth Centuries*, Chicago and London.

Whitcomb, Donald (1979), 'The City of Istakhr and the Marvdasht plain', in *Akten des VII. International Kongresses für iranische Kunst und Archäologie, München, 7–10 September 1976*, Berlin, pp. 363–70.

— (1985), *Before the Roses and the Nightingales: Excavations at Qasr-i Abu Nasr, Old Shiraz*, Metropolitan Museum of Art, New York.

— (1988), 'A Fatimid residence at 'Aqaba, Jordan', *ADAJ* 32, 1988: 207–24.

— (1989), 'Evidence for the Umayyad period from the Aqaba excavations', in Bakhit and Schick, eds, pp. 164–84.

— (1994a), 'The *misr* of Ayla: Settlement at 'Aqaba in the early Islamic period', in King and Cameron, eds, pp. 155–70.

— (1994b), 'The Ayla mosque', *Fondation Max van Berchem Bulletin* 8: 3–5.

— (1994c), *Aqaba, 'Port of Palestine on the China Sea'*, Amman.

— (2000), 'Archaeological research at hadir Qinnasrin, 1998', *Archéologie Islamique* 10: 7–28.

— (2002), 'Khirbet al-Karak identified with Sinnabra', *Al-'Usur al-Wusta* 14.1: 1–6.

— (2006), 'The walls of Early Islamic Ayla: Defence or symbol?', in Kennedy, ed., pp. 61–74.

—, ed (2004), *Changing Social Identity with the Spread of Islam: Archaeological Perspectives*, Oriental Institute Seminars 1, Chicago.

Whitcomb, Donald and Janet Johnson (1979), *Quseir al-Qadim 1978: Preliminary Report*, Cairo and Princeton.

— (1982), *Quseir al-Qadim 1980: Preliminary Report*, Malibu.

Whitehouse, David (1972), 'Chinese porcelain in medieval Europe', *Medieval Archaeology* 16: 63–78.

— (1973a), 'Chinese stoneware from Siraf: The earliest finds', in Norman Hammond, ed., *South Asian Archaeology: Papers from the First International Conference of South Asian Archaeologists Held in the University of Cambridge*, Park Ridge, pp. 241–55.

— (1973b), 'Maritime trade in the Gulf: The eleventh and twelfth centuries', *World Archaeology* 14.3: 328–34.

— (1975), 'The decline of Siraf', in F. Bagherzadeh, ed., *Proceedings of the Third Annual Symposium on Archaeological Research in Iran*, Tehran, pp. 263–70.

— (1980), *The Congregational Mosque and Other Mosques from the Ninth to the Twelfth Centuries*, Siraf III, London.

— (1997), 'Islamic pottery and Christian Europe from the tenth to the fifteenth century. The thirteenth Gerald Dunning Memorial lecture', *Medieval Ceramics* 21: 3–12.

— (2001), 'East Africa and the maritime trade of the Indian Ocean, AD 800–1500', in B. Amoretti, ed., *Islam in East Africa: New Sources*, Rome, pp. 411–24.

Whitehouse, David and Andrew Williamson (1973), 'Sasanian maritime trade', *Iran* 11: 29–49.

Wightman, G. (1989), *The Damascus Gate, Jerusalem*, BAR International Series 591, Oxford.

Wilkinson, Charles (1973), *Nishapur: Pottery of the Early Islamic Period*, Greenwich.
— (1986). *Nishapur: Some Early Islamic Buildings and Their Decoration*, New York.
Wilkinson, J. C. (1980), 'Darb Zubayda architectural documentation program. B. Darb Zubayda-1979: The water resources', *Atlal* 4: 51–68.
— (2002), 'The origins of the aflaj in Oman', in Morony, ed., pp. 285–302 (reprinted from the *Journal of Oman Studies* 6, 1983: 177–94).
Wilkinson, John (1992), 'Column capitals in the Haram al-Sharif', in Raby and Johns, eds, pp. 125–39.
Wilkinson, T. J. (1975), 'Sohar ancient fields project. Interim report no.1', *Journal of Oman Studies* 1: 159–64. Also 2 (1976): 75–80; 3 (1977): 13–16.
— (1980), 'Water mills of the Batinah coast of Oman', *PSAS* 10: 127–32.
— (1998), 'Water and human settlement in the Balikh valley, Syria: Investigations from 1992–1995', *Journal of Field Archaeology* 25.1: 63–87.
Williamson, Andrew (1972), 'Persian Gulf commerce in the Sassanian period and the first two centuries of Islam', *Bastan Chenasi va Honar-e Islam* 9–10: 97–109.
— (1987), 'Regional distribution of mediaeval Persian pottery in the light of recent investigations', in Allan and Roberts, eds, pp. 11–22.
Willey, Peter (2004), *Eagle's Nest: Ismaili Castles in Iran and Syria*, Ismaili Heritage Series 10, London and New York.
Wulff, Hans (1966), *The Traditional Crafts of Persia. Their Development, Technology, and Influence on Eastern and Western Civilizations*, Cambridge, MA and London.
Wulzinger, Karl, Paul Wittek and Friedrich Sarre (1935), *Das islamische Milet*, Berlin and Leipzig.
Yenisehiroglu, Filiz (2005), 'L'Archéologie historique de l'émpire ottoman: Bilan et perspectives', *Turcica* 37: 245–65.
Zarinebaf, Fariba, John Bennet and Jack Davis (2005), *A Historical and Economic Geography of Ottoman Greece: The Southwestern Morea in the 18th Century*, Hesperia Supplement 34, Princeton.
Ziadeh, Ghada (1995), 'Ethno-history and "reverse chronology" at Ti'innik, a Palestinian village', *Antiquity* 69: 999–1008.
Zozaya, Juan (1996), 'Fortification building in al-Andalus', in *Madrider Beiträge* 24: *Spanien under der Orient im frühen under hohen Mittelalter. Kolloquium Berlin, 1991*, pp. 55–74.
— (1998), 'The Islamic consolidation in al-Andalus (8th–10th c.): An archaeological perspective', in Gayraud, ed., pp. 245–58.

Index